BIG
STICKS

By William Curran

**Mitts:
A Celebration
of the
Art of
Fielding**

ACKNOWLEDGMENTS

SPACE AVAILABLE DOES not permit me to acknowledge individually the many persons—librarians, retired ballplayers, baseball writers, members of SABR, relatives, colleagues, and friends—who have contributed significantly to the making of this book. Let them be assured that my appreciation, though expressed in general terms, is nonetheless sincere. For assistance of somewhat greater magnitude I would like to thank the following by name: the staff of the National Baseball Library at Cooperstown, New York, especially senior research associate Bill Deane for answering unerringly a multitude of questions on baseball history; the staff of the Silverton, Oregon, public library for permitting me access to the intellectual resources of a nation through the twin modern miracles of computer links and interlibrary loans; the staff of the Oregon State Library for miscellaneous assistance over many months; Ralph Winnie for unfailing generosity in lending portions of his splendid personal library of baseball books; Jim O'Donnell, Brad Willett, and Bob Jones for helping shepherd the manuscript through several transformations; Mark Rucker for assistance in selecting photos; my agents, Sherry Robb and Bart Andrews, for their patience; and, finally, my indefatigable editors Jane Meara and Abigail Stackpole for—well, everything.

CONTENTS

INTRODUCTION

THE EPIC HITTING binge began with the suddenness of a summer squall. Two years earlier, in the war-shortened, lackluster season of 1918, the major leagues had batted an identical .254. This was close to what the two had averaged since the American League belatedly joined the National in adopting the foul strike rule back in 1903. But now, in 1920, with the majors back on their normal schedule of 154 games, National League batters hit .270. American Leaguers soared to .283. More startling than the increase in batting averages was the surge in home runs, up 46 percent over the major-league totals for 1917, the most recent season of regulation length.

Conditioned to a style of baseball in which an adequate lead might be built on a walk, a sacrifice, a steal, and a fielder's choice, the fan of 1920 must have looked on in approval and amazement as runs scored by the half dozen and base hits showered the still-new steel-and-concrete ball parks like cherry blossoms in a high wind.

But enthusiasm in the bleachers was fueled by more than the increase in base hits and scoring. Baseball offense had developed a new and exciting dimension—the home run. Thanks to George Herman "Babe" Ruth, star-pitcher-turned-outfielder, the once rare but always exciting long ball was coming into its own as a strategic weapon. Having set a new major-league home-run record of 29 in 1919, Ruth followed with an incomprehensible 54 in 1920; incomprehensible because two seasons earlier he had tied for the major-league leadership with 11, a typical winning total for the years leading up to World War I.

Attendance figures rose as dramatically as batting averages. Thrilled by Ruth's home-run exploits and the general expansion in hitting, Americans who had rarely attended a ball game before competed with veteran fans for the best seats at the ballpark. In 1920 the New York Yankees, featuring the recently purchased Babe Ruth, set a major-league home-attendance record of 1,298,422. Three seasons earlier the club had drawn 330,294. In that tumultuous season of 1920 there must have been moments, perhaps during the seventh inning of a 15-to-13 slugfest, when the happy fan pinched himself and asked whether things could get any better. They could. And they did.

In 1921, the National League, a trifle slow to catch up with the American in the changing fashion in batting, boosted its league average to .289 and almost doubled its output of home runs. The following year, for the first time in the new age, National Leaguers outhit and outslugged their rivals. Collectively, the major leagues hit 1,055 home runs in 1922. It represented an increase of 68 percent over a span of five years.

On August 25, 1922, the disciples of what was called scientific baseball, the old-fashioned, low-scoring, defense-minded game, may have experienced their ultimate nightmare. At Chicago's Wrigley Field, the Cubs nosed out the Philadelphia Phillies, 26 to 23. Going into the eighth inning the Cubs held a 26-to-9 lead but barely managed to hang on for the win. Between them the teams made 51 hits.

In 1922, St. Louis Browns right fielder Jack Tobin, a scant 142 pounds as he stepped from the shower, startled fans at Sportsman's Park by hitting 13 home runs from his leadoff spot in the batting order. In more than half the seasons from 1904 to 1918, Tobin's total would have made little Jack the major-league home-run king. In 1922 he finished sixteenth.

What really signaled the spread of home-run fever was that by 1922 not one but three batters—Ken Williams of St. Louis and Clarence "Tilly" Walker of Philadelphia in the American League, and Rogers Hornsby of St. Louis in the National League—actually outhomered the mighty Babe Ruth. (Owing to a spring suspension and other misadventures, Ruth missed a third of the season and had one of the poorest years of his career—.315 batting average, 35 home runs, 99 runs batted in.)

Paradoxically, in the early twenties, batters were not only hitting the ball harder than ever, they were hitting for very high averages. While Ruth was compiling an astounding 113 home runs for 1920 and 1921, he batted .377. When Rogers Hornsby hit 42 home runs in 1922 to set a new National League record, he batted .401. Such performances flew in the face of reigning doctrine that if a batter consistently took a hefty cut at the ball, particularly if he consciously tried for home runs, his batting average would drop. It remains doctrine to this day, strongly supported by experience. Why the precept failed among batters of the 1920s has never been satisfactorily explained.

The highly conservative *Baseball Magazine,* one of the two or three most influential baseball journals of the 1920s, was inclined to fuss editorially about such unaccountable changes. "In five short years," a late 1921 editorial ran, "the number of total bases have [sic] risen in the major leagues more than 30 percent. How are we to reconcile the fact that slugging has not resulted in a falling off of batting? On the contrary, slugging such as the game has not witnessed for many years has been accompanied by soaring batting averages." Prudently, the editors ventured no conclusion.

Veteran New York Giant manager John McGraw thought that the young players of the 1920s were simply smarter than their predecessors, a surprisingly generous assessment for a man whose own playing days had ended in 1902. The great right-hander Grover Cleveland Alexander, then with the Chicago Cubs, remarked sourly that the quality of pitching had declined alarmingly. He attributed the falloff to the coddling of young pitchers. But even "Aleck" was not getting batters out as easily as he had before World War I. Rogers Hornsby, one of the shrewdest observers of the game as well as one of its greatest hitters, pointed out that it was largely the men who were already baseball's best hitters who had taken up the new fashion of slugging.

Oddly, no one at the time seems to have taken into account the increased physical size of the players. When young Babe Ruth reported to the Boston Red Sox in 1914 at six feet two inches, few major leaguers were his equal. By the early 1920s, however, players of Babe's size were more common, and spidery little slap-hitters like Pittsburgh's five-feet-four-inch Walter "Rabbit" Maranville were rapidly disappearing from the game.

It is important to understand what is intended by the term *slugging* as used in 1921. Slugging suggested a manner of addressing the pitch as much as the actual achievement of long hits. Before World War I, most players, particularly rookies, were urged, indeed ordered, to bat "scientifically," that is, to choke up on the bat and push the ball toward holes in the infield or to plunk it just over the infielders' heads. It was viewed as the high-percentage approach to batting. Contrariwise, a batter who held the bat close to the knob, swung as hard as he could, and trusted to luck where the ball might land was said to be slugging. Slugging was the natural, or unlettered, approach to batting, in essence, "the sandlot style."

As mysterious as the soaring batting averages among sluggers was the fact that many of the hardest swingers did not strike out often. Major-league strikeout totals declined even as home-run records were being set. Premier power hitters such as Rogers Hornsby, Ken Williams, the Philadelphia Athletics' Al Simmons, and Washington's Leon "Goose" Goslin rarely struck out more than 30 to 40 times a season. The acknowledged whiff king of his generation, Babe Ruth achieved 90 strikeouts just twice, with a career high of 93. In the ranks of nonsluggers, Cleveland shortstop Joe Sewell in 1925 fanned only 4 times in 608 at-bats. Whatever the reason, batters of the 1920s made contact most of the time.

While *Baseball Magazine* fretted about the purity of the game, batting averages and home-run totals continued to rise. Except for 1921, every season from 1920 through 1925 produced at least one .400 hitter. In 1922 there were three. In "slack" 1921, Rogers Hornsby stayed well above .400 from the first week of the season to the last, only to falter in the final few games and finish at .397. Expectations of fan and player had changed so dramatically in the space of a couple of seasons that Hornsby was moved to offer a public explanation for his dereliction.

In an interview with *Baseball Magazine* at the close of the 1921 season, Hornsby charged his last-minute slump to the rainy weather in St. Louis during the Cardinals' final series against Pittsburgh. The slugger explained that while he had no trouble getting wood on Pirate pitching, he was not able to drive a sodden ball with his customary élan.

By 1925 both leagues had pushed their batting averages above .290 and their collective home runs approached 1,300. On some clubs, guys batting only .310 were dropped to seventh place in the order and fans stopped asking for their autographs. Sluggers began to yawn. "Who are the hardest pitchers you have to hit against?" a writer asked Hornsby in 1924, after "Rajah" had batted .424. "There are no hard pitchers to hit," answered the batting champion. Arrogance? Yes, that, but likely plain truth as well.

Major leaguers and their fans weren't the only ones having fun. Like an echo of Verdun, the postwar batting barrage had enveloped every park in Organized Baseball. In rickety wooden ballparks from Fall River to Fresno, outfield fences stood at risk of being reduced to kindling under the impact of base hits. It must have been a great time to be alive and hold a season pass to the local ballyard.

Actually, not everyone in baseball could have been enjoying the new order. There were the pitchers, remember. In 1917, major-league pitchers had a composite earned-run average of 2.68, a figure typical of the period before World War I, when the man with the toeplate dominated the game. Five seasons later, in 1922, the big-league ERA went above 4.00, a level that would become unpleasantly familiar to a whole generation of pitchers. By 1925, when hitters were just getting their second wind, the collective ERA reached a towering 4.33. That summer, in the seclusion of many a Pullman upper berth, rookie pitchers must have contemplated a career change.

Providentially, young pitchers of 1925 were no more clairvoyant than are stock analysts. Worse times lay ahead. In fact, by 1930, in a schedule of 154 games, the sixteen major-league clubs would score a horrific 13,695 runs, an average of 11.1 a game. Sluggers that year would hit 1,565 home runs. While the total may not impress today's fan, who lives in a nebula of home runs and little else, it was two and a half times the number hit in 1920, when the long ball first came into fashion. In the crowning indignity to pitchers, the National League batters in 1930 would hit over .300 and pile up almost 20,000 total bases. In this improbable season George "Showboat" Fisher, a rookie outfielder with the St. Louis Cardinals, batted .374 in 92 games, sported a slugging average of .587, and drove in 61 runs. His reward was to be shipped back to the minors for additional seasoning.

At center stage throughout this extravagant decade and casting the longest shadow in the history of baseball is the familiar but sometimes incongruous figure of Babe Ruth. The silhouette in the batter's box may be Falstaff's, but the performance rivals Hercules'. If a man can be said to play baseball with genius, Babe Ruth did so. Dozens of his contemporaries have testified that anything that can be done on a baseball field Ruth could do and do well. Pitch, hit, hit with power, bunt, run bases, field, throw, and, if need be, coach on the baseline.

From 1919 through 1921 Ruth dominated baseball as no athlete had ever before dominated a professional sport. Consider that in 1920 he hit more home runs than did fourteen of the fifteen other major-league teams. Baseball elder statesman Branch Rickey said in the 1960s that to match Ruth's dominance over his contemporaries a modern player would have to hit about 180 home runs a season. As the 1920s progressed, other players, quick to adopt Ruth's power ethos, began to match, or nearly match, some of the Babe's individual feats. But when it came to cumulative records or breaking new ground, Ruth and his big bat always stayed a step or two ahead of the crowd.

Throughout the 1920s, hard-core patrons of the low-scoring, intellectualized game—"inside baseball"—protested the swelling game scores and especially the rising home-run totals. Mass-circulation magazines ran jeremiads with titles like "Baseball Shudders at the Home Run Menace," "The Growing Problem of the Home Run," and "More Home Runs?" Newspaper editorials demanded that "something be done" and warned of a threat to the integrity of the national pastime, perhaps the republic itself. But presumably even conservative fans, whatever their misgivings about the power game, continued to frequent the ballpark. It was, after all, the only game in town.

In fact, the scientific game had not disappeared at all. There were simply fewer low-scoring games. It's true that in the 1920s base stealing declined rapidly as an offensive weapon. At the same time, the principal features of inside baseball—the sacrifice bunt, the squeeze play, the hit-and-run—along with a variety of defensive strategies—had never lost favor and are still in use today.

What brought on the eruption of power hitting in the 1920s? In all likelihood it was born of a combination of causes. Regrettably, many baseball historians cling to the hoary theory of a conspiracy by baseball owners to introduce a livelier ball. (In the 1920s it was widely known as the "rabbit" ball because, it was alleged, the ball hopped from the bat with alacrity.) The most popular version of the conspiracy tale has avaricious major-league owners meeting in secret in a smoke-filled hotel room (the date varies from 1919 to 1921) and ordering an obsequious manufacturer to liven the ball in the interest of fattening batting averages and increasing home runs. The reason for secrecy is never made clear.

Be assured, no such meeting ever took place. Nor was an order to doctor the ball ever given. Between the introduction of the cork center in 1910 and the cushioned-cork center in 1926, no change whatever was made in specifications for the official major-league baseball. It is entirely possible that the ball used in 1919 was a trifle livelier than its prewar counterpart. But, if so, the change was accident rather than design and could have resulted from the availability of better-quality materials following World War I.

It would be naïve to conclude from the high batting averages of the 1920s that the old-timers were better hitters than our modern players. More likely the reverse is true. At all events, it is difficult to compare performances from one era with those of another, since conditions of play are sometimes significantly different.

A sabermetrician—the new computer-equipped baseball analyst—who derives his title from that admirable fellowship, the Society for American Baseball Research (SABR), may conclude from his number crunching that Wade Boggs is a cinch to have batted .435 in the mid-1920s. I have no trouble with the conjecture. Boggs is a great hitter. But let's make the study complete. We will have Boggs play with the training, nutrition, medical care, and coaching of the 1920s.

First let's deprive Boggs of the services of Ted Williams as a special batting coach. Rookies of the 1920s rarely received individual instruction at any stage of their careers, and, in fact, had to fight for a chance to get into the batting cage to take a few practice licks at the ball.

Next we'll take away Wade's batting helmet and batting gloves. We should also trim him down physically to the size of the average third baseman in 1925, let's say 5 feet 10 and 170 pounds. And no diet of lemon chicken. Chicken was an expensive commodity in the twenties, not something that even a big-league ballplayer could afford more than once a week. And while we're at it, we'll have Boggs play three to five consecutive doubleheaders in the afternoon heat of September. After the games let him try to get a night's rest in St. Louis or Washington at a hotel equipped with a small room fan, if any fan at all. You get the drift.

Although the modern ballplayer enjoys advantages over his 1920s predecessor in physical comforts and instruction, today's game is almost certainly harder to play well. It may be the reason that the majors can't find enough genuine big-league talent to man twenty-six teams despite a doubling of the national population and the addition of blacks and Latin Americans to the player pool. In any case, the computer wielder needs to remind himself periodically that no matter how many numbers he punches into his machine, a flesh-and-blood Ruth, Hornsby, or Ty Cobb will never actually face Roger Clemens or Dwight Gooden. We cannot know how well the old-timers would have done. We know only that the best of them handled the challenges of their own generation admirably.

There seems to have been a particular boyish innocence and enthusiasm about ballplayers of the 1920s. In *The Glory of Their Times*, that grand old American League slugger Goose Goslin confesses to Lawrence Ritter, "I never could wait for spring to come so that I could get out there and swat those baseballs. . . . I'd have paid *them* to let me play." Once during batting practice before an exhibition game in Los Angeles, Babe Ruth patiently hit 125 balls into the stands. He knew that the West Coast crowd had turned out not so much for the ball game as to see him sock baseballs. Babe, who dearly loved to hit, was prepared to indulge them as long as he had strength in his arms.

Allowing for the inclination to hyperbole that often accompanies nostalgia, the plentiful memoirs of American life in the 1920s describe a near childlike exuberance and optimism. Dr. Émile Coué's mantra was on many tongues—"Every day in every way, I'm getting better and better." And in the workplace George Babbitt's boosterism was the order of the day. Life seemed no more worrisome than a 3-and-0 pitch.

A story that illustrates how the carefree attitude of the era extended to the ballpark involves, appropriately enough, Babe Ruth. In a game at Philadelphia's Shibe Park in 1930, Ruth, a left-handed swinger, hit 3 home runs, something he had never before achieved in a regular-season game although he had done it twice in the World Series. With a chance to hit 4 homers in a single game, Babe impishly took one turn at the plate batting right-handed. After taking 2 called strikes, he thought more seriously of the situation, switched to his normal side, and promptly struck out. It was the act of a carefree adolescent. No manager today would permit it. Possibly it was Babe's way of underscoring that big-league baseball is, after all, only a game, even for a player earning more money than the president.

"Perhaps nostalgia blurs the recollection," Harold Seymour writes in *Baseball: The Golden Age,* "but having read early baseball literature and spent summer days in a major-league park in the 1920s, I am left with a sense of the deeper emotional attachments and less inhibited loyalties of the fans of those times. Parks were smaller and more intimate. Fans felt closer to the teams and the players."

Periodically, a TV commercial will invoke the atmosphere of a 1920s ballpark to lend cachet to the sponsor's product, however tenuous the connection with baseball. There is the wistful little boy in knickers, the kindly old man, presumably the grandfather, muted sunshine, a decorous crowd, peanut and hot dog vendors, and, implicitly, a lively ballgame, featuring lots of hitting. Pure Norman Rockwell? I'll let you in on a secret. I lived close enough to the period to say with some assurance that it was indeed that pleasant. Grass, sunshine, proximity to the players. No bat night, no helmet night, no night. No exploding scoreboards, no instant replay, no organ music, no roar of jet planes overhead. No sound except the chirp of vendors, the crack of the bat, and the cheering of the crowd. It brings to mind a line from Fred Stein's charming memoir of New York's Polo Grounds in the 1930s, *Under Coogan's Bluff:* "There was nothing on the menu but baseball and that's the way we liked it."

ONE

BABE PULLS THE TRIGGER

"Babe Ruth could hit a ball so hard and so far that it was sometimes hard to believe your eyes."
—SAMUEL POND "SAD SAM" JONES

ON A CHILLY April morning in 1919, at the Tampa, Florida, fairgrounds, Babe Ruth, the brash, young left-handed pitching ace of the Boston Red Sox, led off the top of the second inning against the New York Giants in the first game of the spring exhibition schedule. Already as famous for his slugging as for his snapping curve and pinpoint control, Ruth had been playing the outfield and first base between pitching starts since the beginning of the truncated 1918 season.

Ruth stepped into a fastball from Giant right-hander "Columbia George" Smith and drove it well beyond the boundary of the playing field, which was located in the broad infield of the local racetrack. According to witnesses, the ball sailed over a stand of coconut palms bordering the far side of the track in right-center, and landed in a plowed field, where it finally rolled to a stop.

By the time disbelieving spectators were slipping weakly back into their seats, the young slugger had circled the bases and was sitting on the bench. Although there were some experienced baseball hands present, including a dozen or more reporters from

New York and Boston, none had ever seen a baseball hit so far and with such force. Chances are that no one *anywhere* had ever seen a ball hit so hard.

On the following morning, April 5, the venerable W. O. "Bill" McGeehan, who covered the Giants for the New York *Tribune,* reported to his readers up north that Ruth's blow had traveled so high "it came down coated with ice." The more matter-of-fact Fred Lieb of the New York *Press* organized a group of baseball writers, including Frank Graham of the New York *Sun* and Paul Shannon of the Boston *Globe,* and with the aid of a surveyor's glass attempted to measure the length of the home run. Assisted by Giant right fielder Ross Youngs, who directed the group as best he could to the spot where he had retrieved the ball, Lieb and his colleagues calculated the blast at 625 feet, including the roll. If the figure seems to make a mockery of the laws of physics, it is possible that the shaken Youngs erred slightly in his spotting.

Four years later, in his baseball autobiography, John McGraw, never on friendly terms with Ruth, cited the Tampa home run as the longest hit he had seen in his thirty years in the big leagues. Without explaining how he arrives at the figure, McGraw gives the distance as 587 feet. Recalling the episode in his own memoirs many years later, Ed Barrow, who was the Boston manager in 1919, came up with a figure of 579 feet. Witnesses may remember slightly different distances, but even the most conservative agree that the Babe's shot in the Tampa exhibition game was airborne for about 525 feet. To put the event into perspective, the average big-league home run today travels about 365 feet—and this is with a ball widely believed to be much livelier than the one hit by Ruth in 1919.

Chances are the only one not surprised by the Paul Bunyan clout was Ruth himself. When it came to extolling his talents, Babe would make Dizzy Dean and Muhammad Ali appear self-effacing. Early in 1919, Ruth boasted to the sporting press that in the coming season he would demolish every home run record on the books. Although still thought of primarily as a pitcher, Babe had been hitting tape-measure homers around the American League since he first arrived in 1915. Moreover, while doing emergency part-time service in the Red Sox outfield in 1918, he tied for the major-league home run leadership.

Baseball writers in and outside Boston reacted to the colorful Ruth's late-winter bluster with an indulgent chuckle and granted him an outside chance at matching Ralph "Socks" Seybold's American League home-run record of 16, set with Philadelphia in 1902, before the league adopted the foul strike rule. Everyone agreed that Babe hit a long ball. At the same time, reporters knew that the game's best players, including some tough pitchers, would be back from wartime service. (As a married man Ruth had been draft exempt.) In the new season Babe wouldn't have the easy pickings he had enjoyed in 1918. In a cautionary note, *The Sporting News,* self-appointed guardian of the game's welfare, urged Ruth not to try for home runs lest his batting average suffer. In that era, batting average was the principal criterion for determining a player's worth.

It is doubtful that Ruth kept abreast of press chat. His formal education was meager and his intellectual curiosity nonexistent. Babe was by choice a stranger to the printed word. In later years he would confess that he had read only one book in his life. It had been ghostwritten for his by-line. In any case, in the winter of 1919 Babe was preoccupied. As a star pitcher and batter for a World Championship team, he was demanding more money from the Red Sox—a lot more. Spring training was well along when, on March 21, a stubborn Ruth finally signed a three-year contract at ten thousand dollars a year. Ten thousand dollars was a handsome sum in 1919 and Boston owner Harry Frazee had yielded to Ruth's demands with reluctance and not a little bitterness. An absentee baseball owner based in New York, Frazee's principal business was producing Broadway plays. As long as he owned the Red Sox, he never reconciled himself to the idea that a mere ballplayer should command a salary equal to that paid to a top-flight actor.

Ruth's epic home run in his first time at bat in the spring schedule made the young slugger the focus of attention among writers and fans along the exhibition route as the Red Sox traveled north. In Charleston, South Carolina, Babe wowed spectators by swinging so hard at a pitch that he wrenched an ankle and had to be carried from the field. The Charleston crowd murmured a question that would be heard often in the years ahead whenever the Babe missed on a mighty swing: What if he had connected? Even while striking out Ruth was a sensation.

On April 18, in the next-to-last spring exhibition game, the Red Sox played the Baltimore Orioles in Baltimore. The Orioles were then in the Class AA International League, the highest minor-league classification of the time. The game was of special significance to Ruth, a Baltimore native, for this was the first time he would play before the hometown fans in a big-league uniform. Responding to the occasion, Babe hit 4 home runs in 4 official at-bats. In his other two plate appearances he was walked intentionally. The Red Sox won the game, 12 to 3. True, Ruth's extraordinary performance was against minor-league pitching and in an exhibition game. But the Orioles of 1919 were the most powerful minor-league team in the country, possibly the greatest of all time, and would go on to win seven consecutive International League pennants.

After the game, in an uncharacteristic burst of modesty, Ruth attempted to explain his awesome performance to excited reporters. "It's a gift," the Babe said quietly. It proved to be one of his most enduring statements.

The opening of baseball season must have been particularly welcome in the spring of 1919. The country had been through a bad winter and some even worse years. A participant in World War I for nineteen months, its troops in serious combat only in the final five, the United States suffered an appalling 349,000 casualties. More punishing than the war itself was the pandemic of Spanish influenza, which struck in the autumn of 1918 and lingered for eight or nine months. Worldwide, the disease killed about 25 million people, more than had died in four years of combat. In the United States about 20 million contracted the virus, and of these more than half a million died, a staggering 194,000 in October alone.

To make flu sufferers and their families feel worse, shortly after the Armistice in November 1918, consumer prices, high during the war, took off like an escaped hydrogen balloon. Inflation was stimulated in part by chronic shortages of domestic necessities, notably flour and sugar, sometimes heating fuel. In response Americans did what they had been forbidden to do through nineteen months of war. They went on strike. In the early months of 1919 it seemed that everyone was on strike: streetcar conductors, steelworkers, seamstresses, coal miners, bakers, elevator operators, and thousands more. Outside Midwest factories, armed strikers and scabs fought, sometimes with guns. In Boston, city police staged an unprecedented (and probably justified) walkout, and in New York even stage actors took to the picket lines to protest rising prices. Before the end of the year the United States Department of Labor would record more than 3,600 separate strikes. To add to the discomfort of Americans on the picket line or sniffling in unheated bedrooms, the eastern half of the country experienced the coldest, wettest spring in forty-five years.

Consistent with the pessimism that afflicted the American spirit that spring was the decision by major-league owners to limit the 1919 baseball schedule to 140 games. The owners reasoned that war-weary fans were not yet ready to support the conventional 154-game schedule. As a corporate judgment, it paved the way for the development of the Edsel and Corfam shoes. In fact, the country was hungry for diversion, baseball in particular. Fans would turn out in record numbers.

Boston Red Sox fans were not alone in looking forward to the season with a degree of confidence. On Chicago's South Side, White Sox supporters hailed the return of key players who had been absent in the service or in war industries. The World Champion White Sox squad of 1917 was back virtually intact. Cleveland fans too were not without hopes for victory. In 1918 the Indians had finished a strong second and might have won had the schedule not been summarily canceled at the end of August by order of the secretary of war, Newton Baker.

In New York, even the traditionally threadbare Yankees were flexing their muscles since being taken over by a couple of ambitious millionaires, brewer Jacob Ruppert and construction engineer Tillinghast "Cap" Huston. And, of course, in the National League, the perennially powerful New York Giants had to be considered contenders at the beginning of any season. Cincinnati, with its great pitching staff, also looked formidable.

A year earlier, his team critically short of left-handed hitting because of the war, Red Sox manager Ed Barrow had reluctantly pressed Ruth, the league's best left-handed pitcher, into part-time service as an outfielder. The experiment proved an outstanding success. In 95 games as a pitcher and outfielder, Ruth batted .300 and drove in 66 runs. More than half of the Babe's 95 hits had been for extra bases, and his 11 home runs won him a tie for the major-league lead with the Athletics' full-time center fielder, Tilly Walker. In fact, Ruth should have had 12 homers and a clear title, but under 1918 rules the extra-inning game-ending home run he hit on July 8 was ruled a triple because the winning run scored ahead of him. (In 1920, Organized Baseball would adopt the present rule, which counts all runs scoring on a sudden-death homer.)

As a pitcher in the abbreviated 1918 season, Ruth had appeared in 20 games and won 13 of them. He pitched 19 complete games and posted an earned-run average of 2.22. Then, in the World Series, the slick left-hander started 2 games, won both, and pitched a total of sixteen scoreless innings as Boston nailed down its fifth World Championship in 5 outings.

In the face of Ruth's versatility, Barrow confronted a tough decision for 1919. Other managers might have muttered enviously, "I should have such problems," but the dilemma was nonetheless real. A longtime practitioner of inside baseball, the Boston manager was hesitant to put a former 20-game winner at risk in the outfield now that the wartime emergency was past. In Barrow's experience, home runs had never played a significant role in baseball strategy. But Boston team captain Harry Hooper strongly urged Barrow to continue playing Ruth in the outfield between pitching starts. With misgivings, the manager consented.

In defense of Barrow's caution, it must be said that in the spring of 1919 Ruth was essentially unproven as an everyday player. Up to 1918 he had hit a total of 9 home runs, all as a pitcher. True, several of those early homers were tape-measure shots and had attracted wide attention. It was also true that in his years as a pitcher Babe had hit for a high average. On the other hand, all of his 1918 homers had come before July 1. It might turn out that at best Ruth was a streak hitter.

Whatever reservations Barrow had about playing Ruth every day seemed to be confirmed when the regular season opened.

Babe got off to a terrible start. After 14 games he was batting a puny .198 and had only 1 home run, a tainted inside-the-park effort that could easily have been ruled a single and a 3-base error. Restless Boston fans called for Barrow to abandon the experiment and return Ruth to his pitching duties full time. This was not, after all, wartime baseball. In the end, however, the manager held to the promise he had made to team captain Hooper. When not scheduled to pitch, Ruth remained in left field.

In future seasons fans and writers would accept that it was a convention for Ruth to get off to a slow start. Convinced that spring training did nothing to improve his play, the Babe annually devoted his energies to off-field and after-dark activities—drinking, overeating, gambling, and philandering with local belles. It often took him several weeks of the regular season to shake the effects of the spring bacchanal and get into a routine of hitting baseballs. The 1919 season was a paradigm.

By mid-May Ruth was starting to round into shape and had raised his batting average to .290. On May 20, with more than one fifth of the shortened schedule gone, Babe hit his first legitimate home run of the season. It came at Sportsman's Park in St. Louis, where the ball sailed completely over the right-field pavilion to land on Grand Avenue. In keeping with Ruth's uncanny flair for exploiting the big moment, this blow was a game-winning grand slam, hit on a day that he was pitching. Going the full nine innings, Babe scattered 9 hits as he beat the Browns, 6 to 4. The performance was classic Ruth.

As the end of May approached, the Boston superstar was doing a creditable job of holding down two positions, but he remained well behind his virtuoso pace of 1918. Of greater concern to Red Sox fans was the plight of the team. They were playing less than .500 ball and had recently slipped into the second division. The situation had to be somewhat embarrassing for Ruth, who enjoyed the security of a fat multiyear contract. With a quarter of the schedule played, the man who had pledged to break every home-run record known had hit just one fair ball over the fence and was batting barely well enough to hold his position as a starting outfielder.

If Ruth and the Red Sox had been unproductive in the spring, others in the league were not. Untroubled by the unseasonable cold, the Chicago White Sox, led by the hard-hitting "Shoeless Joe" Jackson and pitchers Ed Cicotte and Claud "Lefty" Williams, threatened to make a runaway of the American League race. In Detroit, Ty Cobb was hitting .377 and had a leg up on his twelfth batting championship in thirteen years. Cobb's teammate Bobby Veach, close behind, was challenging the batting champ, hit for hit. George Sisler, brilliant first baseman for the rising St. Louis Browns, appeared headed for his best season ever.

In the National League John McGraw had gone to the whip right out of the starting gate, and by the end of May succeeded in flogging a strong but aging Giant lineup to a 5-game lead. If "Little Napoleon," as McGraw was styled in the New York press, could work a few miracles with his thin pitching staff, it looked as though October might bring a replay of the somewhat bitter 1917 World Series, which the Giants had lost to the Chicago White Sox, 4 games to 2.

British historian Paul Johnson asserts that the birth of the modern world can be fixed precisely at 12:38 hours GCT on the afternoon of May 29, 1919, when astronomer Arthur Eddington tested empirically Albert Einstein's Special Theory of Relativity during a solar eclipse in the South Atlantic. Eddington joyously proclaimed to the world the correctness of Einstein's hypothesis, and man's understanding of the universe was altered forever.

Babe Ruth would have been among the last people on earth to be aware of such an event, but perhaps, at some profound level of the unconscious, this most natural of athletes sensed the cosmic character of the moment. In any case, on the following afternoon Ruth hit a long home run off the Athletics' Scott Perry at Shibe Park in Philadelphia and with it began an unprecedented display of power hitting, a performance that stamped him as the first truly modern ballplayer. In the four months that followed, Ruth would stand the baseball world on its head and affect the economics of all professional sports.

At about the same time as his home run off Perry, Ruth forced a clarification of his role with the Red Sox, and it may have been what helped him get on track. Although he had not played up to the high standards he customarily set himself, Babe enjoyed being a regular outfielder and was increasingly unhappy at having to pitch every fourth day. He went to Barrow and asked to be relieved of pitching duties.

"How come?" the manager asked.

"I'm tired all the time," Ruth complained.

"Have you tried sleep?" the unsympathetic Barrow responded to baseball's most notorious night owl. But Babe's request was reasonable, and in the end the hard-nosed manager relented and took Ruth out of the rotation. In his fifth season in the majors, Babe had become a full-time outfielder.

There is some evidence, just enough to be tantalizing, that since young Ruth was a pitcher and not expected to hit anyway, his first manager with the Red Sox, Bill Carrigan, may have turned the spirited rookie loose at the plate. (Babe probably wouldn't have accepted direction anyway.) Given free rein in his ninth spot in the order, Babe held his big bat down at the knob, dug in, and swung with all his might. Later he told writer Grantland Rice, "I copied my swing after Joe Jackson's because his was the perfectest."

Although Ruth may have modeled his swing on Jackson's, he didn't hit in quite the same way. Jackson was a level swinger, a consistent hitter of line drives though he hit the ball very hard. Occasionally, Shoeless Joe's "ropes" simply carried out of the ballpark. But Jackson was not a home-run hitter. Ruth, on the other hand, was a confirmed uppercutter at bat. He consciously tried to loft the ball, and, since he hit it with such force, quite a few of those towering drives cleared the fence.

In any case, Carrigan's rookie pitcher batted .315 in 1915 and more than half his 29 hits went for extra bases. He also hit 4 home runs. Cleveland outfielder Robert "Braggo" Roth, who played in 109 games that year, led the American League in home runs with 7. Ruth also drove in 21 runs in his 92 at-bats and had a slugging average of .576. He never changed his batting style thereafter.

In May 1919, once relieved by Barrow from the pressures of having to pitch every fourth day, Ruth's hitting improved. In June he pushed his batting average well above .300. On June 30 he hit his seventh home run and second grand slam of the year—in a

losing cause. It came off New York Yankee ace right-hander Bob
Shawkey and landed in the upper deck in right field at the Polo
Grounds, just about where Babe had hit his first major-league
home run back in 1915. Although Ruth was leading the league,
he was actually behind his pace of 1918, when he was not even
a full-time player.

Outside Boston Ruth's hitting was attracting no more than
polite attention. At home Red Sox fans had little else to amuse
them, since the team was in sixth place and sinking rapidly. As
July opened, most baseball writers may have dismissed the possibility of Ruth's setting a new home-run record. With just 7 to
his credit, it looked as though Babe would be lucky if he retained
the league leadership.

In July the weather finally improved. Players stopped blowing
on their hands and fans doffed their topcoats and unbuttoned
their suit jackets. The warming seemed to have a magical effect
on Ruth. On July 5, for the first time in his career, he hit 2 home
runs in one game, a feat he would duplicate sixty-nine times before he retired. On July 12 at Chicago's Comiskey Park, he hit
home run number 11 to tie his 1918 mark. Then, at Cleveland
on the eighteenth, he staged a one-man batting circus.

When the stumbling Red Sox took the field at League Park
that hot July day, they stood 0 and 9 in their season series with
the Indians, the only team in the league with a realistic chance
of catching front-running Chicago. Boston had every reason to be
relaxed. In the fourth inning, with a man on and the Sox trailing
by 1, Ruth hit a long home run to put his team ahead. At the end
of seven innings, the teams were tied at 3, but in the bottom of
the eighth the Indians scored 4 times to go ahead. It looked as
though Cleveland had locked up its tenth win of the year over
the hapless Sox and would gain ground against Chicago.

In the top of the ninth, Boston pushed across a run and loaded
the bases with 2 out and Ruth coming to the plate. In a percentage move, Cleveland manager Lee Fohl signaled for lanky left-
hander Fritz Coumbe to come in and pitch to the left-handed
Ruth. Coumbe threw a breaking pitch. The partisan crowd gasped
as Babe missed with one of his most ferocious swings. Then
Coumbe, or more likely his catcher, Steve O'Neill, made a mis-

take that Ruth's opponents would learn never to make. The left-hander came back with the same pitch. Ruth hit it completely out of League Park, across Lexington Avenue, and onto the roof of a commercial laundry on the south side of the street. It was Babe's third grand slam in eight weeks, and with it the Ruth legend took a geometric leap forward.

When the Red Sox held the Indians in the bottom of the ninth to win 8 to 7, choleric Cleveland owner James Dunn fired manager Fohl on the spot and appointed center fielder and team captain Tristram "Tris" Speaker to succeed him. Curiously, Ruth's blow may have helped shorten Coumbe's career as well. A 13-game winner in 1918, the left-hander was soon on his way out of baseball.

In Detroit on July 21, Ruth chalked up homer number 14 off the Tigers' crafty right-hander Howard Ehmke. It was reported as the longest ball ever hit at Navin Field. Similar stories came from all over the league. Longest homer ever at St. Louis. Longest at Chicago. At Cleveland. At New York. Babe was not only hitting them often, he was hitting them out of sight.

An interesting footnote to Ruth's revolutionary display of power was that he tended to hit his home runs off the league's best pitchers: Bob Shawkey of the Yanks; George "Hooks" Dauss, Howard Ehmke and Hubert "Dutch" Leonard of Detroit; Dickie Kerr and Lefty Williams of Chicago; Urban Shocker of St. Louis. Babe didn't care who was throwing. And he treated right-handers and lefties with equal disdain.

At home in Fenway Park on July 29, Ruth hit one about 480 feet to dead-center field off Detroit left-hander Dutch Leonard for home run number 16 to tie Socks Seybold's seventeen-year-old American League record. In all, the Boston phenom had hit 9 home runs in July for the greatest month that any slugger of the century had ever had. Just two years earlier, in 1917, 9 home runs would have won him a share in the league title. And here the Red Sox still had two months left on the schedule.

Ironically, in the middle of this most productive month for the young slugger, manager Barrow had been forced to recall Babe to the mound for emergency pitching duty. On July 8, moody right-hander Carl Mays had jumped the team and remained AWOL for more than two weeks. Partly for reasons of league politics, Mays was rewarded for his rebellion by being sold to the newly rich and increasingly powerful New York Yankees. When teenage right-hander Waite Hoyt was added to the Red Sox rotation on July 31, Babe was returned to the outfield full time.

Amid the hoopla generated by Ruth's batting feats, the pennant races were not entirely lost sight of by the fans, especially not in the National League, where the fired-up Cincinnati Reds were overtaking the wilting Giants. Nor had Ty Cobb, Joe Jackson, George Sisler, and others stopped hitting the ball solidly. Yet, suddenly Babe Ruth was the center of national attention. Everywhere the Red Sox played, fans crowded the ballpark in hopes of seeing the fugitive pitcher bust one.

As would happen a number of times in Ruth's career when he was on the threshold of a home-run record, he hit a dry spell in August. He was keeping his batting average up with timely singles and doubles, but for a period of more than two weeks he hit no home runs. Then, on August 14, Babe tagged Chicago's Dickie Kerr for number 17 at Comiskey Park to break Seybold's American League record. Two days later, before leaving Chicago, Ruth hit a ball completely over the right-field bleachers and onto South Wentworth Avenue, the longest drive ever seen in that city. It must have been the home run that novelist James T. Farrell recalls in his memoir, *My Baseball Diary.* "In 1919," Farrell writes, "I saw him hit a ball over the right-field bleachers in Comiskey Park."

Ruth's bat was hot again. On August 17 he hit homer number 19 off the St. Louis Browns' ace, Urban Shocker, at Sportsman's Park, and on the twenty-third at Detroit he recorded his fourth grand slam of the season to establish a major-league record that would stand for thirty-six years. Before the Red Sox had left Detroit Ruth hit 3 more home runs, to give him 7 in twelve days. The next mark for Babe to shoot at was the 24 homers hit by Clifford "Gavvy" Cravath of the Phillies in 1915, a very high total for the era, although most were hit at Philadelphia's pint-sized Baker Bowl. As August drew to a close, baseball fans everywhere blissfully surrendered to Babe Ruth mania. War, Spanish flu, and cold weather seemed far behind. Inflation and strikes remained, but they were outside the ballpark, where they could be temporarily dismissed.

After his unparalleled display of power in Detroit, Ruth let his bat cool for a week while fans drummed their fingers, waiting for him to tie Cravath, the National League's star home-run hitter. It almost seemed as though the Babe were biding his time, waiting for the most appropriate moment to put the senior league in its place. Had it been within his power, he could scarcely have chosen a better one. Labor Day doubleheader. Fenway Park. Enthusiastic hometown crowd. It was also a day when Ruth had been announced as a spot starter. Weakened by the loss of both Ruth and Carl Mays from the starting rotation, Boston's pitching staff was collapsing from the strain of having to absorb late-season doubleheaders. It prompted Barrow to call on Ruth to help out on special occasions.

Pitching the first game, Ruth beat Washington, 2 to 1. He drove in Boston's first run with a triple and later scored the winning run himself. No homer. As the nightcap got under way, the suspense must have been great among Boston fans. In the top of the seventh Washington scored to tie the game at 1. In the bottom half of the inning, with 1 out, Red Sox center fielder Braggo Roth walked. Now was the time. Ruth drove a fastball from James "Grunting Jim" Shaw, one of the league's best right-handers, more than 400 feet into the right-field bleachers to put the Sox ahead for good. It was home run number 24, and it tied Babe with the popular Cravath. An appreciative hometown crowd almost shook Fenway Park from its footings.

With four weeks to go in the season, Ruth was a cinch to pass Cravath's mark. He did it within four days. With twenty-three days at his disposal, it was simply a question of how high Babe would push his total for the year.

In the pennant races, Cincinnati had widened its lead over the second-place Giants to 8 games, and it appeared safe for the Rhinelanders to print World Series tickets. In the American League, Cleveland was driving hard to close the gap with Chicago. As for the powerful White Sox, it looked as though they were dawdling, daring the second-place Indians to give it a try.

Operating on the premise that the hyperactive Ruth performed better when faced with a challenge, a few enterprising writers began to search the baseball archives for new goals for the big guy. It must have taken digging, since in 1919 baseball records were not nearly as complete and accessible as they are today. The first thing the reporters brought to light was the pre-1900 home-run record of 25 by Washington's John "Buck" Free-man, set when the Senators were still in the National League and a dozen years before Griffith Stadium was built. Already tied with Freeman, the Babe laid the old first baseman's record to rest al-most as fast as it had been identified when he clipped Herbert "Lefty" Thormahlen of the Yankees for number 26.

Burrowing further into yellowing box scores, some re-searcher came up with the obscure (and anomalous) record of 27 home runs hit by Chicago White Stocking third baseman Ed-ward "Ned" Williamson way back in 1884. In that year the White Stockings, forerunners of the Cubs, played at Lake Front Park at Michigan Avenue and Washington Street, where renovation a year earlier had reduced the distance to the left-field fence to 180 feet. Until 1884 a ball hit over the fence at Lake Front had been a ground-rule double. (In 1883 Williamson had 49 doubles in 98 games—and 2 home runs.) For reasons unknown, the Lake Front Park ground rule was changed for the season of 1884. Any ball clearing the fence that year was counted as a home run.

Four Chicago players of 1884 were credited with 21 or more homers, unheard-of numbers in that era. Williamson, a fine third baseman but generally light hitter, led the league with 27, all but 2 hit at home. In the following season the White Stockings moved to West Side Park on Congress Street, where the distance to the foul pole in left was a more-challenging 216 feet and the fence was twice as high. That season Williamson hit 3 homers.

Tainted or not, Williamson's mark was in the record book. It gave Ruth something to aim for, and apparently he welcomed the challenge. At this point any home-run record must have looked puny to Babe.

Once again Ruth lapsed into one of his suspenseful dry spells. A week went by. Public anxiety mounted, especially among Bos-ton fans. Ten days and nothing. (Not quite nothing, actually, since Babe maintained his place among the league's top ten batters at

.325.) Eleven days. With only a week to go in the season his home-run total remained at 26.

As a late-season revenue generator for a sixth-place team, the Red Sox front office had designated Saturday, September 20, Babe Ruth Day and announced that the slugger would pitch the first game of a doubleheader against the league-leading White Sox. Fenway Park overflowed for the occasion. On Jersey Street thousands jostled one another as they sought scarce tickets from scalpers. It was the sort of setting that Ruth would revel in throughout his career. For Babe, there was no such thing as too much limelight or too much adulation. Before the first game Boston admirers presented their hero with a carload of gifts, including a diamond ring. Flint-hearted Red Sox owner Harry Frazee limited his contribution to a ten-cent cigar.

Outside Fenway Park, Boston was still feeling the effects of the police strike. In the steel towns of Pennsylvania, Ohio, Indiana, and Illinois, labor troubles had reached the flash point. Striking steel workers and strike breakers were actually shooting one another. In Washington, some officials muttered that the country might have to be put under martial law. Inside the ballpark, however, you would not have suspected that there was grave social unrest in the nation. Here, nothing was important except Babe Ruth Day and the possibility of a new all-time home-run mark.

Despite his impressive outing on Labor Day, Ruth's pitching arm was rusty. After blowing a 3-run lead and letting Chicago tie the game in the sixth inning, he had to be relieved. Disappointed, the Babe went to left field to finish the game. Then, with 1 out in the bottom of the ninth, he came to bat with local fans exhorting him to "paahk one on the Common, Babe." Metaphorically, he did. He hit a tremendous home run over the left-center-field wall off Lefty Williams to beat the White Sox, 4 to 3.

At the point where the ball left the park, the wall was 37 feet high and more than 400 feet from the plate. As the home run cleared the barrier with plenty to spare, the cheers of the partisan crowd must have been heard on the far side of the Charles. Players on both teams were bug-eyed. For a left-handed batter to hit such a blow to left field off one of the best left-handed pitchers in the league defied baseball norms. Between games White

Sox third baseman George "Buck" Weaver visited the Red Sox dugout to tell Ruth, "That was the greatest poke I've ever seen."

When the cheering had died down, some Calvinist in the press box reminded everyone that although Ruth had tied Williamson, he had not yet passed him. And there were just six games left in the abbreviated season. It would have rivaled the Tea Party in Boston lore had Ruth set the new all-time record in the second game of the doubleheader. Life rarely generates such scenarios.

It was more fitting that Ruth waited until September 24, when the Red Sox were at the Polo Grounds in New York for their final series with the Yankees. This was the park where he had hit his first major-league home run and where, in the future, he would achieve his greatest fame. When, in the top of the ninth with his team trailing by a run, Ruth hit number 28 over the roof of the second deck in right field off the Yankees' 20-game winner, Bob Shawkey, it became official. Babe Ruth had passed Williamson to become the greatest home-run hitter of all time and all places, including Cook County, Illinois.

In a Ruthian grace note, on Saturday, September 27, in the next-to-last game of the season, Babe hit number 29 off Rip Jordan at spacious Griffith Stadium in Washington. Predictably, it was hailed as the longest home run ever hit in Washington, and it gave the Babe a home run in each park in the league for the season, something that had never before been achieved.

Ruth appeared in only 130 games in 1919. Had the major leagues played a full schedule of 154, it is reasonable to assume that he would have hit 30 or more home runs. In any case, 29 proved enough to mesmerize the country. The Babe's closest rival in either league was the doughty thirty-eight-year-old Gavvy Cravath of the Phillies, with 12. No one else had more than 10. A new kind of sports king had been crowned, one truly larger than life.

Partly forgotten in the excitement generated by Ruth's home-run exploits was the fact that in his first year as a regular outfielder he batted .322. In the National League that year, it would have made him batting champion. In his own league it was good enough for ninth spot. In addition to his sensational hitting, Ruth also led all major-league outfielders in fielding percentage. He made only 2 errors and had 16 assists in 246 chances. To round out his extraordinary year, he won 9 of 14 decisions as a pitcher for a team that finished 21½ games out of first place. Here was Frank Merriwell made flesh.

In the seasons immediately ahead, the influence of Ruth's new style of hitting on other players would be unmistakable. Many batters of appropriate size and strength—Bob Meusel of the Yankees, his brother Emil "Irish" Meusel of the Phillies, George Kelly of the Giants, Harry Heilmann of the Tigers, Rogers Hornsby of the Cardinals, and others—committed themselves to the free swing and the long ball without suffering loss to their batting averages.

More profound and far-reaching effects of Ruth's 1919 season are less easy to measure. Throughout the country there had to be college, high school, and even sandlot ballplayers pondering the Babe's performance. What their coaches had been telling them was obviously not true. Choking up on the bat and trying to poke the ball past an infielder was clearly not the only way to a high average, success, and fame on the diamond, especially if you had broad shoulders. We can guess that many strong young hands began to slide down to the knob of the bat as cheap spikes or sneakers dug in at the plate. Within a year seventeen-year-old Henry Louis Gehrig, a pitcher and sometime first baseman at New York's High School of Commerce, who would someday be Ruth's teammate, broke up a schoolboy championship game at Chicago's Wrigley Field with a grand-slam home run. The national pastime had turned a corner.

In the excitement stirred by Ruth's slugging, it looked as though the 1919 World Series might prove an anticlimax. The Chicago White Sox were a prohibitive favorite to beat a patchwork Cincinnati team with good pitching that had managed to finish 9 games ahead of the New York Giants. Handicapped by a two-man pitching staff, Giant manager John McGraw had been additionally hampered by the presence on the roster of a couple of corrupt players, Hal Chase and Heinie Zimmerman, ironically both former batting champions. It took guts for McGraw to fire the two in September on suspicion of fixing games. In any case, by midsummer, Cincinnati's superior pitching had made itself evident and the Reds won easily.

The White Sox's modest 3½-game margin over the hard-driving Cleveland Indians obscured the ease with which the Sox had, in fact, taken the pennant. In the light of history it seems entirely possible that some Chicago players may have been dogging it in the final months of the season.

Cincinnati's upset victory in the Series, 5 games to 3 (the major leagues were experimenting with a best-of-nine formula), caught everyone off guard and set tongues to wagging about the validity of the results. Many persons who attended the series, however, testified that they noted nothing in the Sox's performance that could be pointed to as flagrant dereliction. Still, the question remained, how was it possible that a team like the Reds could beat Lefty Williams *three* times and the superb Ed Cicotte twice? The Black Sox had been consummately subtle in their betrayal. Almost a year would pass before the truth about the rigged World Series was uncovered.

While no one approached Ruth in home-run power, 1919 was a banner year for hitters, especially in the American League. Detroit's Ty Cobb won his twelfth batting title with an average of .384, his highest mark in six years. Three other American Leaguers finished above .350: Detroit's Bobby Veach, Chicago's Joe Jackson, and St. Louis's George Sisler. American League batters made almost the same total of hits in a schedule of 140 games as they had in the regular schedule of 1917.

The National Leaguers improved their numbers too, but in less spectacular fashion. A modest .321 was enough to win the batting championship for Cincinnati's center fielder Edd Roush, but the league had doubled the number of its .300 hitters since 1917.

It remains a mystery why for a couple of seasons the National League lagged behind the American in improved batting. Except for the color of the stitching (red and black for the National, red and blue for the American), the ball used was identical in both leagues. It might be argued that National Leaguers were deprived of direct contact with Babe Ruth and his new style, but they saw him in spring training and knew what he was up to. It may be significant that the National League was traditionally the more conservative and dominated by veteran managers like John McGraw, Brooklyn's Wilbert Robinson, Boston's George Stallings, and St. Louis's Branch Rickey—men you would expect to be cautious about giving their young players freedom to bat as they wished.

Perhaps the biggest winners in 1919 were the people who held stock in major-league clubs. Attendance was phenomenal. Here again, the American League led the way, with a paid attendance of 3,654,236, an increase of 22 percent over what the league had drawn in 1917. Had the American League been playing a conventional schedule of 154 games, they certainly would have gone over the 4 million mark.

The National League, up 18 percent from their 1917 attendance, was not exactly feeling pain financially, except over the loss of those fourteen playing dates. With a normal schedule they would have drawn well over 3 million. To illustrate the power of tradition, the second-place New York Giants outdrew everyone in the majors both at home and on the road. Their 708,000 at home was the highest figure for the decade.

Much of the record increase in American League attendance in 1919 may be ascribed to postwar exuberance, but the drawing power of Ruth's hitting must have played a role as well. With no pennant race to speak of except during a brief slump by the White Sox in June, four American League clubs—Chicago, Cleveland, New York, and Detroit—drew well over half a million at home. The also-ran Red Sox were not far behind. We can only guess what the league's attendance might have been had Ruth gotten off to a strong start instead of languishing until July.

Attendance in 1919 was also helped by the long-overdue legalization of Sunday baseball in New York. Incredibly, until the New York legislature passed a bill in April 1919 providing for local option, baseball—indeed virtually all recreational activities—had been forbidden on Sunday by law. The ban meant that you couldn't even play catch in your backyard. As soon as Governor Al Smith signed the new bill, the New York City Council approved baseball on Sundays after two P.M. On May 4, more than 35,000 New Yorkers crowded the Polo Grounds to enjoy the novelty. At Brooklyn's Ebbets Field on the same day, there was a capacity crowd of 25,000.

Sunday baseball had long been legal in St. Louis, Chicago, and

Cincinnati, where large German and Roman Catholic populations held a Continental view of the Sabbath. Before the end of World War I, democracy had gradually triumphed over Sabbatarianism in Washington, D.C., Detroit, and Cleveland as well. New York was emancipated in 1919. But Massachusetts clung to its Blue Law for another decade, and Pennsylvania until 1934.

In Boston, Ruth's long-ball heroics in 1919 may have salved some of the disappointment at the Red Sox's sixth-place finish. Still, Sox fans were accustomed to championships, not second-division finishes. With a pitching staff that included Herb Pennock, "Sad Sam" Jones, Waite Hoyt, and Allan Russell, and with Babe Ruth leading the attack, there was good reason to expect that the team would do much better in 1920. Little did Hub fans suspect what horror the future held for them.

On the day after Christmas, Harry Frazee closed a deal with New York Yankee owners Ruppert and Huston in which he sold Ruth's contract for a reported $100,000 in cash plus a loan of $300,000 against a mortgage on Fenway Park. In a perverse gesture of deference to the Christmas season, Frazee held up public announcement of the deal until early January. But the pact was irrevocable. Babe Ruth and his booming bat were on their way to New York and the Polo Grounds. The twenties were about to roar.

TWO

THE
YEAR OF
WONDERS

"If I'd just tried for them dinky singles I
could've batted around six hundred."
—BABE RUTH

ACCORDING TO THE Gregorian calendar, the decade of the 1920s
would not begin, strictly speaking, until 12:01 A.M. on January 1,
1921. In January 1920, however, most Americans didn't concern
themselves with such arithmetical subtleties. It was enough for
them that after a troubling decade, a significant integer in the
date had changed and seemed to offer them a fresh start.

The year opened with the trace of a smile on its face, perhaps
a sardonic one, but a smile nonetheless. The bulk of the nation's
strikes had been settled or had fizzled out. Postwar inflation showed
small but encouraging signs that it had peaked. Above all, the war
to end wars had been won, the peace nailed down after a fashion,
and the doughboys were home again in clean, comfortable, boun-
tiful America, where they belonged. The future held infinite
promise, particularly for the young, white, and sound of limb.
Not for nothing has the period of the 1920s been called "the last
brief holiday from fear."

As regards America's pleasure principle, on January 6 and 16
two stories broke that would directly impinge upon it. On the
sixth the Boston Red Sox belatedly revealed the sale of Babe Ruth

to the New York Yankees. Ten days later the Eighteenth Amendment to the United States Constitution, prohibiting "the sale, manufacture, or transportation of alcoholic beverages," became law, since exactly one year earlier it had been ratified by three quarters of the states. The country was in store for some unprecedented slugging and defiant drinking.

In spite of the record price paid, the Yankees' deal for Ruth must rank as the most profitable ever made by a major-league club. The Babe would help transform what had a few years earlier been a down-at-the-heels franchise into the colossus of professional sports.

When the sale was announced, Ruth protested noisily (his customary style) that he was happy in Boston and, in fact, might quit the game in favor of a business career rather than report to New York. It is doubtful that he fooled anyone. *The Sporting News,* for example, headlined the story, RUTH'S LIKING FOR BOSTON IS PATHETIC. The Babe could not have been thoroughly happy in Boston. Owner Harry Frazee was a tightwad and made little effort to conceal his contempt for ballplayers. Besides, the Hub was too small an arena for Ruth's gargantuan talents and ego.

In all likelihood Ruth was angling for a share of the purchase price, a common maneuver among players at the time. For all his apparent lack of sophistication, the new home-run king had a keen sense of his value at the ticket window. He was probably the first player of this century to hire a publicist and agent of sorts, a man named John Igoe. Under baseball rules then in force, however, Ruth had to negotiate his contract in person.

The Yankee owners—New York National Guard Colonel Jacob Ruppert, courtly heir to a New York City brewing fortune, and Army Reserve Colonel Tillinghast L'Hommedieu Huston, a homespun Hoosier engineer—were a pair of open-handed millionaires who desperately wanted a winner in New York. The colonels quickly demonstrated how simple it is to persuade even the most homesick ballplayer to report to a new club. They tore up Ruth's existing three-year contract and doubled his annual salary to $20,000. Moreover, the new contract stipulated that the big left-hander was not required to pitch a single inning to earn the pay. Huston had scarcely hung up the phone before Ruth booked a Boston & Maine sleeper for New York.

At the winter meetings in December 1919, the major leagues had approved a long-overdue piece of internal legislation, one that would profoundly influence the future of baseball: They outlawed the noisome spitball along with its cousins, the licorice ball, the slippery elm ball, the emery ball, the mud ball, and others. It is more accurate to say that the baseball elders *virtually* outlawed the trick pitches. The initial ruling was that for the 1920 season only, each club might designate two of its pitchers to continue to use trick deliveries. At the end of the season, the wet one and its fellows were to be banished forever.

Perhaps fearing to be charged with unfair labor practice (something they engaged in constantly anyway) the owners ultimately fudged their decision. For the 1921 season and beyond, they added a grandfather clause to the prohibition. The second ruling permitted eight National League and nine American League spitball pitchers to register as incapable of holding their jobs if deprived of the special pitch. The seventeen were authorized to use trick pitches without penalty for the remainder of their careers. In other words, about 20 percent of the starting pitchers in the majors would continue to throw the spitter legally and God knows how many illegally. Still, some rule was better than no rule, and on balance even the qualified stricture must have aided the hitters greatly.

The Yankees' 1920 spring-training camp at Jacksonville, Florida, proved to be the most exciting that the club had ever known. No fewer than thirteen New York writers were assigned to cover the team. As long as Ruth was present, even a press corps of that size had little trouble generating copy. In fact, the writers had to hustle to cover all of the Babe's spring activities, a policy that condemned them to some sleepless nights. On the eve of the season's opener at Philadelphia, presumably indifferent to a throbbing head and red-rimmed eyes, Ruth assured reporters that he would hit 50 home runs. Asked to comment on his undistinguished performance in spring exhibition games (.314 BA, 1 homer), the fun-loving slugger said, "Spring training doesn't mean a thing."

There is an oft-repeated story of Ruth's 1920 life-style that involves Frank "Ping" Bodie, one of the first Italian-Americans to achieve stardom in the big leagues. Bodie was assigned to room with Ruth during spring training. One day a New York baseball writer stopped Bodie in the hotel lobby. "Tell me, Ping," the reporter asked, "what kind of a guy is Ruth, really?"

"Sorry, I have no idea," Bodie answered.

Miffed at what appeared to be a brush-off from the normally jovial and accessible San Franciscan, the reporter responded sharply. "Well, you room with him, don't you?"

"Wrong," Bodie said. "I room with his suitcase."

When the season opened, Ruth repeated his listless start of 1919. More than two weeks passed and he failed to hit a home run. This time he did not have the excuse that he was tired from having to pitch. New York fans grew restless. Owners Ruppert and Huston too may have been feeling uneasy about their enormous investment. Actually, there was not a thing to worry about. The Babe was just catching up on lost sleep and steaming the last of the mint julep out of his system. On Saturday, May 1, at the Polo Grounds, he hit his first home run as a Yankee. Appropriately, it came against the Red Sox and a former pitching mate, Herb Pennock, one of the slickest left-handers in the history of the game.

On the same afternoon at Braves Field in Boston, the Braves and the Brooklyn Robins (nicknamed for their colorful manager Wilbert Robinson) played a twenty-six-inning 1-to-1 tie, the longest big-league game on record. Brooklyn's Leon Cadore and Boston's Joe Oeschger pitched the entire game. The Robins scored once in the fifth inning, and the Braves tied it in the sixth. After that it was all zeroes until the umpire was forced to call the game because of darkness. Symbolically, this odd contest rang down the curtain on two decades of low-scoring games. In the 1920s, hits and runs would be plentiful regardless of how close the contests.

Having broken the ice against Pennock, Ruth went on a tear and hit 12 home runs in May, improving on the major-league record he had set in July 1919. Again, as in 1919, most of his homers came against the league's strongest pitchers: Sad Sam Jones, Dickie Kerr, Lefty Williams, Dutch Leonard, Hooks Dauss, Joe Bush, and others. The Babe's shot off his old pitching rival, the great Walter Johnson, in the second game of the Memorial Day doubleheader hit the façade above the upper deck in right field at the Polo Grounds, and, in the words of one New York writer, "almost tore away part of the roof." Comfortably settled into his new surroundings, Ruth was on his way to what John Thorn and Pete Palmer in *The Hidden Game of Baseball* have assessed as "the best [season] any mortal ever had."

Of the first 16 home runs Ruth hit at the Polo Grounds in 1920, all went over the roof or into the second deck. Only one other man had ever cleared that roof—Joe Jackson—and that was back in 1915. By the end of May the groundskeepers at the Polo Grounds had extended the foul poles to the roof of the park to initiate that custom in the major leagues.

Ruth established himself early on not only as a hitter of long home runs but also as the creator of the highest pop flies ever seen. The phenomenon may have been the result of his pronounced uppercut swing. In any case, the "sky-pop" became a Ruth trademark. Understandably, such towering flies were hard to catch, especially in the afternoon sunshine, and over the years Ruth and his fans enjoyed many laughs as bewildered fielders staggered about trying to guess the point of reentry.

Jimmy Dykes, an excellent second baseman with the Philadelphia Athletics, was an early victim of a Ruth sky-pop. Dykes lurched uncertainly, trying to draw a bead on the ball. By the time it fell behind the embarrassed infielder untouched, Ruth stood on second, laughing. But the laugh was on Babe. The scorer ruled the play an error.

In the spring of 1920 Ruth wasn't the only one in the Yankee batting order hitting home runs. Several of his new teammates—Ping Bodie, Bob Meusel, Wally Pipp, Aaron Ward, Del Pratt—must have been studying the Babe's style throughout that thunderous May. Ruth made swinging from the heels look easy—and profitable. As June opened everyone wanted to get into the act. On the third, Ping Bodie hit a grand slam to beat Philadelphia. On the following day, second baseman Del Pratt hit another grand slam as the New Yorkers beat the Athletics a second time. The Yankees collected 13 homers in five days. For the month they hit a record 27, including another 12 by Ruth.

Despite the Yankees' record pace in home runs, they held no

monopoly on the long ball. The Ruth fever was spreading. At Philadelphia on June 23, as the Athletics pounded the Detroit Tigers 15 to 9, the two clubs collected 8 home runs between them, an unheard-of total for a single game. In 1917 that would have been well over a week's production of homers for the entire league. "The real hero of this season," a New York writer commented, "will be the man who can . . . pitch a no-hitter." Appropriately, that hero turned out to be Walter Johnson, who no-hit the Boston Red Sox on July 1, the first of only nine no-hitters pitched in the majors during the 1920s.

In 1919 cartoonist Robert "Believe It or Not" Ripley had waggishly labeled the Yankee batting order of Roger Peckinpaugh, Wally Pipp, Frank "Home Run" Baker, Del Pratt, and Ping Bodie "Murderers' Row." Collectively they batted .289 for the year and had 34 homers, impressive numbers for the time. With the addition in 1920 of Babe Ruth and rookie slugger Bob Meusel, the Yankees had turned into a real Murderers' Row, a team tradition that would culminate in the fabled batting order of 1927.

The burst of home runs by Ruth and the Yankees in May and June sent New Yorkers into a baseball frenzy. The old brass turnstiles at the Polo Grounds went into a free spin as thousands of newly won fans rushed to see the sluggers in action. In the afternoon game of a doubleheader on May 31, the Yankees set a new major-league single-game attendance record of 38,688. It was the custom in the case of scheduled doubleheaders (Memorial Day, July Fourth, Labor Day) to play the first game in the morning, empty the park, and charge a second admission for the afternoon. Since the Yankees had drawn more than 11,000 for the morning game, it meant that they sold about 50,000 tickets for the day. For those times, it added up to an extraordinarily profitable one. In the first week of June, Ruth and his supporting cast would play before more than 150,000, about half of what the Yankees had drawn for the entire 1917 season.

On June 7 the Yankees took their power circus on the road. With Ruth as the major attraction, the team's swing around the league resembled the triumphal procession of a monarch and his courtiers. Fans everywhere seemed as excited about the Babe as those in New York did. On June 13 the Yanks helped set a new single-game attendance record in Cleveland, and on the twentieth, another in St. Louis. In April the Yankees had already helped to set a new single-game record at Boston on the occasion of Ruth's first appearance at Fenway Park in his New York uniform.

Almost seventy years removed from the scene, it is difficult to measure the popular impact of Ruth's early home-run exploits. The bare record suggests that it was phenomenal. As a national athletic hero, the Babe had little competition from stars in other sports, with the possible exception of heavyweight champ Jack Dempsey. And boxing was a sport not quite respectable, not even legal in many states, including New York.

Golf and tennis were essentially country-club activities. Americans who did not belong to private clubs rarely saw them played. Professional football was in its infancy, and the college game was played on campus, essentially off limits for working-class fans. Among the few fully developed professional spectator sports, boxing and horse racing commanded a narrow focus of followers, and these were at the very top and bottom of the social scale. For the bulk of American sports fans—and here we really mean men—baseball was synonymous with sports, and Babe Ruth had become its dominant figure. Still living within the shadow of a terrible war and slowly emerging from three centuries of Puritan-designed torpor, America of 1920 was ripe to be turned on by something—anything. It proved to be the home run and its principal artisan, Babe Ruth.

Quick to sense the national mood, baseball writers busied themselves reinforcing it with gaudy prose about the Babe and his escapades, both on and off the field. Reporters competed in coining silly epithets to characterize Ruthian prowess at bat. Sultan of Swat, Wizard of Wallop, Prince of Punch, Monarch of Maul, Battering Babe, King of Klout, Titan of Thump, Behemoth of Bust, and on and on. Among the dozens that must have rolled from battered typewriters in the smoke-filled press boxes, only Sultan of Swat seems to have stuck.

Much of the sports writing of the early 1920s tended to be playfully baroque anyway. Since not all newspapers of the time granted by-lines to mere baseball writers (a surprising number of whom were Ivy League graduates), it may be that anonymity was an invitation to extravagance in language. An account in the staid *New York Times* on June 3, 1920, of a Yankee win over the Washington Senators opened with this sentence: "The fruitful bat of the unmatchable Babe Ruth carried him still higher into the realm of greatness up under Coogan's Bluff yesterday, the swaggering swat king blistering the ball for three home runs in the double-header with Washington as a crowd of 28,000 people fumed and fussed in the midsummer heat and sang the praises of the fencebuster in as thunderous a community chorus of cheers as ever jarred the eardrums of the gay populace." Imagine how the game might have been described in less distinguished New York journals.

Later the same month, a *Times* reporter (not necessarily the same one) wrote of Ruth: "He has become a national curiosity and the sightseeing Pilgrims who daily flock into Manhattan are as anxious to rest eyes on him as they are to see the Woolworth Building. . . ."

Not everyone was thrilled with, or approved of, the revolutionary increase in home runs. *The Sporting News,* good and gray, reported Ruth's derring-do but without enthusiasm. And demonstrating the hazards of publication lead time for even the most cautious of magazine editors, F. C. Lane, assessing Ruth's 1919 performance in the July 1920 issue of *Baseball Magazine,* wrote: "The probability that he would ever again make twenty-nine home runs in a single season was remote." When the issue went on sale, the Babe already had 24 homers, with three months yet to play.

More important to veteran Yankee fans than Ruth's slugging had to be the realization that for the first time since 1906 their team was a serious contender for the American League pennant. As July opened, the Yankees found themselves in the unfamiliar atmosphere of first place, where they daily had to fight off the challenge of the second-place Cleveland Indians. In hot pursuit of both, just a few games off the pace, was the defending champion, the Chicago White Sox.

In early July, while the Yankees were still on the road, Ruth's home-run bat cooled. But he was hardly in what could be called a slump; he was batting .372. On July 9, back at his beloved Polo

Grounds, Babe found the range again and teed off against Detroit left-hander Red Oldham for homer number 25. Less than a week later he tied his 1919 record of 29. It was only July 15. The Yankees had sixty-one games to play. It meant that every time the Babe came to bat in the next two and a half months he was in position to set a record.

On the weekend of July 17 the rugged Chicago White Sox arrived in New York for an important 6-game series. The Sox were now just 3 games behind the Yankees, who had slipped to second place. New York fans were transported. The Yankee owners themselves could not have contrived a better formula for filling the ballpark. To heighten the excitement in the city, Sir Thomas Lipton, the genial Irish baronet and tea merchant, had arrived in the United States in his sleek sailing yacht, *Shamrock IV,* to challenge for the America's Cup—and he would do it not in snooty, remote Newport, Rhode Island, but right in New York Harbor, under the gaze of the Statue of Liberty.

In the midst of this exhilarating weekend, *The New York Times,* in a highly unscientific poll, concluded that the America's Cup races were generating more interest among sports fans than were Babe Ruth and the crucial White Sox series. Periodic updates of the ball games had been posted on the Seventh Avenue side of the building and news of the yacht race on the Broadway side. The editors noted (and seemed just a bit pleased) that larger crowds gathered on the Broadway side. Still, you can bet that anyone at the Polo Grounds that weekend considered himself lucky to be there.

On the eve of the big series, it is doubtful that there was a baseball fan anywhere who wasn't aware that Ruth's next home run would make him the first man in major-league history to hit 30 in a season. The Babe played to a familiar script. He would keep the fans waiting.

The opening game of the Yankees–White Sox series offered a hint of what baseball would be like for the remainder of this eventful season and indeed for much of the era. It matched New York's Carl Mays and Chicago's Ed Cicotte, the league's two best right-handers after Walter Johnson. Yet, the Yankees beat the visitors, 20 to 5, collecting 21 hits for 40 bases, including 3 home runs. The winners drew not a single walk. For their part the White Sox made 15 hits but had trouble bunching them. They managed 1 walk.

What marks the game as characteristic of the early 1920s is that amid this shower of base hits, 14 of them for extra bases, not a single Yankee batter struck out and only two in the White Sox lineup did. (Also characteristic of the age was the loose fielding—9 errors in the game, 4 by Chicago's star third baseman, Buck Weaver.)

Unhappily for local fans, Ruth contributed no homers to the tidy rout. Who cared that the Babe was 3 for 5 and was batting over .375? The fans, especially new fans, had come in hopes of seeing him set a home-run record. That afternoon 36,000 went home on the El disappointed.

On Sunday, July 18, 30,000 New Yorkers defied threatening weather lest they miss the big moment. Once more Babe left them frustrated. Between rain showers, the Yankees beat the White Sox a second time, 8 to 4. The batting fireworks were provided by Ping Bodie rather than his elusive roommate, as Ping hit his second grand slam in six weeks and drove in 6 runs. Despite continuing bad weather, again on Monday a crowd of 28,000 hopefuls showed up at the Polo Grounds, this time for a double-header. At last the Sultan of Swat delivered, but as usual he kept his feverish subjects waiting until the second game.

In the first game Ping Bodie homered again as the Yankees won, 8 to 2, to make it three straight over the Sox. In the fourth inning of the nightcap, at long last, Ruth hammered one of left-hander Dickie Kerr's curveballs into the right-center-field bleachers for home run number 30. Fans demonstrated their relief and pleasure by tossing straw hats in the air. No player had ever hit a longer ball at the Polo Grounds save Ruth himself. In the ninth inning Babe hit another homer of more modest dimensions, but despite his effort plus a third Yankee home run by Peckinpaugh, New York lost its first game of the important series, 8 to 5.

Although the Yankees had failed to gain ground on Cleveland, the White Sox series must have brought joy to the club treasurer. Between Saturday and Tuesday, Ruth and his mates had pulled 129,000 fans into a park that seated less than 40,000. It was only

July and the colonels had recouped Ruth's purchase price plus some pocket change.

The Yankees, after hitting a startling 27 home runs in June, increased their total for July to 38. The club had already almost doubled its total of home runs for the entire season of 1919. Nothing approaching the Yanks' early-summer display of power had ever been seen before. But while the New Yorkers may have been rewriting the book on power, they were not the only team meeting the ball squarely. The Indians, White Sox, and Browns all were on a pace that promised to make them the first major-league teams of the twentieth century to bat over .300.

Despite the special burdens that came with his first full year as playing manager, Cleveland center fielder Tris Speaker was having the greatest season of his already outstanding career. In addition to himself Speaker had six .300 hitters in the lineup. "Spoke" had come to the majors with the Boston Red Sox in 1909 and quickly established himself as one of the five best hitters in baseball along with Cobb, Jackson, Pittsburgh's Honus Wagner, and Cleveland's Napoleon Lajoie. In 1916, when Speaker batted .386, he interrupted Cobb's string of nine consecutive batting titles.

In addition to being an outstanding hitter, Speaker was universally regarded as the greatest center fielder in baseball, a man who played so shallow that he occasionally made putouts at second base. As the 1920s progressed, however, and the long ball became the fashion, even Spoke found himself forced to play deeper.

In St. Louis, George Sisler, the Browns' remarkably graceful first baseman, was batting well over .400, a pace he would hold for the rest of the season. In addition, after five years in the majors, "Gorgeous George" had turned into something of a slugger. His teammates were not nodding at the plate either. The entire St. Louis outfield of Jack Tobin, Ken Williams, and William "Baby Doll" Jacobson was batting over .350.

To no one's surprise, Chicago's Joe Jackson, the prototype natural hitter, was keeping his average close to .380. In midsummer it must have been unimaginable, especially among adoring White Sox fans, that 1920 would be Shoeless Joe's final season in

Organized Baseball. Alluding to the Black Sox conspiracy, James T. Farrell wrote years later, "The defection of Joe Jackson hurt Chicago fans more than did that of any of the others."

Jackson's teammate Eddie Collins, who unlike Joe batted scientifically, was also hitting close to .380 and would finish the season with the highest average of his distinguished career. The new era, it appears, was kind to every type of batter. Collins, one of the finest second basemen in baseball history, had averaged .324 since breaking in with the Philadelphia Athletics in 1908. From 1920 until his retirement from regular play in 1927, he would bat .346. Collins, the White Sox field captain, was so patently incorruptible that the gamblers who fixed the 1919 World Series never even considered approaching him.

In the National League, where Ruth's trick of uppercutting the ball seemed slower to catch on, home-run production in 1920 remained modest. Plain old contact hitting, however, was very much in style and batting averages climbed rapidly. In particular, Rogers Hornsby was putting on an exhibition that would see his 1919 average of .318 increase by more than 50 percentage points.

Ironically, it was Ty Cobb, the undisputed master of the base hit, who appeared momentarily disoriented by the changes under way in baseball. After skipping spring training to avoid the discomforts of the exhibition schedule, Cobb had gotten off to the worst start of his career. It was early May before he pulled his batting average above .200. On the Tigers' first visit to the Polo Grounds late in the month, the New York writers were merciless in reminding "The Georgia Peach" that he had been displaced by Babe Ruth as the greatest name in baseball. While Ruth was blasting a couple of game-winning homers to go with an assortment of lesser hits, Cobb had only a single to show for the 3-game series. If Cobb was feeling the pain of dethronement, he nevertheless maintained his silence and his dignity. The sophisticated New York writers should have known better than to pen an obituary for Ty Cobb. In spite of sustaining the worst injury of his career in June, one that kept him on crutches for a month, the fiery Georgian would finish with a respectable .334 batting average and produce 147 runs in 112 games.

By midsummer, as major-league batters continued to hit home runs in record numbers, charges surfaced that the owners had introduced a rabbit ball. The complaint came largely from base-ball writers. One whimsical plaintiff suggested that if you held a baseball to your ear, you could hear the rabbit's heartbeat. Babe Ruth, hardly a disinterested party, told Frank McNeill of the New York *Evening Sun* that stories about a juiced-up ball were "a lot of bunk" and that it was the same ball that he had been hitting 400 feet and more since back in 1915. Well, maybe Babe didn't say *bunk* exactly, but the *Sun* was a family paper and, anyway, the readers were in no doubt about Babe's position.

Ruth was not the only player to dispute that there had been a change in the ball. Rogers Hornsby declared flatly, "The lively ball is a myth." In the press boxes, however, denials fell on deaf ears. By 1921 the charges of ball tampering would reach levels of hysteria.

At the end of July Ruth had 37 homers. If he maintained the pace, he would hit 61 for the season. The idea was incredible (though probably not to Ruth himself). At this point, the country went Babe Ruth crazy. In American League cities, people who had never before been within a mile of the ballpark fought for tickets whenever it was announced that the Yankees were com-ing to town. Parks filled hours before game time so that fans would not miss Babe taking batting practice. A few newcomers to base-ball were known to leave a game as soon as it appeared that Ruth had taken his last turn at bat. Wherever the Babe hit a homer, fans cheered wildly, even if it had been struck against the home team. Frequently spectators fainted.

At least one hormonal response to a Ruth home run was med-ically documented. In a deadpan report to the press, a consor-tium of nerve specialists, acting under the aegis of the United Hospital Fund, explained what happened when one of the Babe's drives cleared the fence: "The superenal gland affects the insolu-ble glycogen so as to change it to glucose; the thyroid gland af-fects the body's proteid metabolism so as to supply new proteid substances for those which are broken down, and the crowd, dis-playing mass emotional instability, acting along the familiar line of mob psychology, brings about a general demonstration in which individual participation is wholly involuntary." In short, when one fan went nuts, they all did.

As was bound to happen in the course of such a season, on

August 19 at the Polo Grounds, a fan collapsed from the excitement and died as Ruth hit home run number 43 over the right-
field grandstand roof off Ray Caldwell of Cleveland.

Ruth's exploits were viewed as so extraordinary that he was
sought by medical research organizations for testing. Eagerly they
charted responses and reflexes and found him exceeding the ceil-
ings of their scales. "One man in a million," a Columbia University Medical School test assessed him. In Ohio a professor of physics
named Hodges spent weeks ciphering on foolscap and announced to the nation that his calculations showed the Babe generating 44 horsepower every time he leaned on one of those
fastballs. In fact, Hodges said, they were leaving the bat at a ve-
locity of 500 feet per second.

Though it is doubtful that Ruth ever read Professor Hodges's
monograph, on occasion he expressed to reporters his fear that
one day he would kill a pitcher with a line drive. Before we dis-
miss Babe's furrowed brow as another instance of Ruthian mega-
lomania, let's consider unscientific but perhaps more convincing
evidence of how hard he could hit a baseball. A more sober and
reflective witness than George Sisler can hardly be imagined. In
a book written after his retirement, Sisler tells of being a spectator at Game Four of the 1926 World Series between the Yankees
and the Cardinals at Sportsman's Park. In the sixth inning, Ruth,
who already had 2 homers in the game, hit a line drive off Cardinal reliever Herman Bell. Sisler confesses that for just an instant
he felt that if St. Louis center fielder Taylor Douthit had gotten a
good jump he might scoop the sinking drive off his shoe tops. In
fact, the ball kept rising until it came to rest in the bleachers a
good 430 feet from the plate.

An equally reliable witness, veteran baseball writer Tom Meany,
describes in one of his books his immediate reaction to Ruth's
famous called-shot homer in Game Three of the 1932 World Series between the Yankees and the Chicago Cubs. As Ruth made
contact with the pitch Meany was honestly convinced that Chicago second baseman Billy Herman would make an easy catch of
the line drive on the grass behind second. The ball sailed over
the Wrigley Field tiny bleachers, 445 feet away—the first ball
ever to clear them.

Finally, there is the barroom tale that Ruth hit a ball between the legs of Washington pitcher Hod Lisenbee that carried over the center fielder's head. No, not even the immortal Babe could play so fast and loose with gravity. I am sufficiently awed by credible witnesses affirming that the ball passed under Lisenbee and carried to center field before landing.

In our media-suffused age, when celebrities appear at times to outnumber autograph seekers, it is hard to imagine the magnitude of Ruth's impact not only on the sports page but also on the entire realm of feature news. There was only one medium— print. But there was a lot of it. New York City, for example, had thirteen daily newspapers, not counting those in foreign languages, and it was not unusual for cities of 20,000 population to have two.

In addition to newspapers, there were, perhaps, two dozen periodicals with national circulation. Almost all were true magazines, that is, general interest, unlike today's mass of periodicals, most of which address single interests. In the 1920s there was nothing incongruous in an article on Ruth appearing in the *Literary Digest*.

At a rough estimate, fewer than 5 million Americans ever actually *saw* Ruth play in a major-league game. Yet, except for military and political heroes, his may have been the first celebrity name in the country's history to become a household word. His fame spanned all classes, age groups, and ethnic communities. The nickname Bambino, for example, is said to have originated among new immigrants from Italy. Manufacturers fought for Ruth's endorsement of their products, regardless of whether the product was connected with sports. Politicians sought his vote and women his favor. He is not known to have turned many of them away.

For several years after 1920, it must have been difficult to pick up a newspaper or periodical during baseball season without encountering a story on the Sultan of Swat. In a syndicated feature, "What Ruth Did Today," which appeared in hundreds of papers, his every activity on the field was tabulated for an eager public. Not infrequently his escapades made the front page, especially when he suffered one of his frequent (and mostly minor) injuries.

As a case in point, on July 6, 1920, while traveling by automobile from Washington to Philadelphia, Ruth, a notoriously careless driver, rolled his brand new touring car. With him were his wife and three teammates, but miraculously no one was seriously hurt. Inevitably, an excited informant persuaded the press that Ruth had been killed. When word was flashed to the world, at least one London paper responded with a prominent obituary.

Some historian—Thucydides, or maybe it was Macaulay—observed that extraordinary men are likely to surface in times uniquely compatible with their talents. The idea often touches off debate on whether the man helped create the time or the time the man. Certainly, Babe Ruth did not create the Roaring Twenties. Neither did the decade create him. He had been a big-league star since 1915. Yet, while his revolutionary bat and supernova personality might have been welcome in any period of baseball history, the Sultan of Swat appeared at precisely the right moment. Even his dramatic mid-career switch from pitcher to outfielder was timed perfectly. Ruth's incomparable batting skills and genius for self-promotion not only had a major influence on the future of baseball and indeed all professional sports but affected national attitudes concerning the use of leisure in a democratic society as well. All this may seem a bit much to lay on the ebullient, guileless Babe, but there is no denying that he left a Ruthian-size dent in American social history.

As the 1920 season entered the hot days of August, Yankee home-run bats quieted. Except for those by Ruth, whose pace had slowed somewhat, the team hit just 5 homers during the month. Yet, Babe was anything but docile at the plate. On August 4 he was hitting .394. To show the kind of season it was, .394 made him an also-ran in the batting race. On the same date, Speaker was batting .414, Sisler .403, and Joe Jackson .397.

At about this point in the season American League pitchers became convinced that Ruth had no weakness. He had seen his last good pitch and would wind up drawing 148 bases on balls. No official record of intentional walks was kept until 1955, but newspaper accounts of games in 1920 suggest that many—perhaps a third—of Ruth's passes were ordered from the opposition bench.

By midsummer the Babe must have been arm-weary from

poking hits into left field to thwart a defense pulled far to the right. During August the Bambino managed only 7 home runs, but when he clipped Jim Shaw in Washington on the fourteenth, Ruth had, for the second year running, hit homers in every park in the league.

Although the National League had no individual hero like Babe Ruth to excite fans, it did come up with a lively pennant race. Defending champion Cincinnati and the surprising Brooklyn Robins played eyeball to eyeball from May to September. And the Giants, who in June faced the specter of finishing last, put on a stretch drive that threatened to duplicate that of the Miracle Braves of 1914. Unfortunately for McGraw, his team had waited too long to get started and the Giants finished seven games behind a spunky Brooklyn squad. The slumping Reds wound up a disappointing third.

The fatal beaning of Cleveland shortstop Ray Chapman in mid-August at the Polo Grounds cast a temporary pall over what promised to be one of the most joyous seasons in baseball history. But in a perverse way the fatality proved a boon to batters by hastening the adoption of a major-league policy that would keep fresh, clean baseballs in play for the future.

On Monday, August 16, a dull, drizzly day, Chapman, a right-handed batter, led off for the Indians in the top of the fifth inning. He batted from an exaggerated crouch and was a notorious plate-crowder. The Yankee pitcher, surly right-hander Carl Mays, was widely known to have no compunctions about throwing at batters who claimed too much of the plate. He had already hit five during the season. Even under the best weather conditions, Mays's odd underhand delivery was difficult to follow, and on this day, the ball, wet from the intermittent rain, was muddy and discolored.

According to witnesses—there were thousands, of course—Chapman seemed to lose sight of the ball. He appeared frozen as the pitch streaked toward his head, which hung out over the plate. The ball struck him in the left temple with a nauseating pop that was heard throughout much of the park. Ruth heard the sound from left field. Chapman was helped to his feet, walked a few steps, then collapsed. He was carried from the field to St.

Lawrence Hospital, where he died the following morning of a
massive skull fracture.

Many in the Cleveland organization, possibly including Chapman's close friend Tris Speaker, were convinced that Mays had
thrown at their teammate deliberately. It was a charge generated
by emotion, and there was little beyond Mays's bad reputation to
support it. The pitch had definitely been in the strike zone. Unfortunately, so had Chapman's head. Nevertheless, in their bitterness, a few of the Indian players warned publicly that Mays should
not show his face in Cleveland again. Manager Speaker, on the
other hand, whatever his convictions about Mays's culpability,
wisely held his tongue.

On the Yankees' September visit to Cleveland, manager Miller
Huggins prudently left Mays behind. If the episode affected the
moody pitcher, he gave no evidence of it on the mound. He went
on to win 26 games in 1920, and increased that to 27 the following year.

For a few days after Chapman's death, big-city dailies ran editorials decrying the time-honored but barbarous custom of the
beanball. *The New York Times* called for the official adoption of
batting helmets. Back in 1906, the clever and resourceful Roger
Bresnahan, catcher for the New York Giants and inventor of
shin guards, had designed and patented a practical batting helmet. At the time, no one was interested. Nor were there takers
in 1920. Batting helmets would not come into widespread use in
the majors until the mid-1950s, and were not made mandatory
until 1973.

As Ruth, Sisler, Hornsby, and others pounded the ball with
increasing fury through mid-season in 1920, charges by the press
of ball tampering could no longer be ignored. A group identified
only as "friends of Babe Ruth" gathered a number of the baseballs
that Ruth had actually hit into the stands that spring and took
them for testing to the United States Bureau of Standards in
Washington, D.C. The bureau had considerable experience in
testing baseballs. In 1917 they had dissected thousands, submit-
ted by a number of manufacturers, before deciding which represented the best buy for the government for use by wartime
servicemen.

Using the elaborate equipment remaining from 1917, including bouncing wells, propulsion tubes, impact walls, etc., the Bureau put the Ruth home-run balls to the test. On August 21 they
released their findings. The official ball of 1920, the bureau announced, was in no respect different from that of 1917. Nothing
had been done to the ball that would cause it to be livelier than
those used in past seasons.

While the frequency of home runs may have declined as summer waned—even for Ruth—hitting did not. In September, the
increase in runs and base hits appeared headed for a climax. On
September 11 the St. Louis Browns swept a doubleheader against
the Washington Senators, 13 to 6 and 17 to 2. On the following
day in Philadelphia, the Phillies beat the defending champion
Cincinnati Reds, 21 to 10. There were 30 hits, 14 for extra bases,
but only 1 home run. A sign of the times, the Reds made 9 errors.
Typically, only one of the Phillies struck out, and three of
the Reds.

On the fifteenth, the Browns were back at it, pounding out
22 hits as they clobbered the Boston Red Sox, 18 to 5. Again,
only 1 home run. One Brownie struck out. Possibly the late-summer outburst in both leagues was stimulated in part by the new
policy of keeping a clean ball in play at all times.

George Sisler and his Brownie mates were unrelenting. On
the seventeenth they battered the Philadelphia Athletics, 17 to 8.
The teams shared 39 hits, 24 for St. Louis. No home runs in the
game. One St. Louis batter struck out. Hits, hits, hits. Weary pitchers must have prayed for the season to end. On the same day in
Detroit, the Tigers beat the Red Sox, 14 to 13 in thirteen innings.
There was 1 homer, and the inevitable 8 errors, 5 by the victo-
rious Tigers.

That afternoon in Boston, the St. Louis Cardinals made 12
consecutive hits while beating the Braves in a modest 9-to-4 contest. The consecutive-hit streak is still the major-league record
though it has been tied once. Cardinal batters were just warming
up. On the twenty-seventh at Chicago they banged out 25 hits
against the Cubs. The days of inside baseball seemed eons in
the past.

On September 13 Ruth hit home run number 49 off Howard

Ehmke at Detroit. It brought him within one of fulfilling his spring pledge to the baseball writers. Concurrently, the Yankees regained first place from the Indians as the American League race turned frenetic. New York, Cleveland, and Chicago were running what amounted to a dead heat. The margin between first place and third stood at .0034.

On the threshold of a home-run milestone—this time a historic 50—Ruth experienced one of his dry spells. Ten days passed. No homers for the Babe. Worse, the Yanks slipped to third place in the standings. They may, in fact, have fatally damaged their pennant chances two weeks earlier during an exhibition game at Pittsburgh's Forbes Field.

Playing schedules of the early 1920s provided for a generous number of open dates. With Ruth in the lineup the Yankees were in great demand to play exhibition games on these days, especially in cities where the Babe had not been seen before. Even for the rich Yankees, a guaranteed capacity crowd was too tempting to pass up. In Pittsburgh on September 8, the Bambino delighted 29,000 National League fans by hitting the longest home run ever seen at Forbes Field. But the game proved costly. Ping Bodie, having the best season of his career, broke an ankle sliding and was lost to the team. Sadly, this popular player never regained his form, and the meaningless exhibition game in effect forced an end to his big-league career.

On September 24 at the Polo Grounds, after a lapse of eleven days, Ruth nailed Cuban rookie José Acosta of the Senators for home run number 50. Before the crowd had a chance to savor the moment, Babe hit number 51 off reliever Jim Shaw. Although the Sultan of Swat had made history again, the Yankees were by this date effectively out of the pennant race.

In the National League the Giants too were finished. Despite their sensational rise from seventh place in mid-July to second in early September, McGraw's men found the fired-up Brooklyn Robins too much to overcome. In one stretch in the final month the Robins won sixteen of eighteen. Brooklyn may have had the only pitching staff in baseball not getting cuffed around that historic September.

Early in the month a rumor of game-fixing had surfaced in

Chicago, involving the Cubs and the Phillies. Cub president William Veeck, Sr., conducted a private investigation, and when that proved fruitless, he faintheartedly called upon the press to help ferret out the truth. By this time the matter had attracted the attention of the state's attorney, who summoned a special Cook County Grand Jury. Perhaps made nervous by signs that a grand jury investigation was under way right in their own town, the enormously talented but suspiciously languid White Sox suddenly caught fire. Through September 23 they won 7 straight and passed the sagging Yankees. Soon the hot Sox had run their record to 11 out of 12, including 2 out of 3 over the league-leading Indians. Chicago was within a hairbreadth of taking the American League lead and probably the pennant.

But it was too late. The Cook County Grand Jury had expanded its investigation beyond the Cubs-Phillies question. Besides, they were too busy to notice that the White Sox were madly piling up brownie points. On September 27, almost a full year after the World Series fix, the Black Sox scandal broke in the press. The Sox owner Charles A. Comiskey suspended seven of the players named—Cicotte, Williams, Jackson, Weaver, Oscar "Happy" Felsch, Charles "Swede" Risberg, and Fred McMullin. Former first baseman Charles "Chick" Gandil, the alleged ringleader, had quit baseball after the 1919 season. Toward the end of October the grand jury handed up indictments on all eight on charges of conspiracy.

Ultimately a newly created Commissioner of Baseball, Kenesaw Mountain Landis, would ban the eight conspirators from the professional game for life. In any case, Chicago's season was down the tubes. Cleveland, the good guys, won the pennant by 2 games. The Yankees finished third, 3 games out of first. One cynic suggested that the reason the White Sox played so enthusiastically for the last two weeks of the season was to be in position to throw another World Series.

When it was evident that both the Yankees and the Giants were out of contention, a few New York baseball writers proposed a City Series. Such series had been played twice in the past, in 1910 and in 1914, both won by the Giants. With Ruth present, a man who had helped generate a record 1,289,422 home admissions during the season, a postseason series between land-lord and tenant at the Polo Grounds, baseball's largest park, would both please the fans and bring in a pile of money. Wisely, National League president John Heydler vetoed the idea. Neighboring Brooklyn was in the World Series, and a concurrent baseball attraction in New York, especially one featuring Babe Ruth, was certain to steal the Robins' thunder. It simply would not be fair.

In the Yankees' final series in Philadelphia, from September 27 through 29, Ruth rounded off his incredible performance by hitting 2 more home runs, to bring his total for the season to 54. He had bettered his major-league record of 1919 by 25. George Sisler, the runner-up in the majors, finished with 19.

In November, when the statisticians donned their green eye shades and totaled up the damage for 1920, they learned, among other things, that the American League had scored almost 1,000 more runs than had the National and had made 523 more hits. Still, both leagues batted with unprecedented vigor. In the American League forty-two batters finished above .300, twenty-nine of them regulars. In the National, twenty finished in the magic circle, thirteen of them regulars. Things had changed since 1917, when both leagues batted under .250.

Two American League teams, Cleveland and St. Louis, batted over .300, the first major-league teams in the twentieth century to do so. The Chicago White Sox finished at a handsome .295, and the irony is that we can't be sure that every Sox batter was putting forth his best effort. Understandably, American League pitchers had a much higher earned-run average, 3.79 against 3.13 for the National League. In home runs the Yankees established a modern team record with 115, almost half of which belonged to Ruth. That total made the Yankees one of only two major-league teams to outhomer the Babe (the Phillies were the other).

Despite being outgunned by the American League, especially in home runs, National League hitters had not idled away the summer boning their bats. They hit a respectable .270. In particular, league batting champion Rogers Hornsby, who posted a robust .370, served notice that painful days lay ahead for National League pitchers.

Philadelphia Phillies veteran Fred "Cy" Williams led the National League in home runs with what now appears a puny 15. When you consider, however, that Sisler was the major-league runner-up to Ruth with only 19, Williams was not far off the pace for normal hitters. Everyone seemed to be a step or two short of mastering Ruth's knack of getting the ball well up into the air, or whatever magic it was that he employed. That would change— quickly. Three seasons hence, at age thirty-six, Cy Williams would almost triple his 1920 output of home runs, as emerging sluggers in both leagues performed like feats.

In 1920 fans reaffirmed their approval of the increase in hitting. More than 9 million paid their way into major-league parks to surpass by a comfortable margin the old record of 7.25 million, established way back in 1909.

As for Ruth, no athlete had ever before dominated a professional sport as he did baseball in 1920. Although the raw numbers tell only part of the story of his dominance, they are nonetheless impressive in themselves. In addition to hitting an epic 54 home runs, Ruth batted .376, scored 158 runs, drove in 137, and compiled a slugging average of .847. More than half his hits went for extra bases. Babe's 148 walks outdistanced by 51 his nearest competitor in either league. And for good measure he led the Yankees in stolen bases with 14. It's worth noting too that Babe missed a dozen games in the Yankee schedule.

Most of these impressive numbers the Babe himself would later top by comfortable margins, including the stolen-base figure. Two, however, remain unequaled: his slugging average of .847 and his home-run percentage of 11.8. John Thorn and Pete Palmer have calculated that at the Polo Grounds in 1920 Ruth had a slugging average of .985. In the face of such an achievement the term *astonishing* is a pale assessment.

Among the statistical surprises of the season, George Sisler, who hit .407 to win the American League batting title, actually topped the fabulous Ruth in total bases, 399 to 388. Sisler was helped considerably by the 257 hits he rolled up, still the major-league record for a season of any length.

In a one-sided World Series, second of the experimental best-of-nine formula, the Cleveland Indians, still grieving for Ray Chapman and wearing black armbands, beat Brooklyn, 5 games

to 2. Chapman's replacement, twenty-one-year-old Joe Sewell, fresh
from the University of Alabama, made 6 errors in the Series and
batted only .174. The charged-up Indians didn't need his help.
Playing manager Speaker, who had batted .388 for the season, hit
.320 during the Series and led his team in hits and runs scored.

The 1920 World Series is probably best remembered for an
unassisted triple play in Game Five by Cleveland second baseman
Bill Wambsganss, the only one in World Series history. Game Five
was remarkable in other ways. In the bottom of the first inning,
Cleveland right fielder Elmer Smith hit the first grand-slam home
run in World Series history, and in the fourth inning Cleveland's
31-game winner, Jim Bagby, became the first pitcher to hit a World
Series home run. What more could happen? What a year!

THREE

OF
RABBIT BALLS
AND THE
POWER
OF MYTH

> "American fans fervently wish to believe that some great intelligence presides over everything, that some superbrain is in charge. In a pinch it is even reassuring to believe in conspiracy theories. More terrible if *no one* were in control."
>
> —JOHN DIZIKES
> *Sportsmen & Gamesmen*

THE BASEBALL'S FREQUENTLY noted perfection of form is a Platonic conceit. Despite the ball's being mass-produced, its measurements can never be precise. Neither can its condition remain constant past the moment when the umpire, acting under official baseball rules, lifts it from its sealed package to rub it gently with blue mud from the Delaware River and reduce the gloss. This nagging mutability may be at the root of all the controversy ever generated over a baseball's behavior in flight. As Martin Quigley shrewdly observed in his minor classic, *The Crooked Pitch,* "Every throw in baseball is made with a ball that is not quite like any ball ever thrown before."

If Ruth benefited from a rabbit ball being sneaked into play in 1919, he was the only one in Organized Baseball to cash in. Just two of his Red Sox teammates hit any homers at all, a grand total of 4 between them. Ruth's closest pursuers in the home-run derby—Tilly Walker, George Sisler, and Home Run Baker—each had 10, a typical total for league leaders before World War I.

The initial reaction of baseball officialdom to an allegation of conspiracy to liven the ball was bewilderment. True, hitting had increased in the first postwar season, especially in the American League. Yet, the American Leaguers fell 5 percentage points short of the .273 they had batted in 1911, a year when the official ball had indeed been made livelier—by inadvertence—with the introduction of the cork center. Not even the 1919 home-run totals, up sharply from the war years, matched the 515 hit in the majors in 1911. Finally, National League batters, swinging at the same baseball, performed only slightly better than they had in 1917, the last "normal" season. In short, except for Ruth's 29 home runs, nothing extraordinary had shown up in the batting records for 1919.

Someone—it may have been American League president Byron Bancroft Johnson—suggested that if the ball was livelier in 1919, perhaps it could be attributed to the postwar availability of better-quality materials, particularly Australian wool. It was a sober and reasonable supposition. The response of those who cherished the idea of a conspiracy to corrupt the baseball was to turn the Australian-wool explanation into a running joke. This must have begun early, perhaps in the spring of 1920, because by June 3 of that year a New York reporter writes of a home run by Ping Bodie, "Ping jarred the ball right where the Australian wool was thickest," confident that even the most unperceptive among his subway readers could not miss the cynical allusion. As late as the 1930s, baseball writers continued to make mocking references to Australian wool, and my impression is that anyone could convulse a 1920s speakeasy gathering merely by uttering the words.

Once launched, the notion of a conspiracy to adulterate the baseball grew like morels in a damp wood lot. From 1920 onward, no laboratory testing of the ball, no sworn deposition from the manufacturer, the owners, or the workers on the production line, no opinion from veteran managers or responsible ballplayers, could shake popular conviction that a plot had been hatched in a smoke-filled hotel room to hop up the official baseball. In fact, this tireless devotion to the chimera of a rabbit ball continues to the present day.

To understand why successive generations have cherished the notion of a corrupted ball as the only possible reason for an expansion in hitting, it may help to trace briefly the origins of the standardized baseball.

Before 1860 most baseballs were made, we assume, entirely by hand and mostly at home. There is no record of even informal rules governing size. On average, the ball of the period before the Civil War was probably slightly smaller than today's eleven-inch softball. It was, in other words, a convenient size for the male hand, yet big enough to offer a fair target on its way to the plate.

By custom, the core of most early baseballs consisted of what was then known as India rubber—caoutchouc—an unrefined form of latex used in, among other things, the manufacture of pencil erasers. It was the same crude rubber that Cortez found the Aztecs bouncing playfully and tossing from hand to hand when he arrived in Mexico in 1519. The first known use for rubber was in sports.

It is likely that the India-rubber core in the baseballs of the 1840s and 1850s was crudely formed and varied considerably in size. This core was wound in wool or cotton yarn and shaped by hand until the whole was approximately spherical. The two- or four-piece leather cover was stitched by hand and made as tight as possible. Sometimes the cover was soaked before stitching so that it would shrink and become tighter. There are reports of balls being made with a core of lead, perhaps for reasons of economy. Doubtless some homemade balls had no core at all. The durability and liveliness of early baseballs must have varied greatly from village to village and artisan to artisan.

Early in the history of the game, and in the best American tradition, a few men set themselves up to fashion baseballs in volume and for profit. Although information about methods of production is fragmentary, the first ball manufacturers are thought to have limited the size of the rubber core to about one and a half ounces. But ball tampering—or rumors thereof—surfaced almost from the outset. Tradition has it that as the popularity of the game spread and baseball was no longer the exclusive province of gentlemen and collegians, there was demand for a livelier ball.

Whatever the truth about a blue-collar penchant for baseballs with zip, we know that by 1860 balls made with cores of two and a half to three ounces of rubber were not uncommon. After the Civil War we hear of manufacturers using as much as five or six ounces, essentially a crude blob of rubber wrapped in a leather cover.

In the spring of 1865, just as the Civil War was ending, young Benjamin Shibe of Philadelphia, a carriage driver and leather worker, approached Alfred J. Reach, English-born star player for Colonel Tom Fitzgerald's Athletics Baseball Club, with a proposal for manufacturing a standardized baseball. Reach, a left-handed second baseman and sometime catcher, was one of the best known ballplayers of his day. It looks as though Shibe wanted Reach to contribute a famous sports name, some consumer data, and perhaps a spot of cash, while he himself manufactured the ball. The meeting was fruitful. By April of the following year, Reach and Shibe had established a small factory and sporting-goods store on Philadelphia's Chestnut Street.

An experienced mechanic, Shibe quickly discovered that, with a product wholly dependent upon hand labor, it was close to impossible to hold to exact specifications for size and weight, regardless of how desirable such standards might be. Allowing himself realistic tolerances, he modified the specs for the new ball. In part they read, ". . . not less than nine nor more than nine and one-quarter inches and weigh not less than five nor more than five and one-quarter ounces." Almost a century and a quarter later, Shibe's specifications for size and weight remain in force for all baseballs used in the professional game.

While Ben Shibe may have been the first to produce a standardized baseball—and that is by no means certain—it was not a patentable idea. By the early 1870s a number of sporting-goods manufacturers were turning out standardized balls for a rapidly expanding retail market. It meant that when the National League

was established in 1876, following the dissolution of the first professional league, the National Association of Professional Base Ball
Players, there was a scramble to corner the limited but prestigious business. The charter of the new league provided that the
league secretary, in this case Nicholas Young, should have the
responsibility for obtaining baseballs for the eight clubs. Apparently Young found it expedient to contract with a single supplier,
creating, in effect, an "official" big-league ball.

In a 1940 interview for *Nation's Business*, Ben Shibe's son
Tom told a reporter that it was the A. J. Reach Company who
won that first contract in 1876 to supply the new league with
baseballs. Although customarily such a contract was sought for
profit, the deal in this instance was that Reach would supply the
baseballs free of charge. The offer may well have swayed Young's
decision. The advantage to the manufacturer, of course, was that
he could advertise that his was the only ball approved for use in
the only major professional league, and presumably every youngster in America would covet a Reach ball.

If Tom Shibe's story is accurate, Ben Shibe and Reach must
have assumed that the exclusive contract with the National League
put them at a considerable advantage in winning the hearts and
purses of young America. At about this time, however, enter the
lanky figure of premier right-handed pitcher Albert Goodwill
Spalding, who would exercise a profound influence over the development of professional baseball. That influence included
shrouding in mystery the process of manufacturing balls.

Spalding's record of 207 wins against 56 losses in the five-
year history of the National Association confirms that he was a
pretty crafty pitcher. He proved to be an even craftier businessman. While still the dominant star of the Association, young
Spalding became a key figure in Chicago businessman William
Hulbert's efforts to establish the National League. For persuading
most of his Boston teammates to jump to the new league, Spalding was rewarded by being named field manager of the Chicago
franchise (a club he would eventually own). Proximity to the
National League's Chicago headquarters plus his close acquain-
tanceship with founder Hulbert were to give Spalding considerable leverage in league affairs.

Spalding served only two years as manager of the Chicago

White Stockings. At the close of the 1877 season, barely twenty-seven, A.G., as he was called, hung up his spikes to devote himself to business. A year earlier, with his brother Walter as partner, Spalding had begun a retail sporting-goods operation. The new firm, A. G. Spalding & Brother, opened its first store on Chicago's Randolph Street, not far from National League headquarters. (With the appearance of a brother-in-law in 1879, the corporate name was pluralized to Brothers.)

From the beginning, Spalding seemed ready to acknowledge that what he was selling was less expertise in the design and development of sports equipment than his name and reputation as a former big-league star. Unlike Reach and Shibe, Spalding Brothers avoided, where possible, the actual process of manufacturing the merchandise that bore their name. Instead, they licensed others to make the products for them.

Because of A.G.'s fame as a pitcher, the baseball early became the most important item in the Spalding Brothers line—symbolically, at least, if not in terms of revenue. The company adopted the baseball as its trademark. But the Spaldings had neither the know-how nor the capital equipment to produce the balls. From the beginning they farmed out the task, initially to Louis Mahn of Boston, where Spalding had won his greatest fame, and later, sometime around 1880, to Reach and Shibe. On the long association that followed between Spalding and the A. J. Reach Company hangs a tale that serves to both fuel and confuse the debate over the lively ball in our century.

In his biography of A. G. Spalding, Arthur Bartlett records that the young entrepreneur, a man of considerable personal charm, had a stock response for persons who inquired too closely where the Spalding Brothers baseballs were manufactured. With a mischievous grin A.G. would reply, "We make them evenings in the attic at home." The answer was intended at once to disarm the questioner and to invite a change of subject. It became Spalding's policy to avoid public scrutiny of his business operations and to keep secret all mergers and partnerships he entered into, not unusual behavior among nineteenth-century American businessmen.

By 1878, in a bold move and perhaps aided by his influence

in National League councils, Spalding had won the contract to supply the league with baseballs. A. G. went a step beyond the custom of supplying balls free of charge. He offered to pay the league a dollar a dozen for using them. The new policy quickly scared off the competition and the Spaldings would win the National League contract annually for the next ninety-five years.

About two years after A. J. Reach had been licensed to make baseballs for Spalding, the manufacturer won the contract to supply the newly formed American Association, the second major league. Now obligated to meet the needs of the two big leagues in addition to servicing their retail business, Reach and Shibe found production capacity seriously strained. To finance urgently needed plant expansion they turned to Spalding. For an investment of fifteen thousand dollars, A. G. Spalding & Brothers in 1885 received half-interest in the Reach Company.

At Spalding's insistence the partnership was kept secret, and A. G. encouraged Shibe and Reach to promote their products as though the two companies were in vigorous competition. He even supported the idea of the Reach Company's publishing a rival annual baseball guide. In 1892 Spalding acquired controlling interest in A. J. Reach, and it may have been about this time that A. G. Spalding & Brothers began to claim in their advertising that they had supplied the official ball for the National League from the time of the league's founding in 1876. Eventually Spalding acquired control of several other companies in the sporting-goods field, including Wright & Ditson and Peck & Snyder. By the mid-1890s A.G. had put together a monster sports-equipment conglomerate. In order to sustain the illusion of competition, however, he insisted in all cases that the company taken over maintain its corporate identity and continue to operate under the same officers.

It's surprising that more people didn't wonder aloud how the Spaldings were able to advertise their products in the annual baseball guide of their "competitor" Reach, even as Reach advertised its wares in the Spalding publication. The same was true for Wright & Ditson, who once asserted in an ad published in the Spalding guide that their league baseball was equal in quality to any ball made. As Bartlett observes, the claim was indisputable, since the Wright & Ditson ball was coming from the same source as that of Spalding and Reach.

Curiously, for many years only persons in the inner circles of the sporting-goods business were aware of the common manufacturing operation. Most fans and even sportswriters assumed that the Spalding and Reach balls were made in separate places and had distinct characteristics, including the degree of liveliness. What is astonishing is that the illusion survived up to and beyond World War II. It may be less the result of Spalding's addiction to secrecy than of the baseball public's penchant for self-deception. In *A. G. Spalding and the Rise of Baseball,* Professor Peter Levine recounts a story from *The Sporting News* of December 1886 that confirms that the misconception had a long history. "Two unnamed professional ballplayers, experts in their field, swore they could tell the difference between Spalding and Reach baseballs just by touching them. 'The joke of all this,' the story went, 'is that the balls . . . are made at the same factory and of the same material. One basket is marked "Spalding" and another "Reach." This is the only difference between them.' "

Even someone as astute as Ban Johnson, founder of the American League, may have been taken in. At any rate, when the new league was forming, Johnson approached Ben Shibe and said that if Shibe would back a Philadelphia franchise, the A. J. Reach Company could have an exclusive contract to supply the balls. With Spalding's approval, Shibe accepted the offer, and Reach began its long association with the American League, much as Spalding Brothers had long been allied with the National. It is hard to believe that Johnson could have been long in discovering that the baseballs for both leagues came out of the same bin—not that it really made any difference.

Not everyone was ignorant of the identity of Reach and Spalding baseballs. Bartlett cites a casual meeting at Spalding's New York store in 1892 between Henry "Father" Chadwick, the pioneer baseball writer, and Al Reach. Evidently there had been complaints from players about the quality of the Spalding National League ball that year. In his newspaper column Chadwick reported, "I saw Al Reach in Spalding's store last week, and I asked him what was the cause of complaints of the balls in use this season. He said he could not account for it except on the basis of an experiment Mr. Shibe had been trying in oiling the covers. The balls this year are made the same as before."

We don't know why Ben Shibe experimented with oiling the covers in 1892. Most likely it had something to do with increasing durability of the ball. A ball was expected to last the game in those days. In any case, Shibe was renowned as a devoted craftsman, a man who took pride in delivering the best product possible. Right up to his death in 1922, he worked to improve the quality of the baseball.

In 1883 Shibe had introduced the practice of treating the yarn with a kind of rubber cement so that the ball would hold its shape better. The new process also permitted the cover to move slightly without affecting the yarn underneath. In 1901 the Reach Company installed machines to wind the yarn. Besides speeding production, the shift from hand winding to machines must have helped to achieve a more uniform quality in the ball. But the most significant innovation by far came in 1910 with the introduction of Shibe's cork center.

As always, the purpose of the new feature was to improve serviceability. The core, consisting of a tiny ball of cork encased in thin hemispheres of black rubber, was designed to create a baseball that would hold its shape better under game conditions. Though clearly unintended, the cork center, it was discovered, also made the ball more lively. No secret was made of the fact, and given the woeful state of big-league batting at the time, no one complained about the ancillary benefit.

It is worth considering briefly what had brought batters to low estate before Shibe's cork center offered a temporary respite. Back in 1893, when the baseball rules committee increased the pitching distance from fifty feet to sixty feet six inches, hitting surged just as the committee intended that it should. In the seasons immediately following the rule change, National League teams (the American Association had folded) commonly scored more than 1,000 runs in a schedule of only 130 games. Four-hundred hitters became as common as they would be again in the 1920s. In 1894, four men finished above .400, three from the Philadelphia Phillies. That year the Phils had nothing but .300 hitters or

better from the leadoff man through the pitcher, and they finished with an all-time high team batting average of .349. Boston
center fielder Hugh Duffy led the league in batting with .438, also
an all-time record.

Bear in mind that even though the pitching distance had been
lengthened ten and a half feet, Duffy and his teammates were
flailing away at a ball once proudly described by a manufacturer
as "professional" and "dead" to distinguish it from the inferior
and much livelier ball sold to schoolboys, the "nickel rocket."
Once the pitchers had adjusted to the increased pitching distance, however, the official ball's lack of resiliency made itself
evident again. In fact, by the turn of the century (1901, that is)
batting averages began to slide alarmingly. What happened?

At least a couple of things. First, and most important, in 1901
the National League adopted the foul strike rule. Thereafter, the
first two foul balls became strikes, where formerly they had
counted as nothing. The new rule clearly reduced the plate life
of a lot of free-swingers. (The American League waited until 1903
to adopt the rule, with predictable results.) I can't believe, however, that the foul strike rule alone was enough to bring on the
catastrophe that overtook the hitters for the better part of two
decades. The real villain, it seems to me, was the spitball and its
variations. We may never know the full catalog of alien substances applied to the ball in those dark years. It was not only
the unpredictable flight of the trick pitches on their way to the
plate that caused the batters grief but also the discoloration and
the unspecified weight added by saliva, licorice, hair tonic, chew-
ing gum, mud, grass, and who knows what else caked into the
seams. The term *loading up,* long associated with the spitball,
carried literal import. Difficult to hit, the weighted spitball probably didn't carry well off the bat either.

In keeping with its sinister character, the spitball's origins are
shadowy. It may have started with Frank Corridon, a right-handed
pitcher with the Providence Club of the Eastern League, who
back around 1902 demonstrated the enigmatic flight of the wet
one for teammate George Hildebrand, an outfielder. Hildebrand,
later to become an American League umpire, carried the technique with him to Sacramento in the Pacific Coast League, where,

according to legend, he taught it to sore-armed teammate Elmer
Stricklett and saved Stricklett's pitching career. Stricklett, heart
brimming with gratitude at being promoted to the majors, in turn
taught the trick pitch to others.

It makes better sense to me to assume that Corridon was the
vector, since he made it to the majors sooner than Stricklett and
had a longer career. There may even have been a third culprit,
one never identified, who introduced the spitter earlier. At all
events, the vice spread rapidly. By 1904 the spitter and its kin
were in full flower in the big leagues. In that year New York
Highlander right-hander John "Happy Jack" Chesbro improved
his record from 21 and 15 to 41 and 12. Chesbro probably hadn't
known what happiness really was before he acquired the wet
one. Alas, the Goddess Nemesis is never far from scenes of pre-
mature rejoicing. On the final day of the 1904 season, in the ninth
inning of a key game with the Boston Pilgrims, Happy Jack un-
corked a wild pitch—probably an errant spitter—and with it went
the game, victory number 42, *and* the American League pennant.
Unfortunately, Chesbro's downfall was not enough to dissuade
other spitball devotees. In 1908, the Chicago White Sox's Big Ed
Walsh hawked his way to 40 wins. For big-league hitters, night
had fallen with a vengeance.

When at last trick pitches were proscribed in 1920, American
League umpire Billy Evans, esteemed as something of a scholar
in that trade, predicted that league batting averages would rise
from 20 to 25 percentage points. In time they did just that.

Believers in a rabbit-ball conspiracy have made much of testimony from fleet-footed outfielders like Tris Speaker and Edd
Roush, who traditionally played shallow, that around 1920 fly balls
they would normally have run down without difficulty were sailing over their heads. There is another dimension to the observation. The late Edd Roush once told me that after the departure
of the spitball it was noticeably easier to throw an unadulterated
ball because it was so much lighter. In the heyday of the spitter,
he said, trying to throw out a runner at third with a ball laden
with five innings' accumulation of saliva, tobacco, and mud was
like trying to cut him down with a lead shot. The same ball was
not likely to travel far when hit, either.

Understandably, the decline in hitting in the early 1900s produced a share of complaints about dull games and recommenda-
tions for a quick fix. Not everyone reveled in the refined skills
that characterized scientific batting and inside baseball. A favorite
proposal among those who wanted more bang in the game was
to move the pitcher back another three feet, putting him midway
between home and second. In the years before World War I,
Branch Rickey, for example, was an enthusiastic lobbyist for this
change. Francis Richter, editor of *Sporting Life,* thought outfielders should be stripped of their gloves. Others advocated revocation of the foul strike rule. There was even a vote for an early
form of the designated-hitter rule. Oddly, few voices—none iden-
tifiable—called for livening the ball. In any case, the bulk of fans
seemed reasonably satisfied with the game as it was, and so the
hitters remained shackled until the banishment of the spitter and
the arrival of Babe Ruth.

Of course, the first move toward making life more bearable
for the batters—the introduction of the cork-center ball—was
happenstance. Late in the 1910 season, the cork-center ball was
tested under game conditions and used intermittently in the World
Series as well. It proved satisfactory enough so that the National
Commission gave the OK for its adoption in 1911. Hitting took a
spectacular turn upward, especially in the American League, where
the league average jumped by 30 percentage points. Detroit's Ty
Cobb batted .420, the highest mark he would ever achieve.
Cleveland rookie Joe Jackson hit .408. The number of .300 hitters
in the American League increased from eight to twenty-seven, in
the National from eight to sixteen.

Pitchers' earned-run averages rose. In the American League
the collective ERA jumped from 2.53 in 1910 to 3.34 in 1911.
While the National League's gain in batting average was modest,
run production increased 10 percent and home runs were up an
eye-opening 32 percent to 316, a level the league would not
achieve again until the halcyon days of the early 1920s. It looked
as though the cork-center ball had helped the batters to overcome, in part, the curse of trick pitches.

The batting holiday continued through the season of 1912,
but then something happened that has yet to be explained. The

pitchers began to reassert the tyranny they had exercised before 1911. By 1914 hitters were back where they had started. Properly, 1911 should be known among fans and baseball historians as Year One of the Lively Ball Era. Instead, pitchers managed to forestall the new order until 1919, when Babe Ruth popularized a batting style that could not be denied, spitball or no.

When American League batting dropped from .262 in 1912 to .256 in 1913, the editors of the *Reach Guide* for 1914 observed that "a slight decline was well distributed due to gradual adjustments." Adjustments to what? They don't say. With equal vagueness the editors note that, in the National League, "both batters and pitchers have adjusted themselves to conditions." As late as 1916 the guides attribute the steady decline in hitting to "stabilization." What is most significant is that at no time do the editors show disapproval or disappointment at the falloff in offense. It is hard to avoid the inference that at the time most writers and fans viewed low batting averages as the norm. The increase in hitting from 1911 through 1912 may have been written off as an aberration, albeit a pleasant one. What a pity that we can't question half a dozen regular catchers from that period about what happened.

When the batting revolution began in earnest in 1920, accompanied by public accusations of ball tampering, the response of the baseball establishment was at first surprise, then hurt, finally defensiveness. The *Reach Official Base Ball Guide* for 1920 actually boasts of the increase in hitting in 1919 and suggests that it is "partly due to 'Uncle Ben' Shibe's great invention of 1910 of the cork centered ball." The *Spalding Guide* for 1921 titles its wrap-up of the 1920 season "Record Year for Records" and marvels at how hard the ball was being hit. "The infielders were being hustled harder than they have been hustled since the days of the liveliest ball," the editors observe. Further, they opine that the long-overdue proscription of freak deliveries "stimulated players to bat the ball as they had not batted it in years." These cannot be the words of men covering up a plot. And to what purpose?

In 1921, responding to allegations that the ball had been livened surreptitiously, the eminently honest and reasonable National League president, John Heydler, a former sportswriter and statistician, ordered an investigation. Once Heydler determined that, in fact, the ball had not been tampered with, he announced his finding. But in a year in which Ruth was on his way to 59 home runs, Heydler was wasting his breath. If his effort achieved anything among the plaintiffs, it was to mark him as partner to the plot.

In 1922 the *Reach Guide* ran a full-page ad in an effort to curb the uproar. "We never experiment with our patrons," it read. "There has been no change in the construction of the CORK CENTER BALL since we introduced it in 1910." The chorus of "Tell it to the Marines" could be heard from Maine to Florida.

Old Ben Shibe himself was among the first to deny publicly that he had made the slightest change in the ball. It must have been confusing and frustrating for the eighty-one-year-old "father" of the standardized ball to be confronted with accusations that he seemed helpless to refute as long as Ruth and his imitators were hitting dozens of Reach balls over the fence. When Shibe died two years later, in 1922, the controversy was still gathering force, and old Ben probably went to his grave unaware that he was dealing with a phenomenon too powerful to submit to reason or evidence—the force of myth. For that is precisely what the alleged secret agreement to enliven the ball had become.

Surprisingly few reporters of the time showed themselves resourceful enough to visit the Reach Company's Philadelphia plant and check for possible tampering with specifications for the official ball. Of the handful that made the effort, none emerged with the damning evidence that conspiracy advocates coveted. For that reason, perhaps, the stories didn't attract a lot of readers. In 1926, for example, a staff writer from *Popular Mechanics* toured the Reach production line and found nothing suspicious. Among other things, he reports what at least a few had known for a long time, that the two major-league balls were identical, differing only in the color of the stitching. Reviewing contemporary popular notions of exactly how the rabbit took up residence in the ball the reporter adds: "We can accept any of these theories if we care, but in the last analysis, about the only basis we have for believing that the ball is more lively now than formerly is the increasing number of home runs and the longer hits being made. And even that is far from sound evidence."

Among firsthand reports of visits to the Reach factory is a 1929 story by Edward Burns of the Chicago Tribune Press Service. It was nine years after the first alarms, but debate had been rekindled by a renewed surge in hitting in the 1929 season. The light tone of Burns's article suggests that he had been through this exercise before and really didn't expect to uncover chicanery. Styling himself "Old Sleuth," Burns recounts a tour of the plant under the guidance of Tom Shibe. At the time, Shibe was president of the Philadelphia Athletics as well as chief executive officer of the A. J. Reach Company (owned by Spalding, of course).

Among other stations on the production line, Burns and Shibe visited the bouncing well, where balls were tested for resiliency by being dropped from a point eight feet six inches above an iron-slab floor. To meet standards of quality control, Shibe explained, each ball must rebound exactly three feet eight inches. Burns chose a dozen new balls at random. All bounced three feet eight inches.

Shibe couldn't resist needling the good-natured reporter. He asked: "You didn't see them putting Mexican jumping-beans inside the ball at any time, did you?"

"No," Burns responded, "but are you sure there aren't some hidden passageways or something?"

Shibe concluded the tour on a more serious note. "You've seen them making baseballs just as they have been doing since 1910. Absolutely no change. . . . The ball could be made more lively, I suppose, but you can see for yourself what an expensive outlay would be involved in changing machinery and materials."

Strictly speaking, Tom Shibe's claim of "absolutely no change" was not true. In 1926, Reach (and, naturally, Spalding) introduced the cushioned-cork center. The modification involved inserting a tiny washer of red rubber—the "cushion"—between the hemispheres of black rubber surrounding the cork center, and encasing the whole in a thin sphere of red rubber. In effect, the cushion was an interior flange of the red rubber casing and bonded both inner and outer casings to the cork center to strengthen the entire core of the ball. The new feature was widely advertised by

Reach and Spalding as evidence of their continuing effort to produce the most serviceable baseball possible.

To illustrate the ball-tampering paranoia that held sway in the
1920s, baseball writer Arthur Mann, in an article entitled "The
Dead Ball and the New Game," which appeared in the August
1926 issue of *Baseball Magazine,* charged that the manufacturer
had, in fact, conspired to deaden the ball by inserting "an extra
piece of rubber." Although Mann was absurd in charging conspiracy, he was correct about the rubber. However tiny, the cushion
was extra. It was also true that in the 1926 season, offensive statistics would take a substantial dip in both leagues. (For the first
time in five seasons no major leaguer batted .400.) But in the
following year Ruth socked 60 cushioned-cork-center balls into
the seats, and by 1928 the two leagues were back to their old
tricks. In that year they hit almost 1,100 homers.

An unshakable assumption on the part of rabbit-ball theorists
has been that livening or deadening a baseball is somehow a simple process. "The whole matter of liveliness is due to tighter
winding," one baseball writer assured the fans in the mid-1920s.
"The machines which wind the ball can be set to wind tight or
loose. If the balls are wound tight, they will travel high, wide and
handsome; if wound loosely, they won't go far." The testimony
of the manufacturer that livening the ball would involve expensive changes in both machinery and materials is brushed aside as
so much establishment rhetoric.

To inform myself on the state of the art, I talked with Roger
Lueckenhoff, manager for quality control in the engineering department at Rawlings Sporting Goods, present supplier of balls
for the major leagues. A former semipro baseball player who has
been involved in the manufacture of baseballs since 1948—"sew-
ing balls," in the jargon of the trade—Lueckenhoff is the benefi-
ciary of more sophisticated machinery than the Shibes used, and
perhaps better quality materials as well. He concedes that the
ball could be made more lively, but not without affecting the
official specifications for circumference and weight. "To make a
significant change in the liveliness of the ball," he says, "my concern would be what happens to the other specifications, the other
physical tolerances that are locked in." Furthermore, Lueckenhoff

categorically rejects the idea that in the 1920s—or any other period—a change in the liveliness of the ball could be effected in
absolutely secrecy. He testifies that in the four decades he has
been involved in the manufacture of baseballs, there has been no
change whatever in the process except for the switch from
horsehide covers to cowhide. To make that change, Rawlings first
had to convince Organized Baseball beyond the shadow of a doubt
that the cowhide cover would not affect performance. "It's well
to remember," Lueckenhoff says, "that no baseball has ever performed by itself. It must first be hit with a bat."

One of the most puzzling aspects of the rabbit-ball dispute of
the 1920s is the apparent absence of protests from the pitchers.
There must have been complaints, of course, considering the
shelling that many pitchers were taking. Yet, their grievances seem
not to have attained prominence, either in the daily press or in
the memoirs of star players from the period.

On the other hand, there is well-documented testimony from
at least one pitcher on the other side of the debate. Vean Gregg,
an ace left-hander for Cleveland before World War I, came back
in 1925 after seven years of retirement to become a spot starter
and reliever for the Washington Senators. It's not surprising that
reporters descended on the forty-year-old pitcher with questions
about the lively ball. Gregg may have disappointed some of them
when he assured G. H. Dacy of *Baseball Magazine* that the ball
of 1925 was not one bit livelier than the one he had thrown
before the war. The veteran left-hander offered the opinion during a season when both leagues were on their way to .292 batting
averages and four teams would bat over .300.

Even among the working press, for the most part zealous
guardians of the rabbit-ball myth, an occasional voice of reason
was raised. As early as June 1921, F. C. Lane, conservative editor
of *Baseball Magazine* and not an unqualified admirer of Babe
Ruth, identifies the Babe as the cause rather than the effect of
"the lively ball era." Lane writes: "The livelier ball may have influenced the situation to some extent. But the livelier ball is a thing
so elusive that it offers the scantiest evidence. For example, the
manufacturers claim that the ball in use last year was no livelier
than the ball employed some seasons ago. The manufacturers ought

to know what they are talking about, and we can see no reason why they should deceive the public on this point. . . . We are irresistibly impelled, therefore, to see in Babe Ruth the true cause for the amazing advance in home runs."

A few years later an editorial in *Popular Mechanics* observed:

> There are two factors which may well account for the longer hits that are now being made. One is the increasing tendency to take a freer swing at the ball and not rely on chopping at it for a well-placed hit, as was formerly more common. The other is the ban which was placed on the various freak deliveries shortly before the great epidemic of home runs.

The explanation offered by *Popular Mechanics* is so patently sensible that it is difficult to understand why this suggestion and others like it were not enough to lay to rest the whole debate over the rabbit ball. There can be only one reason. Myth is rooted in imagination and emotion; it is by nature impervious to common-sense rebuttal. For example, from 1920 to the present, something that has characterized conspiracy advocates is the categorical rejection of test results that support a manufacturer's contention that nothing has been done to make the ball livelier. It began with the popular dismissal of the United States Bureau of Standards test in 1920.

In 1929, New York Giant manager John McGraw persuaded prestigious *Scientific American* to conduct a test of the ball then in use. In reporting the result, associate editor Louis S. Treadwell raises a point that would win favor today with Rawlings's Roger Lueckenhoff. Any test of the ball, Treadwell contends, is by implication an assessment of recent batting records and playing conditions as well.

Compared to the exhaustive tests administered by the Bureau of Standards in 1920, Treadwell's screening must be described as sketchy. He conducted a straightforward comparison of resiliency between the 1929 ball and that of 1924, a season whose batting statistics are typical of the first half of the decade. Apparently, the test was intended to substantiate or refute charges that the ball of 1929 had been made even livelier than the "stitched golf ball" of the early twenties. Treadwell's test was simply not comprehensive enough to settle that question, but what results he got should have been of interest to anyone concerned with baseball.

Although Treadwell used only National League balls in his test, he reminds the reader that all major-league baseballs have the same source and are identical, a fact that some baseball writers would dispute for another decade.

Treadwell's comparison of the balls for liveliness proved inconclusive. Despite having lain in its box for five years, the 1924 ball seemed a trifle peppier than the newer model. The most significant result of the test was to demonstrate that the slightest use—literally one bounce—will rob a new ball of some resiliency. In brief, the newer the ball, the greater the advantage to the batter. The finding supports the conjecture that the explosion in offense in the 1920s owed much to the practice of keeping a fresh ball in play. Treadwell cites a game in the spring of 1929 in which ten dozen new balls were used.

Additionally, Treadwell calls attention to testimony from bat manufacturers that the majority of ballplayers, amateur as well as professional, had abandoned the old thick-handled "choke" bat, once favored by scientific hitters such as Ty Cobb, and shifted to the thinner handle pioneered by Babe Ruth. "Also, it is an undeniable fact," Treadwell goes on, "that since 1919 when Ruth made 29 home runs . . . the average 'sand lot' player has been imbued with the idea that the so-called 'slugger' is the one who gets ahead. . . . The leagues are now filled with batters who have, during their professional careers, studied and strived for long hits." The editor concludes his analysis of the lively-ball flap with detachment and reason. "The greater number of .300 hitters is explained more reasonably," he writes, "by a combination of all changed conditions co-incident with the advance in skill in the game, together with a slight increase in the liveliness of the ball."

Despite the best efforts of such responsible journalists as Treadwell and Burns, by the early 1940s the rabbit-ball conspiracy tale had assumed the sanctity and immutability of scripture. We find as excellent and respected a baseball reporter as Frank Graham writing in his history of the New York Yankees, "The

craze for home runs spread—and fattened on a lively ball introduced surreptitiously into the American League. (The National
League got it the next year.) Somebody apparently figured that if
one Babe Ruth was so popular, ten Babe Ruths would be ten
times as popular and, accordingly, hopped up the ball." Obviously, Graham had not investigated the matter but simply re-
peats "what everybody knows."

Just a few years earlier, in the April 1940 issue of *Nation's
Business,* Edgar Forest Wolfe, a reporter who had visited Reach's
Philadelphia plant as early as 1923 in pursuit of evidence of ball
tampering, wrote, "Through the years in which there has been
much controversy concerning the comparative 'liveliness' of the
balls used by the American and National Leagues the balls have
been identical, made by the same process and in the same factory." This fact, if nothing more, should have been part of the
intellectual baggage of every responsible baseball reporter of the
1940s. It obviously wasn't.

In the 1980s the rabbit-ball myth continued to pass from hand
to hand manifestly unexamined. In Tim Considine's *The Language of Sport,* published in 1983, we find under the entry **rabbit ball:** "The lively ball used in modern baseball, first adopted
in 1920 by the American League and one year later by the National League. The rabbit ball . . . was introduced to take advantage of the box office potential of slugger Babe Ruth. . . ."

Even the sixth edition of the *Baseball Encyclopedia* pontifi-
cates, "In this he [Baseball Commissioner Landis] was aided by
baseball's great change in 1920. . . . To take advantage of the
rising popularity of a young star named Babe Ruth, the ball was
made much livelier." I wrote to the editorial director of the *Baseball Encyclopedia,* explained that I was doing a book on batting
in the 1920s, and asked whether his staff could help me to doc-
ument the 1920 decision to make the ball lively. I can't say that
I was surprised when I received no reply.

Hardly a season goes by without some TV baseball announcer
suggesting that once more "they" have secretly livened or dead-
ened the ball, depending upon the home-run totals of the hour.
How long will it go on? Frankly, forever. Like old soldiers, baseball myths never die.

In 1982, in his *History of the National League,* Glenn Dickey raises, indirectly, a question about the lively ball that should have come up two generations earlier. "In retrospect, it seems absurd," Dickey writes, "that baseball officials felt the need to disguise what was going on. The lively ball produced a game that the fans found more exciting and wooing the fans was especially important in the aftermath of the Black Sox scandal." Absurd, indeed. Perhaps that's why in 1925, National League president John Heydler, universally regarded by contemporaries as a man of unassailable character, could respond to a direct question from *Baseball Magazine*'s F. C. Lane with an unequivocal answer. "At no time have the club owners ordered the manufacturer to make the ball livelier," Heydler said. "The only stipulation the club owners have made about the ball is that it be the very best that could be made."

FOUR

THE
HOUSE THAT
BUILT RUTH

"I cried when they took me out of the Polo
Grounds."

—BABE RUTH

WHEN THE NEWLY constructed Yankee Stadium opened for play in
the spring of 1923, writer Fred Lieb, in a parody of the nursery
rhyme, dubbed the gigantic ballpark "The House That Ruth Built."
Lieb's epithet caught the popular fancy and continued in use among
baseball writers until the famous park was dismantled in 1974.
(The present Yankee Stadium stands on the site of the original.)

Lieb's catchy phrase implied, of course, that the impressive
triple-deck ballpark had been paid for with profits generated by
baseball's greatest gate attraction. Certainly, the money that
streamed into the Yankee cash box from 1920 through 1922 must
have been welcome. But as early as 1919, well before Ruth arrived in New York, Ruppert and Huston had drawn up plans for
a baseball park of their own—and the colonels had more than
enough funds to see the project through. What delayed them was
the difficulty in finding a suitable site. They wanted their park to
be in Manhattan. Ultimately they settled for the then remote Bronx.

If Ruth's batting miracles in the early 1920s helped set in
motion construction of the Yankees' showcase in the Bronx, an
even stronger case can be made that the Polo Grounds, whence

the Babe had moved, played the key role in shaping his legend. The much-maligned, much-beloved ballpark was an architectural sport, the result, perhaps, of the restrictions imposed by the hollow in which it was built. The distance to the right-field foul pole was an absurd 256 feet. The right-field wall, however, came away from the line at an obtuse angle, and as you moved toward right-center the distance from the plate increased rapidly. In the power alley it was a healthy 449 feet.

In the years Ruth played at the park, the left-field foul pole was about 285 feet from the plate, the power alley 455. For a straightaway hitter, center field was at best disheartening. If the encyclopedic Philip Lowry is not quite sure what the distance was, we may never know. Five hundred feet would not be far off.

In *The Hidden Game of Baseball*, perhaps the finest statistical analysis of the game ever done, John Thorn and Pete Palmer argue that had Ruth been moved to the Polo Grounds in 1919 and played a conventional schedule of 154 games, he probably would have hit his historic 54 homers a year earlier. Owing to quirky design at Fenway Park, the left-handed Ruth had been shooting at a cavernous right-center-field power alley that varied from 405 to 550 feet. It was a phenomenon know as the "Right Field Belly" and has since been partially eliminated by construction of additional stands and the bullpens. Small wonder that Babe hit only 9 of his record 29 homers at Boston, and of these we know that several went to left field. To this day no batter has ever cleared the right-field roof at Fenway.

Regardless of what park he called home, Babe Ruth was destined to be the dominant player of the 1920s. No fence in Organized Baseball could long contain his giant blows. Yet, the Polo Grounds, with its singular configuration, seemed ideally suited to his talents. In addition, the park served the most populous baseball market in the nation. Viewed in hindsight, the move to New York made Ruth's apotheosis inevitable.

While the Polo Grounds of 1920 may have proved to be the ideal home field for a left-handed superman like Ruth, we must not deceive ourselves that most of the ballparks of the era were small arenas, providentially designed to lend encouragement to the new fashion in hitting. In their musing, elderly baseball fans are apt to speak of the old parks as cozy, intimate. It's true; the old parks *were* cozy. From the grandstands fans often could converse with the players—where there were stands.

Among the thirteen ballparks built new or renovated in steel and concrete between 1909 and 1915, few had a significant number of seats in the outfield, that is, inside the foul lines. Typically, the outfield walls separated the playing field from a city street just beyond. The truth is that the playing area of the towering modern baseball palace, with its circumferential seating, is smaller on average and the fences closer than was the case with parks of the 1920s. Not only did our grandfathers play exclusively on grass, they played on wide expanses of it.

Incidentally, the extensive playing area and the limited seating encouraged one of the regrettable customs of the 1920s—the overflow crowd. On days of important games, when ticket seekers exceeded seating capacity, club owners would permit thousands of standees to occupy the outfield, restrained only by a rope barrier. In most, possibly all, ballparks, a ball hit into the crowd was scored a ground-rule double. Too often the practice caused games to be unfairly won or lost and occasionally resulted in phony records, such as the 23 doubles hit by the Cubs and the Cardinals in a July 1931 game.

In *Green Cathedrals,* an invaluable study of the dimensions of every ballpark ever used by a major or Negro league team, researcher Philip Lowry writes: "When compared to the power-alley and center-field dimensions for the 26 current ballparks . . . the outfield fences of fifty years ago were much farther from the plate than those of today." On average, Lowry calculates, Greenberg, Gehrig, Foxx, DiMaggio, and others were firing away at center-field and power-alley barriers that were 17 percent farther from the plate than are those of today. In the 1920s, before many of the clubs had constructed additional grandstands and bleachers in the outfield, fences were even more distant.

Let's consider specifically how much playing area some of those old parks had. We can safely discount the rumor that outfielders at Boston's Braves Field, the last of the 1909–15 generation of parks to be built, had to dodge tumbleweed when pursuing fly balls. Still, Braves Field was remarkably spacious. The foul poles in both left field and right field were 402 feet, and it was an eye-straining 550 feet to dead center.

There is a story that when the park opened in August 1915, visiting manager John McGraw took one look and predicted that no batter would ever hit a fair ball out of the playing area. For a couple of years McGraw's prediction held up. Then, on May 25, 1917, St. Louis outfielder Walton Cruise, a left-handed batter, managed to muscle a pitch into the "Jury Box," a diminutive segment of bleacher seats that had been built in front of the right-field wall. Curiously, Cruise also became the second batter to reach the Jury Box. He did it again in 1921. It was almost ten years before anyone cleared the left-field fence. With the aid of a brisk southeast wind, New York Giant catcher Frank "Pancho" Snyder accomplished the miracle on May 28, 1925.

Braves Field was the extreme case, of course, but not by a great deal. When Philadelphia's Shibe Park, the first steel-and-concrete park in the majors, opened in 1909, it measured 360 feet at the foul poles in both left and right, 393 in the power alleys, and 515 to straightaway center. In the 1920s new construction reduced the distances to more civilized but still challenging levels—334 in left and right, 405 in the power alleys, and 468 to center.

Pittsburgh's Forbes Field, which opened just eleven weeks after Shibe Park, was another pitcher's dream. It was 360 to left, 376 to right, and 462 to center. The park remained essentially unchanged until 1925, when grandstands were built in right field.

At Washington's Griffith Stadium, built in 1911, the roomy playing area saw no significant change through the park's fifty-four-year history. That's why, as recently as 1945, Washington fans sat through an entire American League schedule without once seeing a hometown batter hit a fair ball over the fence.

Others among the old parks were equally discouraging. Cincinnati's Redland Field was open for eight years before a fair ball cleared any outfield fence. But on a single visit in 1921 to play an exhibition game, Ruth hit two out. Even Ebbets Field, known in its later years as a slugger's paradise, was 419 feet to the left-field foul pole when the first game was played there in 1913.

What a thrill it would be to watch a game in one of the old

parks in baseball's most romantic era. Perhaps, if we borrow a trifle of storybook technology from *Star Trek,* we can can journey through time to that sultry July of 1920, when Ruth, scarcely settled into his locker at the Polo Grounds, had taken professional sports to the threshold of a new age. A cautionary note before you surrender to the time warp. Don't be seduced by the apparent freshness, charm, and innocence of what you encounter—the litter-free and orderly streets of midtown Manhattan, the picturesque green double-decker buses on Fifth Avenue, the clean air, the civility of motorists, the stylishness of the pedestrians, looking like so many extras from the television series *Upstairs, Downstairs.* Like societies in every age, this one has its dark underside, principally economic and social inequities. Pockets of poverty flourish just beyond your field of vision both east and west, closer to the rivers. Below Fourteenth Street, sweatshop employment is the norm, sometimes existing within the shadow of Wall Street towers. In New York and other American cities, the seven-month-old Prohibition Law has begun to breed the largest and most vicious underworld the country had known to that time. And before the month is out, Chicago will explode in the country's worst race riot, when a black teenage swimmer innocently strays across a symbolic barrier separating segregated beaches on Lake Michigan. Our grandfathers may have enjoyed cleaner air, but they had plenty of problems.

In the elegant red-marble lobby of your hotel, however, comfort and decorum rule. The amiable desk clerk informs you that there is a doubleheader between the Yankees and the White Sox scheduled for one-thirty at the Polo Grounds, a genuine doubleheader—two games for a single admission of $1.10. Assuming that, like many visitors to New York, you have come to see Babe Ruth, he recommends that you get to the park early so that you can watch the Babe take batting practice. Just yesterday Ruth hit home runs numbers 30 and 31 to break his own record of 1919 with half a season yet to play.

You are surprised that conversation among the scattered groups of men in the lobby—there are almost no women present—deals not with Ruth or even baseball. Most of the men are discussing business or Republican politics. On June 12 the Grand Old Party nominated the genial, silver-thatched Ohio senator, Warren G. Harding, to lead the nation out of the thicket of Wilsonian internationalism. From snatches of concerned conversation you gather that Harding is a political nobody, whose name was not even among the top dozen candidates going into the convention. And to compound worries for the business community, it looks as though well before the November general election, three quarters of the states will ratify the Nineteenth Amendment to the Constitution, granting women the right to vote.

As you walk west on Forty-Second Street to the Sixth Avenue El station you are surprised at the relatively light traffic on one of America's busiest thoroughfares. Furthermore, motor vehicles are outnumbered by pushcarts and horse-drawn wagons. A recent stable census by the New York Bureau of Sanitation revealed that 75,740 draft horses still make their home in the city, almost half of them in Manhattan.

Another surprise: In a city that has just announced its population as 5,621,151, the sidewalks are not crowded. Not a hint of the cheek-by-jowl nightmare of the 1980s. The answer may be that, in a labor-intensive economy, most New Yorkers are at work rather than walking the streets. Those abroad at this hour strike you as shockingly overdressed for such a hot and humid Tuesday morning. Most men are in heavy dark suits and wear high stiff collars and ties.

The ride north in the dark-green wooden El car, with its open windows and rattan seats, is remarkably pleasant. Not a graffito in sight. In fact, the car is spotless. From this height you become aware that New York of 1920 is still very much a horizontal city, like London or Paris of the 1950s. The Woolworth and Singer buildings, along with other modest skyscrapers, cluster at the lower end of Manhattan like tenpenny nails driven through one end of a board.

In less than twelve minutes the red-faced conductor rasps, "Hunt'n'fifty-fift' Street. Polo Grounds. Last stop." From the El platform you catch a first glimpse of the lush grass inside the park and the reddish-brown perfection of the infield. It is the work of Henry Fabian, the most famous of the big-league groundskeepers. By common consent the Polo Grounds has the finest playing surface in Organized Baseball.

Just inside the turnstiles, you are waylaid by young boys hawking scorecards. "Get your scorecard. Fi' cents. Can't tell the players without a scorecard." What the vendors say is true. Numbering of uniforms is a decade away. The numbers on the scorecard, four pages of crude pulp stock, are flashed on the scoreboard during the game to let you know who is batting and who is at what position in the field. The sale of scorecards is an important source of revenue for the club owners, a fact that will delay the adoption of numbered uniforms.

The Polo Grounds is not yet the storied green horseshoe we remember from film reruns of Bobby Thomson's pennant-winning home run or Willie Mays's World Series catch. The double-deck grandstand forms a rough J, the shank running toward right field. Around the top edge of the upper deck a wooden façade bears heraldic devices representing the teams of the National League.

Where there are not grandstands, the park is enclosed by broad wooden bleachers. The distances to the foul poles look absurdly short and are. Until Ruth popularized the home run, the distance to any outfield fence was not thought to affect the game. A glance at the distant bleacher wall in center field convinces you that no human could hit a ball that far. At least one human can and soon will—Babe Ruth.

Scorecard in hand, you settle into your uncomfortable slotted wooden seat in the lower grandstand between home plate and first base. In this 1920 showcase among ballparks, you find the crude cast-iron armrests rough on the elbows.

The Yankees have started batting practice and a lean right-handed hitter is in the cage taking his cuts. His bat is remarkably thick in the handle, as are most of the bats lying in front of the Yankee dugout. "Who's that?" you ask. Since the starting lineups have not yet been posted, your scorecard is of no help.

"That's Del Pratt," a stout man on your right volunteers. "He belts 'em pretty good."

Which is Ruth? you want to know. "A cinch to spot him," your neighbor says. "He's the biggest thing around. Except this kid Meusel. He's a big one too." The man points with his scorecard. "There's Babe. Behind the cage. Talking to reporters."

You are surprised. What you see is a tall, well-knit young man with thin calves. No suggestion yet of the famous beer belly. In fact, Babe looks like a wide receiver. He leans on a bat with his right hand and talks with animation. It occurs to you that except for the departure of the baggy pants and shorter sleeves on the blouse, the Yankee pinstripes have not changed a great deal over the decades.

The stands are filling rapidly and you are relieved to see many of the men remove their jackets and unbutton their stiff collars. There are few women in the park. With approval you note that the women thoughtfully remove their large straw hats so as not to obstruct the view of fans seated behind them. Churlishly, most of the men keep their hats on. Since the day is intermittently cloudy, you hear complaints in the stands that it might rain before game time.

Now Ruth steps into the batting cage. The crowd buzzes. Many stand. Ruth's yellow bat looks heavy and menacing as he swishes it rhythmically, waiting for the pitch. He stands well back in the box, feet close together, right foot turned in slightly, in what we would today call a closed stance. His chin seems to rest on his right shoulder, which is pointed toward the mound. *Swish, swish* goes the heavy bat. Then high behind the left ear, very still, cocked. The pitcher's toss is a bit outside. With easy stride, Ruth steps toward the plate, brings the big club around in a fluid motion, and lashes the ball on a line into left field. It hits the bleacher wall on three bounces. The next two pitches he fouls off, almost falling from the violence of his swing. Then a booming drive to center field, which is gathered in by one of the Yankee pitchers exercising in the outfield. A line drive to right.

The crowd shows impatience. They did not come out to the park early for a lesson in bat control. They want thunder. At last Ruth steps into a pitch just above the knees. The crack can be heard in every corner of the park. A choked cry rises from the crowd as the ball sails higher than the grandstand roof and heads for the half-filled right-center-field bleachers. It is a stupendous wallop. Ushers scramble to retrieve the baseball. The souvenir ball is still unknown to professional baseball.

Ruth launches another shot. It bangs noisily against the wooden façade above the second deck. A screaming line drive reaches the lower stands in right. Then one off the right-field wall that squibs crazily toward center field. Finally a towering fly that falls just yards short of the distant center-field wall. Laughing, Ruth yields the batting cage to a dark, rotund player (Ping Bodie, you learn) and is quickly surrounded by the reporters with their notebooks. The writers are joined by two photographers, who have the Babe pose wielding his bat.

As Bodie takes his practice swings, the White Sox in their striking dark-blue traveling uniforms begin to stream from the clubhouse gate in center field. The thought had not entered your mind until now. These are the Black Sox! Right in front of you on the vivid grass of the Polo Grounds are the men who threw the 1919 World Series. And you are the only one in the stands who knows who the guilty ones are. Wait, that's naïve. Lots of gamblers must know. And there are those in the press who suspect. For all you know, the well-dressed man in the Palm Beach suit and Panama hat, sitting just behind the Yankees' dugout, could be Arnold Rothstein, the alleged mastermind of the conspiracy.

"Which one is Joe Jackson?" you ask the neatly dressed man on your left who wears a flat straw hat, the kind the British call a boater, and carries a rolled umbrella. You suspect he is a tourist, perhaps from Chicago.

"Actually, I don't know these fellows well," he says, "even though I saw them yesterday and Sunday." Then you spot a lean, hatchet-faced player warming up in front of the third-base boxes. "There he is," you tell your neighbor. "There's Shoeless Joe." But where are Gandil, Risberg, Felsch? You remember that Gandil can't be here. After holding out in the spring, he mysteriously dropped out of baseball. Outfielder Shano Collins is filling in at first. And there's the other Collins, the great Eddie, incipient squirrel pouches in his cheeks already making him easy to spot. And the one with the long chin, that must be Buck Weaver.

When both teams have completed batting and fielding practice, groundkeepers begin to smooth the infield. In front of the press box, located at ground level behind home plate, a stocky man in a brown suit removes his derby and puts a large maroon megaphone to his lips. He is there to announce the batteries for today's game. Public-address systems lie even further into the future than uniform numbers. Jack Quinn has been warming up for the Yankees and Urban "Red" Faber for the Sox. Both men are spitball pitchers, operating at the moment under a one-year dispensation.

There are just two umpires, Ollie Chill behind the plate and George Moriarty on first base. Following a brief meeting of team captains and umpires at home plate to review the ground rules, Umpire Chill bellows, "Play ball," and the Yankees trot onto the field. No obsequious welcoming of politicians and visiting civic groups. No pregame playing of "The Star-Spangled Banner," a custom that will come with the growth of patriotic feeling during World War II. (In fact, Congress will not act on the choice of an official anthem for another eleven years.) Quickly, little Harry "Nemo" Leibold, the White Sox right fielder, steps into the batter's box and the game is on.

These are important games for New York. The Yankees trail Cleveland by a game and a half and the Indians arrive at the Polo Grounds tomorrow for a four-game series. If the locals can sweep today's doubleheader, and if Cleveland should lose in Boston, the leaders would face one another all even. New York fans are on an emotional high, not only about Babe Ruth's home runs but also about the possibility of the Yankees' first pennant in their nineteen-year history. You find yourself stunned at the realization that the team on the field wearing the fabled pinstripes has yet to win a championship.

The Yankees get on the board early. First baseman Wally Pipp punches a single to right. Immediately, first-base umpire Moriarty takes position between first and second, behind Sox second baseman Eddie Collins, so that he can call plays at either base. The next batter, Del Pratt, hits the first pitch to left-center. Maybe it's autosuggestion, but it seems to you that neither Joe Jackson in left nor Happy Felsch in center, two of the league's best outfielders, gets a good jump on the ball. It lands between them. Pratt tries to stretch the hit to three bases, but Felsch cuts him down with a tremendous throw. Pipp scores and the Yanks are one up.

"Felsch shoulda had that one easy," the stout man on your right confides. "If I'm Gleason, I fine the bum twen'y-fi' dollahs." (William "Kid" Gleason is the Chicago manager.)

A fan behind you rasps, "It oughta be fifty dollahs." Could it be, you wonder, that this splendid team, whose treachery of last October remains speculation, continues in the clutches of the gamblers?

The way Quinn is pitching, it looks as though the Yankees' 1 run might hold up. You groan inwardly. What worse luck than to travel back through seven decades to the age of Babe Ruth and get stuck at a pitchers' duel.

In the bottom of the third a spitball gets away from Red Faber and he low-bridges Yankee shortstop Roger Peckinpaugh. The crowd emits a low whistle and you are reminded that Ray Chapman will be fatally beaned in this very batter's box in less than a month.

In the top of the fourth Felsch makes amends for his desultory play in the field by hitting one into the lower deck in right field to tie the score. You realize, when Umpire Chill hands a new white ball to catcher Harold "Muddy" Ruel, what the offices of two spitballers had wrought with the one that Felsch just hit into the seats.

In their half of the fourth the Yankees score 3 times, but the Sox come right back in the fifth to pick up 2 unearned runs on Peckinpaugh's error and make the score 4 to 3, New York. You can't help feeling sorry for the Yankee shortstop. The glove he is playing with looks not much bigger than those you use for garden work. Players in the field are constantly spitting into the palms of their gloves and rubbing in the saliva to keep the leather damp and supple. At the end of each half-inning the fielders toss their gloves on the grass near their positions.

In the bottom of the fifth, with 2 out and no one on, Ruth comes to bat. Faber has already walked the Babe twice intentionally, ignoring jeers from the partisan crowd. In this situation it makes perfect sense to put the big slugger on again, and Faber quickly runs the count to 2-and-0. The crowd boos until the Polo Grounds seems to vibrate. Whether manager Gleason yielded to crowd disapproval or Faber simply slipped up you will never know. In any case, the crack of Ruth's bat meeting the ball can probably be heard up on Edgecombe Avenue, two blocks behind the Polo Grounds.

You have to stand and crane your neck to the right to follow the flight of the ball as it ascends higher and higher, until it disappears over the roof of the second deck in right field and lands somewhere on Manhattan Field, the informal cricket ground just outside the park. The ball must have traveled almost 500 feet. Had Reggie Jackson hit such a shot, he might have stood for a full minute, contemplating the magnificence of it. But this is 1920 and the Babe simply trots the bases with his mincing, pigeon-toed stride, tips his hat to the cheering crowd as he crosses the plate, and retires to the dugout. It is home run number 32 and it puts Ruth 3 beyond his 1919 record with half the schedule yet to play. Despite the applause from 32,000 admirers, Babe takes no curtain call. It would be considered very bad form.

As the vendors work the aisles noisily, you become aware that you are hungry and thirsty. No beer for sale, of course. But the hot dogs smell wonderful. It may be because they contain meat. You signal the vendor. With innocent disregard for niceties of hygiene, the hot dog, devoid of paper wrapping, is passed through a dozen hands until it reaches your seat. It tastes as good as it smells, but the skin is tougher than alligator hide. Even in 1920, you discover, life remains a succession of tradeoffs. To wash down the dog, you settle for a bottle of surprisingly bland orange pop.

Quinn continues to mow down the Sox, and with 2 out in the top of the ninth it looks as if the Yankees are home free. Then Chicago shortstop Swede Risberg, choking up on his bat about six inches, pushes a ground single through the left side of the infield. Quinn kicks the dirt and looks unhappy with himself. Light-hitting Ray Schalk, the Chicago catcher, is standing in. With just one man to get, Muddy Ruel walks to the mound for a short conference. "Strike the bum out," someone shouts, and it hits you that the fans have been remarkably circumspect in their language. By contrast, purple chatter from infielders on both teams is occasionally audible.

Quinn works the canny Schalk too fine and walks him on six pitches. It is only Quinn's second walk of the game. The man with the megaphone reappears to inform the press and anyone else within range of his voice that "Honest Eddie" Murphy will bat for Faber.

Murphy is left-handed and a good hitter. On a 1-and-1 count he grounds to Pipp and fans race for the restrooms. A communal groan halts them in their tracks. Pipp has booted the ground ball that should have ended the game. A voice far back in the stands yells, "Get a basket, Pipp, ya dope."

With the bases loaded the troubled Quinn stands on the mound, shoulders sagging. What surprises you most is that Yankee manager Miller Huggins doesn't go to the mound for a conference. But Quinn is the starting pitcher and an eleven-year veteran in the majors. Starting pitchers are expected to finish. Besides, there's nothing that Huggins could tell his pitcher about how to get hitters out that Quinn doesn't already know.

The Yankee cause is not lost. Nemo Leibold, who is batting .215, is up next. On the downside, your scorecard confirms that Leibold has 2 of the Sox's 8 hits. Demonstrating once again that Quinn's spitter is no mystery to him, Nemo trickles a ground single over second to score Risberg and Schalk with the tying runs. Disgruntled fans settle back in their seats and bite their lips.

Eddie Collins, who has not hit safely in four appearances, promptly singles to right to score Murphy. Chicago leads by 1. Now Buck Weaver rifles the first pitch to right for his fourth hit of the afternoon and the Sox are up by 2. Poor Quinn, victim of 6 unearned runs in the game, is obviously tired.

At long last Huggins appears from the dugout and walks to Umpire Chill to make a pitching change. He does not go to the mound to take the ball. It is not yet the custom and must wait for Casey Stengel to bring the mound ritual to full flower in the 1930s. Huggins simply nods to Quinn and the dejected pitcher heads for the clubhouse in center field. Thirty-two thousand fans rise to give Quinn a round of applause as skinny right-hander Bob McGraw, who has been warming up in the right-field bullpen, walks slowly to the mound to face Joe Jackson.

Far to your left a fan shouts, "Hey, Joe, how do you spell *cat?*" an allusion to Jackson's alleged illiteracy. But every Yankee fan knows that Shoeless Joe doesn't need to read the label on the ball in order to hit it out of the park. Prudently, McGraw walks

Jackson and then induces Felsch to ground to third, where Buck Weaver is called out for interfering with Aaron Ward's attempt to field the ball. Chicago is finally retired, but the Yankees trail, 7 to 5.

Gleason brings in his nifty little left-hander Dickie Kerr, winner of two games in the tainted World Series of last October, to nail down the victory. The five-feet-seven-inch Kerr pitched a complete game just yesterday and won despite giving up 2 record-breaking homers to Ruth. But in 1920 there is no pampering of pitchers. "We hit this bum yest'day," a hoarse voice from the stands counsels. "We'll murder 'im t'day." It starts to look that way.

Third baseman Aaron Ward works Kerr for a walk. Ruel grounds into the hole, where Risberg makes a brilliant stop but has no time to throw. Two on, none out. The crowd howls for runs. A win will pull the Yanks to within 1 game of the league-leading Indians. Huggins sends up popular George "Duffy" Lewis to bat for pitcher McGraw. Now everyone around you is standing and yelling. You become acutely conscious that deodorants are yet to be developed.

Kerr is too careful with Lewis and walks him to load the bases. Yankee fans sense a come-from-behind victory. Now Huggins sends in Wilson "Chick" Fewster to run for the aging Lewis, who represents the winning run. Had the manager known that a few years hence Fewster would win immortality in Brooklyn as one of three Dodger base runners claiming third base, he might have been content with the slower Lewis.

Top of the Yankee order, none out. Peckinpaugh, who needs to atone for that fourth-inning error, lifts a weak fly to Jackson in left. No one moves. Jackson has a rifle arm. Pipp, the other fielding culprit, is due up. But Pipp is a left-handed batter and Huggins inflexibly plays percentage. He sends up the right-handed (but weak-hitting) Sammy Vick to bat for Pipp.

You speculate on what Earl Weaver or Sparky Anderson might have done in the situation. Pipp, one of the league's better hitters, has home-run power. In fact, he has twice led the American League. The right-field porch looms just 256 feet away. So what if Pipp strikes out. Hefting three bats in the on-deck circle is the ever-dangerous Del Pratt. In the hole is Babe Ruth himself.

The worst happens. Vick grounds sharply to Risberg at short. Eddie Collins makes a perfect pivot and relay. Double play. The Yanks are erased. The players run for the clubhouse and the fans stampede for the restrooms.

As you make your unhurried way toward the men's room in the subterranean reaches of the Polo Grounds, you conclude that while the world may have changed dramatically, baseball, remarkably, is little altered. It brings to mind John Thorn's observation: "Baseball seems to exist under a bell jar, oblivious and impervious to the stresses of the world outside."

Shown here in 1877, wearing the uniform of the Pittsburgh Allegheny club,
Edward "Ned" Williamson later starred
with the legendary Chicago White
Stockings. In 1919, when Babe Ruth
broke Williamson's thirty-five-year-old
single-season record for home runs,
baseball at every level entered a new
era. COURTESY OF MARK RUCKER

In 1920, Cleveland's Tris Speaker responded to the pressure of his first full season as playing manager by raising his batting average 92 percentage points. Already thirty-two years old, "Spoke" registered approval of the clean-ball era by hitting .354 for the remaining nine years of his career. COURTESY OF THE CLEVELAND PUBLIC LIBRARY

Shown here in his final year in a Red Sox uniform, a trim Babe Ruth was on his way to making good a preseason pledge to rewrite the book on slugging. For the next sixteen seasons home runs came in record numbers, but never again was Babe in such good physical condition. NATIONAL BASEBALL LIBRARY, COOPERSTOWN, N.Y.

The ill-starred "Shoeless Joe" Jackson makes ready to pull the trigger on what many believed was baseball's most beautiful—and lethal—swing. Young Babe Ruth so admired Jackson's form at the plate that he made it his own. COURTESY OF THE LIBRARY OF CONGRESS

In the unforgettable season of 1920, this frail-looking athlete actually outmuscled Babe Ruth in total bases. An additional scratch single that year would have made the Browns' George Sisler the first batter in history to amass 400 bases in a single season. NATIONAL BASEBALL LIBRARY, COOPERSTOWN, N.Y.

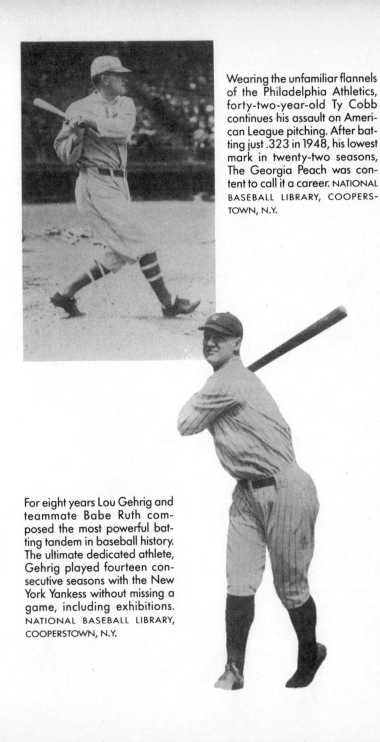

Wearing the unfamiliar flannels of the Philadelphia Athletics, forty-two-year-old Ty Cobb continues his assault on American League pitching. After batting just .323 in 1948, his lowest mark in twenty-two seasons, The Georgia Peach was content to call it a career. NATIONAL BASEBALL LIBRARY, COOPERSTOWN, N.Y.

For eight years Lou Gehrig and teammate Babe Ruth composed the most powerful batting tandem in baseball history. The ultimate dedicated athlete, Gehrig played fourteen consecutive seasons with the New York Yankess without missing a game, including exhibitions. NATIONAL BASEBALL LIBRARY, COOPERSTOWN, N.Y.

Ty Cobb (*left*) and Bobby Veach
in happier days, before Cobb
became Detroit manager. Only
the irascible perfectionist
Cobb would have carped at a
player like Veach, who six times
topped 100 RBI, twice on as few
as 3 home runs. GEORGE BRACE
PHOTO

The imperious Rogers Hornsby
turns congenial and hefts a
Louisville Slugger for the pho-
tographer. That intense gaze
helped "Rajah" to a lifetime
major-league batting average
of .358, second only to Cobb's
.367. GEORGE BRACE PHOTO

The third man, along with Cobb and Veach, in an outfield that batted a record .374 in 1921, Detroit's Harry Heilmann appears to have belted yet another fastball to a distant corner of Navin Field. His free swinging carried "Slug" to four American league batting titles and one .400 season.
COPYRIGHT DETROIT *NEWS*

Frank "Ping" Bodie, born Francesco Pezzolo, was the first of several generations of Italian-Americans to star with the New York Yankees. A member of the Yankees' original Murderers' Row in 1919, Bodie's big-league career was cut short by injury.
NATIONAL BASEBALL LIBRARY, COOPERSTOWN, N.Y.

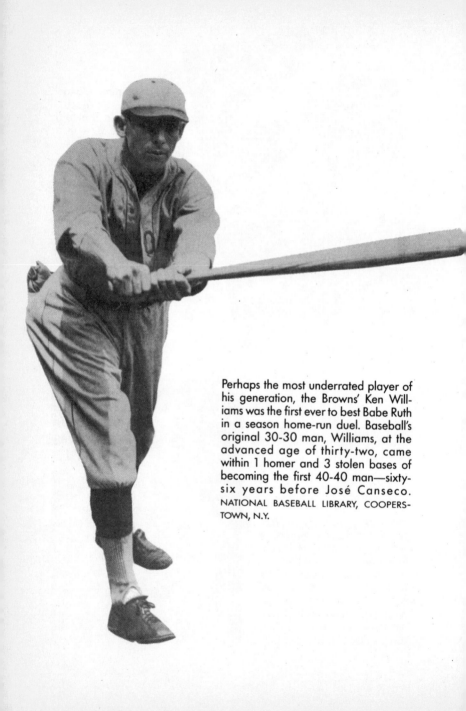

Perhaps the most underrated player of his generation, the Browns' Ken Williams was the first ever to best Babe Ruth in a season home-run duel. Baseball's original 30-30 man, Williams, at the advanced age of thirty-two, came within 1 homer and 3 stolen bases of becoming the first 40-40 man—sixty-six years before José Canseco.

NATIONAL BASEBALL LIBRARY, COOPERSTOWN, N.Y.

FIVE

THUNDER ON THE HARLEM

"Who owns New York, boys?
Who owns New York . . . ?"
—Columbia University Fight Song

IN THE OPINION of conservative baseball writers—and conservatives seem to have been the majority at the time—the salient fact of the 1921 season was the rapid spread of the "Babe Ruth disease." It is interesting to note how often writers of the period employ images of pathology when discussing Ruth's influence on the game. Animal imagery was equally popular. *Baseball Magazine*'s F. C. Lane seemed to delight in deriding Ruth's "gorilla-like strength" or his application of "brute force," as though little skill was required to hit a baseball into the center-field bleachers. In June 1921, Lane ruefully observed that "almost any batter that has it in him to wallop the ball is swinging from the handle of the bat with every ounce of strength that nature placed in his wrists and shoulders. He [Ruth] has not only slugged his way to fame, but he has got everybody else doing it."

Dismissing the importance of soaring attendance throughout baseball, as home-run hitters drew excited new fans, *Baseball Magazine* later sniffed editorially, "The connoisseur is never in the majority. The multitude appreciates the obvious and loses the finesse, even at the ballyard."

A compelling instance of Ruth's influence on other batters can be seen in the career of Ken Williams of the St. Louis Browns. A slender left-handed batter, Williams weighed a full fifty pounds less than Ruth. Initially a classic line-drive hitter in the manner of his teammate George Sisler, Williams hit with enough power in 1920 to collect 10 home runs. It placed him eleventh in the American League. Early in 1921, according to *The Sporting News,* in response to dugout banter, Williams experimented with modifying his batting style to imitate Ruth. Slowly, the Browns' left fielder gained command of what the Babe had so perfectly characterized in his own style—the grooved swing. The result for Williams was 24 home runs in 1921 and 40 percentage points added to his batting average. It made a believer of him and his manager, Lee Fohl. The following year Williams would become the first batter to take the home-run crown from Ruth.

The slowness of National League hitters to adopt the new fashion in batting gave rise years later to the canard that the senior league's owners had been waiting for the American League to field-test the lively ball before making a decision to juice up their own. It is more likely that National League regulars spent the winter of 1920–21 pondering Babe Ruth's 54 home runs and, more important, his new $52,000 salary. Before the first maple leaf turned scarlet in the fall of 1921, National Leaguers had upped their average from .261 to .289, just 3 percentage points below that of their mentors. The real eye-opener of 1921 was that the Nationals increased their home runs 42 percent, essentially achieving parity with the junior league.

In 1921, as National League pitchers watched their collective earned-run average worsen from 3.13 to 3.78, all five of the "licensed" spitball pitchers who were starters turned in winning records. Their combined ERA was only 3.19. William "Spittin' Bill" Doak led the league in both winning percentage and ERA. Burleigh Grimes tied for the lead in total victories.

American League spitballers fared equally well. Red Faber of Chicago, Urban Shocker of St. Louis, and Stan Coveleski of Cleveland were among the top five pitchers in both wins and winning percentage. Faber led in earned-run average with 2.48, against the league's stratospheric 4.28. If there was a rabbit ball loose in 1921, it wasn't feeding in the spitballers' lettuce patch.

Except for periodic and temporary defilement by registered spitball pitchers, most of the baseballs served up to batters in 1921, starting on Opening Day, were clean and white. Before Memorial Day pitchers in both leagues were complaining about having to throw an endless succession of glossy new balls, while batters stood grinning at the plate. In response to the pitchers' plight, in June league presidents Johnson and Heydler agreed to have the umpires rub the gloss from the new balls before each game with dry soil, a practice still in force. Additionally, the league presidents recommended that umpires exercise discretion in putting new balls into play. Since no plate umpire wanted to preside over another fatal beaning with a dirty ball, however, we can guess that the policy was not rigidly enforced.

Though doubtless helpful, deglossing the new baseballs worked no miracles for pitchers. Late in July 1921, *The Sporting News* announced with what sounds like sincere relief that, after a spring of riotous hitting, "major league batting seems to have finally struck 'normalcy.'" At the time eight men were batting over .400 and thirty-five batters in each league were hitting better than .320.

In an early April game at Baker Bowl in 1921, the Phillies bashed the Giants, 11 to 5, and hit 4 home runs in the process. In his account of the game, reporter Jimmy Isaminger of the Philadelphia *North American,* who had broken the Black Sox story the previous autumn, chided the loutish locals for resorting to "brute strength" in overcoming the more artful and, in the reporter's view, classier New Yorkers. Had the conservative Isaminger been privileged to peer into the heart of John McGraw, leader of those "classy" Giants, the writer might have been shocked at what he discovered.

Smarting from three successive second-place finishes, McGraw was rebuilding his team in a new image. Little Napoleon may have been truculent, irascible, vituperative, stubborn, and all the other unpleasant things he has been called—but he was never a fool. The lesson of Babe Ruth, acted out right in McGraw's own ballpark, was not lost on him. Consequently, with the exception of veteran left fielder George Burns, McGraw had completely recycled his pennant winners of 1917. The Giants were still the fastest team in baseball and, as always, they could field well. But now they had a lot more punch at the plate. It was particularly true in the case of their young first baseman, George Kelly, who thrilled Giant fans for a week or two at the opening of the 1921 season by leading Ruth in the home-run derby. Kelly, in fact, went on to win the National League home-run title with a less than Ruthian total of 23.

The tip-off on McGraw's new attitude was that in 1920 he had persuaded the Giants' principal owner, Charles Stoneham, to offer the impoverished St. Louis Cardinals $300,000 in cash for slugger Rogers Hornsby. It was about three times what the Yankees had paid for Ruth and might have purchased control of any one of several major-league franchises. Cardinal general manager and field manager Branch Rickey was the only man alive with the chutzpah to demand that along with the cash the Giants throw in Frankie Frisch, the league's most promising young infielder. The deal fell through, of course, and it was rumored that McGraw's response to Rickey's extortionate demand would have drawn blushes from a longshoreman. It is tempting to speculate what baseball records might look like now if Hornsby had followed Ruth to the Polo Grounds in 1921.

The Giants may have modified their style of play in the twenties, but in other respects they were the Giants of old. When they were not brawling with umpires or other teams, McGraw's playful rowdies sparred with one another in the dugout. In spite of their high spirits, after four months it looked as though the Giants were headed for their fourth consecutive second-place finish. Late in August the New Yorkers trailed high-flying Pittsburgh by 7½ games. The Pirates' combination of speed, defense, and pitching seemed to be too much for McGraw and his power hitters.

But Little Napoleon had not been sitting around waiting for a miracle to bail him out. In June, his team slipping toward third place, he tried to land Cincinnati's star third baseman Heinie Groh, only to have his hand slapped by the new Commissioner of Baseball. The captious and autocratic Landis had detected some irregularity in the offer made for Groh and vetoed the deal. It was a tough break for New York. Acquisition of Groh would have given McGraw the strongest infield in baseball.

Undaunted, in July McGraw dealt with the Phillies for good-field, no-hit utility infielder Johnny Rawlings, veteran outfielder

Casey Stengel, and a backup pitcher. Rawlings was the key man in the deal because McGraw needed to fill a gap in the infield left by the retirement of top-ranked second baseman and team captain Larry Doyle. That's why the Giants had been after Groh. But the canny McGraw also wanted the thirty-one-year-old Stengel, and to land him he gave up young Lance Richbourg, who was fast and could hit well but had little power. The swap of Richbourg for the gimpy Stengel seemed like madness at the time, especially since Casey's bad legs had kept him on the disabled list for most of the season.

Before the week was out, McGraw also sent $75,000 to Seattle for outfielder Bill Cunningham, a hard-hitting right-handed batter, who was the reigning sensation of the Pacific Coast League and was considered the top prospect among minor-league outfielders.

The Seattle Rainiers had scarcely deposited the Giants' $75,000 when McGraw turned once more to the Phillies' slave market. On July 25 he surrendered a bundle of cash and players estimated at $100,000 for star left fielder Emil "Irish" Meusel, brother of the Yankees' Bob Meusel. Philadelphia owner William Baker alibied the deal by charging Meusel with "indifferent performance." Irish was batting .353 at the time of the trade. Meusel, by the way, had not a trace of Hibernian ancestry, but early on a Los Angeles writer decided that Emil looked Irish. And, by golly, he did.

Neither Stengel nor Meusel was the sort of player that McGraw would have given a second look in years past. Casey, who had known his best days in Brooklyn before World War I, was painfully slow. Neither man was Tris Speaker with a glove, and Meusel had a notoriously weak arm. (By a quirk of genes his brother Bob may have had the strongest arm in the history of baseball.) Nevertheless, Stengel and Meusel could hit—and hit with power. That's what McGraw was looking for in the new era. And he was right.

Having completed his deals, McGraw quietly awaited the arrival on August 24 of Pittsburgh manager George Gibson and his laid-back Buccaneers. The Pirates amused themselves between victories with such schoolboy pranks as dropping bags of water from hotel windows on dignified passersby. Led by talented and irrepressible first baseman Charles "Jolly Cholly" Grimm, who kept the boys relaxed by playing his ukulele in the dugout, and their slick-fielding, madcap shortstop, Walter "Rabbit" Maranville, the Pittsburgh pranksters were confident that if they won just 2 of the scheduled 5 games at the Polo Grounds, the pennant race was over.

The grim, reinforced Giants descended on their cocky visitors like a starved cougar on a spring lamb. Pittsburgh blew all 5 games and staggered from the Polo Grounds leading by just 2½ games. The batting star of the series for the Giants was—who else?— Irish Meusel.

The bleeding Bucs retreated across the East River to Ebbets Field, where they promptly lost 3 more. Safely back in Pittsburgh in September, the Pirates protested to the Commissioner that rich teams like the Giants could buy pennant insurance late in the season and negate the patient planning and long-term efforts of poorer clubs. It was a valid complaint and in time led to the establishment of a June 15 trading deadline.

The style of play by the Giants during the Pittsburgh series confirmed that McGraw, who had preached and taught scientific baseball for thirty years, was irrevocably seized by the Babe Ruth disease. For the remaining eleven years of McGraw's tenure, the Giants, whatever their other virtues or shortcomings, would feature power. In confirmation of McGraw's revised tactics, the Giants overtook the Pirates on September 13, and coasted home 4 games in front.

The Yankees, who would hit a record-shattering 134 homers to complement their excellent pitching, had the tougher time making good their October date with the Giants. Tris Speaker's doughty Cleveland Indians, sporting the legend "World Champions" on their 1921 blouses, had declined to approve the script for an all–New York World Series. Before the season, Speaker had picked the Giants to win in the National League and said that he looked forward to meeting them in October. He almost made good the boast.

The Yankees played well all season. Yet, no matter how many runs they scored or home runs they hit, they could not shake the Indians. On August 30 New York opened a 6-game home-and-home series with the Washington Senators. The Yankees won all 6 and scored 59 runs in the process. It was the newly patented Yankee style of attack. But when Miller Huggins and his hulking crew checked the league standings on the morning of September 5, there were the pesky singles hitters from Cleveland just 1 game behind.

On paper the Indians appeared to be no match for the Yankees in any department, including pitching. They were not even as fast as the lumbering New Yorkers, and they would finish the season with only 42 home runs, less than one-third the Yankee total. Still, Speaker had a lot of good contact hitters and they knew how to score runs. As a team they would bat .308 (not enough to lead the league in the new era) and roll up 925 runs, 68 more than in 1920. The Indians' 355 doubles set a major-league record.

When the Indians arrived at the Polo Grounds on September 23 for the crunch series of 1921, the teams were tied in games won and lost, but the Yankees held a percentage-point lead of .002. The odds appeared to favor New York. Two of Cleveland's key men, Speaker and catcher Steve O'Neill, were playing hurt and the Indians' pitching was in disarray.

In the first game New York's young Waite Hoyt outpitched spitballer Stanley Coveleski, 4 to 2, and the Yanks moved a full game ahead in the standings. On the following day Cleveland's George Uhle held the Yankee batters to 4 hits and shut them out, 9 to 0. The Indians had pulled even again. It was a sobering moment for New York.

On Sunday Yankee power finally broke the harness. Before 38,000 ecstatic fans, the New Yorkers buried the Indians, 21 to 7, and they did it without the aid of a Babe Ruth home run. Once more the Yankees held the lead.

The Indians were battered, but they were far from beaten. Since both clubs had expended their first-line pitching, the final game on Monday turned into a bruising, gouging Pier Six brawl, with the lead changing hands several times. When gutsy Cleveland Catcher Steve O'Neill went down swinging for the final out in the ninth, the Yankees lay gasping like a beached whale. But they had won, 8 to 7, thanks largely to 2 home runs and a double by Babe Ruth. The Babe had also driven in 5 runs. Years later Waite Hoyt, whose father-in-law was a New York undertaker, testified that, though it was not reported in the press, at least two fans died of the excitement.

Cleveland left town trailing by 2 games, down 3 in the loss column. With Speaker and O'Neill now forcibly benched and the pitching shot, the Indians folded. New York won by 4½ games. After twenty years in the league, the Yankees were champions.

In both leagues, the 1921 season illustrated that in future it would be difficult for a good team without power to beat a good team with power. Not impossible, just difficult.

No one smiled more broadly over the Yankee victory than cost-conscious Ed Barrow, the new general manager, who had been lured away from the Red Sox over the winter. More than 130,000 had squeezed into the Polo Grounds to watch the Cleveland series, and now Barrow had the pleasure of announcing prices for World Series tickets.

When you look at what Ruth had achieved in 1921, it's a wonder that the Yankees hadn't coasted to the pennant. The Bambino improved his fabulous offensive numbers of 1920 in every category except walks, where he fell just 4 shy. He even stole more bases. Specifically, Ruth batted .378 on 204 hits, including 44 doubles, 16 triples, and 59 homers. His slugging average was .846, a scintilla shy of his all-time mark of .847 in 1920. Babe scored 177 runs and drove in 171. He drew 144 walks and stole 17 bases.

Despite Ruth's impressive achievements in 1921, which included a new major-league home-run record, he had not outperformed the rest of baseball as convincingly as in 1920. Largely for that reason, most baseball historians regard 1920 as the Babe's greatest season.

Significantly, in 1921 five major leaguers other than Ruth—Bob Meusel, "Tilly" Walker, Ken Williams, Rogers Hornsby, and George Kelly—hit more than 20 home runs for the first time in their careers, evidence that the Babe's batting style was spreading.

Although Ruth was now forced to share the spotlight with rising young sluggers, Babe was still hitting the ball farther than anyone else. In park after park, he eclipsed distance records that he had established in the previous two seasons. On successive days in June, for example, the Babe hit 500-foot-plus homers into the left-center-field bleachers at the Polo Grounds. It would be more than half a century before another batter—Joe Adcock of the Milwaukee Braves—reached those distant seats with a fair ball.

On July 18 at Detroit's Navin Field, Ruth hit what may have been the longest home run by any batter in a regular-season game. Reporters resorted to Fred Lieb's 1919 expedient of using surveying instruments to measure the drive and determined that the ball had left the ballpark at 560 feet and was still airborne. Harry Bullion of the Detroit *Free Press,* who was sitting where he could follow the course of the ball, saw it hit a small shed on Trumbull Avenue. Bullion believed that had the ball not collided with the shed, it would have traveled about 590 feet in the air.

It is generally acknowledged that after 1920 pitchers rarely offered Ruth a good pitch to swing at. Witnesses have reported that in the early 1920s some of Babe's longest homers were virtually launched from his shoetops. His search for a decent pitch to hit might have been even more fruitless had he not been followed in the Yankee batting order by young Bob Meusel, the right-handed cleanup hitter. Playing his second year in the majors in 1921, the lanky Californian batted .318, hit 24 homers to tie with Ken Williams for second place in the majors, and drove in 135 runs. The taciturn Meusel pointedly avoided sportswriters, and as a consequence never enjoyed the good press that was the normal lot of a star ballplayer in New York. Despite his great throwing arm, "Long Bob" was at times guilty of lapses in concentration in the field and was known as "Languid Bob" among a few disgruntled fans.

Unlike the fall of 1920, this time the Giants and Yankees didn't need clearance from National League president John Heydler to meet in the dream series. Not only would the entire best-of-nine World Series be played in one city, it would be played in the same ballpark. The press quickly labeled the event the "Nickel World Series," because that was the cost of public transportation from most parts of the city.

Happily for the club owners (under 1921 rules the top three

teams in each league shared in World Series receipts), the sharp recession of spring and summer had run its course. Business was booming, employment was up, and retail prices had begun to skid. Bloomingdale's was offering lightweight men's suits for $23.75. If your budget didn't allow for the cost of the label, you could get approximately the same suit at Saks—34th Street for $13.50. More Americans than ever before enjoyed disposable income and many seemed eager to spend it on leisure-time activities, especially a glamorous sports event like the World Series.

With commercial radio in America barely thirteen months old, New York's radio station WJZ took a daring leap into the future. They arranged to broadcast the Series. Technology for network broadcasting lay years in the future, of course, and WJZ's signal may not have carried much beyond Perth Amboy, New Jersey. Still, the handful of New Yorkers who owned radio receivers must have been thrilled with WJZ's pioneering effort.

Before the Series opened, the New York sporting press hyped it as an epic duel between Babe Ruth and Giant manager John McGraw. It was a bizarre notion: baseball's greatest young slugger pitted against the pudgy, Machiavellian bench manager. But Ruth and McGraw were the two biggest names in baseball and among the game's most volatile personalities, and the contrived matchup made sensational copy. Could "Little Napoleon" outwit the Sultan of Swat in one of baseball's friendliest home-run parks? Since Ruth had hit a mammoth 59 homers in the course of the season, McGraw faced an unprecedented challenge.

Would the Giants dare pitch to the Babe, who had been walked 144 times by American League pitchers? In a transparent effort to rile the notoriously thin-skinned Ruth, McGraw, master of psychological warfare since his earliest years in the game, bellowed for all reporters to hear, "Certainly, we'll pitch to the big bum. Why shouldn't we?" There is no evidence, however, that the ploy had a negative effect on Babe, who was, after all, in his seventh year in the majors and had already played in three World Series.

When Ruth came to bat in the top of the first inning of Game One with a runner on second, 30,000 fans held their breath. The record for World Series home runs was a modest 2, held jointly by Home Run Baker of the Yankees (then playing with the Athletics) and Harry Hooper of the Red Sox. In a 9-game series the Babe could conceivably triple that number. On this at-bat, Ruth singled to center to drive in what would many years later be called a game-winning RBI. Carl Mays shut out the Giants, 3 to 0. There were no homers in the game.

The Yankees won the second game by the same 3-to-0 score. Waite Hoyt limited the Giants to 2 hits. Not only was there no homer in the game, there was not even an extra-base hit. The dream match between the New York titans was looking alarmingly like a replay of the 1905 Series between the Giants and Athletics, when every game ended in a shutout.

Although the Yankees were up by 2 games in the Series, they had gotten a bad break. Ruth scraped his left arm sliding. As happened often in his career when he suffered a break in the skin, Babe's arm became infected. With his arm bandaged, the big slugger played in Game Three and drove in 2 of the Yankees' 5 runs with a single in three official trips to the plate. Unfortunately for the Yankees, Huggins had exhausted his supply of rested pitchers and his team got trounced, 13 to 5. Remarkably, the 20 hits by the Giants in this game remain a World Series record.

Against doctor's orders Ruth insisted on playing in the fourth game, and that afternoon he finally hit his first World Series home run. It was not enough to save the Yanks, who lost, 4 to 2. Still heavily bandaged and brushing aside warnings from the club physician, Ruth played again on Monday in Game Five. He managed a bunt single, and with his heads-up base running helped the Yankees win, 3 to 1.

This was not the Ruth that fans had paid to see, and worse, he was risking his health and future. Reluctantly, but wisely, the Babe sat out the remainder of the Series. The Yankees still had plenty of power hitters in the lineup, including Meusel, Pipp, and Baker, but it wasn't enough to save them. With Ruth out of the way, the Giants swept the next 3 games. It confirmed an axiom of the press that would hold for another decade: "As Ruth goes, so go the Yankees."

By every rule of probability, 1922 should have been Babe Ruth's greatest season. He would be twenty-seven, and playing in

his eighth big-league season. Except for occasional colds and periodic bouts of indigestion resulting from gluttony, he enjoyed
good health. In light of what Babe had achieved in 1920 and
1921, allegedly seeing few good pitches to hit, a goal of 70 home
runs was not out of the question. Fate and poor judgment ruled
otherwise.

In the fall of 1921, as he had done several times in the past,
Ruth organized a postseason barnstorming trip. It was not unusual for a couple of big-name players to enlist the services of a
few journeymen teammates and even some minor leaguers to make
up two squads and tour the provinces, where they could exhibit
themselves in the flesh. Ruth, the biggest entertainment drawing
card in the country, could almost count on making more money
barnstorming than he might in several World Series.

Unfortunately for Babe and his troupe, there was a major-league
rule barring members of championship teams from all postseason
play other than the World Series. It was rumored that the rule
had been inspired by the owners' fear that their high-priced
champions might blow a game to one of the independent black
teams that barnstormers sometimes faced, perhaps in a place like
Cuba. It would shatter the illusion of white superiority. The alleged motive is just absurd enough to be true.

Commissioner Landis, in office little more than a year and not
feeling entirely secure, warned Ruth and the other Yankee players not to carry out their projected barnstorming schedule. Landis admitted publicly that he thought the prohibition was silly. It
was, nevertheless, a regulation of Organized Baseball, and as
Commissioner he was obligated to enforce it.

Sensing that Landis was not bluffing, the lesser Yankees withdrew from the tour. Ruth, a knee-jerk flouter of authority, paid
no attention to the Commissioner's interdiction, nor did his la-
conic teammate Bob Meusel. Ironically, the tour was a bust, mostly
because the barnstormers ran into bad weather. The sluggers made
so little money that they canceled the tour halfway through. Still,
they had gone far enough to provoke a showdown with the fledgling Commissioner. Landis was forced to act and act decisively or
turn in his official seal.

Never one to hand out light sentences—he had once fined
Standard Oil almost $30 million—Landis withheld World Series

checks from the culprits and suspended them for thirty-nine days
of the 1922 season, one fourth of the schedule. The judge had
made his point. For the remainder of Ruth's playing days, he would
continue to defy managers, umpires, and smaller fry, but he never
again crossed the Commissioner. At Landis's urging, the owners
withdrew the prohibition against barnstorming by pennant winners at their next winter meeting.

It was nothing short of miraculous that the absence of Ruth
and Meusel until May 20 did not scuttle the Yankees' pennant
chances in 1922. Thanks to the acquisition over the winter of
two more top-flight pitchers from the Fenway feeding pen—Sad
Sam Jones and "Bullet" Joe Bush—the Yankees boasted what must
have been the strongest pitching staff of the 1920s. Good pitching kept them in contention. In fact, by the time the delinquent
outfielders returned to the lineup, the Yankees were playing .666
ball and were firmly established in first place. But, of course, they
couldn't be expected to maintain that pace on pitching alone.
Over the long haul the team needed both Ruth and Meusel.

Characteristically, having treated the period of suspension as
an extension of his spring training, which meant no training at
all, Ruth was not in shape when he was reinstated. In addition,
he had turned sullen and touchy. To his considerable loss, Babe
tended to take out his unhappiness on umpires. The 1922 season
became a nightmare of suspensions, fines, minor injuries, fist fights
with teammates, and general frustration. For the first time in Ruth's
career, he heard cheers replaced by jeers. Since the Babe's temperament allowed for nothing but adulation, the change crushed
his spirits.

It is a measure of Ruth's irrepressible talent that under the
circumstances he managed a season average of .315 and hit 35
home runs in 110 games. For the first time since he had become
an outfielder he drove in fewer than 100 runs (99, to be exact.)
By Ruth's standards it was a miserable season. Worst of all, he
suffered the humiliation of finishing fourth in the major-league
home-run derby. The Cardinals' Rogers Hornsby, who had hit only
21 homers in 1921, finished with 42 to lead the majors. Others
were getting uncomfortably close to what had been the Babe's
exclusive domain.

Just as they had been involved in a season-long rumble with

Cleveland in 1921, the Yankees of 1922 found themselves unable to shake off the upstart St. Louis Browns. The Browns had discovered dynamite in their bats. Through midsummer New York and St. Louis were alternately in and out of first place. Clearly, it was time for money barons Ruppert and Huston to turn to their Boston fiefdom for salvation. On July 23, for $50,000 cash and a tumbrel of inconsequential baseball flesh, New York acquired Joseph "Jumping Joe" Dugan, the league's best third baseman, and the aging but still potent Elmer Smith. Smith had been heartlessly banished by the Indians to the Siberia of Boston over the winter. Between seasons the Yankees had also snagged light-hitting but slick-fielding shortstop Everett Scott from Boston. Unquestionably, the addition of Dugan gave the New Yorkers one of the top defensive infields in the league.

With their shored-up infield and always classy pitching, the Yankees took a slim lead over the Browns in mid-August and held on tenaciously until October. New York staggered across the finish line ahead by just 1 game.

Meanwhile, John McGraw, after five years of tinkering with lineups, dealing for new talent, and tongue-lashing desultory players, fashioned the kind of season he felt he deserved. Except for a brief moment in July, when they were overtaken by the surging St. Louis Cardinals, the Giants led from start to finish. The only real excitement in the National League in 1922 proved to be the fight for second place among Cincinnati, Pittsburgh, and St. Louis, who finished within a game of one another. Actually, everyone around the league had a little fun. Batters hit .292 to beat out the American Leaguers by 8 percentage points.

McGraw's 1922 squad may have been the finest he ever put together. It might be more accurate to say that it was the strongest McGraw team ever to win a pennant. At last he had succeeded in reacquiring from Cincinnati, whence he had let him slip away back in 1913, the league's best third baseman, Heinie Groh. Groh, along with George Kelly at first, Frankie Frisch at second, and Dave Bancroft at short, formed one of the greatest infields of the first half of the century. Kelly, Frisch, and Bancroft were eventually elected to the Hall of Fame.

Like his neighbor Miller Huggins, McGraw was ready by midsummer to dip into the owner's purse to be doubly sure that the pennant didn't get away from him. Having stripped the Phillies of everyone of value, he turned to the Boston Braves. On July 30, for $100,000 in cash and two starting pitchers, the Giants acquired right-handed pitcher Hugh McQuillan.

What McGraw saw in McQuillan other than his youth is not clear. "Handsome Hugh," as he was called, had not been mesmerizing National League batters. Yet, Branch Rickey in St. Louis must have discerned similar good qualities in the right-hander because he publicly protested the deal and threatened to sue to invalidate it on grounds of collusive business practice. At the very least, McGraw was prescient in making the deal for McQuillan because late in August the Giants' "Shufflin' Phil" Douglas, a pathetic drunk but a good spitballer, got himself barred from baseball for life for offering to throw games so that the Cardinals could win. Douglas was 11 and 4 at the time of his departure. The acquisition of McQuillan in July probably saved the pennant for New York.

In 1922 all but one Giant regular batted over .320. The delinquent, ironically, was newly acquired Heinie Groh, an excellent hitter who just had an off year with his bottle bat. In 1921 Heinie had batted .331.

Throughout the season McGraw, borrowing the idea of platooning from Tris Speaker, made almost perfect use in center field of the physically impaired Stengel and the rookie Bill Cunningham. Between them Stengel and Cunningham batted .348 and drove in 81 runs. From the catcher's spot, where Pancho Snyder and Earl Smith shared the work, McGraw realized 14 homers and 90 RBIs plus a .311 batting average.

The Giants could not begin to match bats with the Yankees in home runs, or even with the Cardinals and Phillies in their own league. Neither did they compare with the Yankees in pitching. But McGraw's men were fast, opportunistic, and they knew how to get on base. Like their Series opponents they were an excellent defensive team by the standards of the day.

In October the World Series was once again touted as costing two nickels for travel and six dollars for the best seat. Many Americans in and out of New York City now had the six dollars as well as the two nickels. As he had pledged in 1921, the genial neologist, President Warren G. Harding, was leading the nation back to "normalcy." Despite the fact that Commissioner Landis had ordered a return to the traditional best-of-seven formula for the World Series, the owners anticipated making money from a Standing Room Only Series. They got it—for 4 games.

As in 1921, the oddsmakers favored the Yankees, largely because of the Ruth's presence in the lineup. This time Babe was in good physical condition though his emotional state left much to be desired.

Perhaps Babe's anxiety had escaped the notice of the oddsmakers, but it didn't get by McGraw. The astute Giant manager recognized that Ruth was so eager to succeed, he would likely swing at anything. The book was to pitch the Bambino low and tight and never throw him a fastball. During the Series McGraw planned to call every pitch made to Ruth. Further, Little Napoleon assigned utility infielder Johnny Rawlings to heap verbal abuse on the fretful Babe from the protective shadow of the dugout.

Poor Ruth batted only .118 and hit no homers during a yawner of a Series, which the Yankees lost, 4 games to 0. In Game Two, with the score tied at 3 at the end of ten innings, plate umpire George Hildebrand inexplicably called the game because of darkness. Commissioner Landis, who had been shading his eyes from the sun when the game was called, went into a rage and ordered the day's receipts turned over to charity to save the good name of baseball. The game went into the records as a tie. The Giants won the other 4 with relative ease. The proud and cantankerous McGraw was once again top dog in New York. It would be his last World Championship.

An angry Colonel Huston, who blamed the Yankees' humiliation on Huggins, impulsively sold his interest in the club to Ruppert. Colonel Jake became sole owner, and although his understanding of the game remained sketchy for the rest of his days, the elegant brewer was skillful at hiring talent to get the job done. During Ruppert's tenure, the Yankees would never again be humbled in this fashion.

The following year, 1923, was a dream season for both New York clubs. The Giants were never out of first place, the Yankees only for a day in the first week. It's as close as teams in both leagues have come to leading wire to wire in the same season. For the Yankees the excitement started in the spring with the opening of their new home, Yankee Stadium, an enlarged version of Lenin's tomb. The park had not been built with the idea of winning architectural prizes, however, but to accommodate baseball fans—70,000 of them. It gave the Yankees almost twice the seating capacity they had had at the Polo Grounds.

It was a repentant Ruth who took the field in the spring of 1923. He began the year in proper style by hitting the first home run at Yankee Stadium. When the mood of reform was upon the Babe, no one could appear more contrite and sober. His determination to behave himself in 1923 is reflected in the fact that he played in every one of the Yankees' games.

It's hard to say just how much Ruth's departure from the Polo Grounds affected his home-run production. Conventional wisdom says, a lot. The Babe himself seemed to agree.

Curiously, Yankee Stadium, with its beckoning right-field porch and impossibly spacious left-field power alley, gave the appearance of having been specially designed to accommodate a left-handed slugger like Ruth. (In fact, the layout of the park seems to have been dictated for the most part by the direction of the streets around it and the amount of money that Huston and Ruppert could afford to spend at the time.) In any case, Ruth hit only 41 home runs that year, and although he regained his American League crown, he had to share the major-league lead with the Phillies' Cy Williams.

Before the 1923 season Ruth announced that he was going to improve his batting. He must have had in mind trying to prove that he could hit .400 like Cobb and Sisler. He very nearly did. His .393 was the highest mark of his career. Surely, that effort should have been enough to fetch him a Triple Crown. Not while Detroit's Harry Heilmann was still in the league. "Harry the Horse"—or "Slug," as he was also sometimes known—hit .403. What must a .250 hitter have felt like in such an age? And they existed. White Sox shortstop Harvey McClellan hit only .235 in 550 at-bats in a league that posted an average of .282.

Ruth put one more record out of reach in 1923. He walked 170 times. Joe Sewell of Cleveland was down over the horizon in second place with 98. Although no official record of inten-tional walks was kept, it has been estimated that the Babe re-ceived at least 50.

If anyone in the Yankee lineup was justified in mourning the club's departure from the Polo Grounds, it had to be right-handed slugger Bob Meusel. In his first season at Yankee Stadium, he dis-covered that so-called "Death Valley" in left-center was exactly that. Meusel managed only 9 homers, probably most of them on the road. The change of scenery did no harm to his batting av-erage, however, and in a couple of seasons Long Bob would work out his problems well enough to lead the league in home runs.

In 1923 and later, the Yankees were stereotyped as Murder-ers' Row, but as much as anything it was their superb pitching and excellent fielding that permitted the team to sail home 16 games ahead of the pack. Tormented by the idea that the Boston Red Sox still had a quality pitcher whom they had not claimed, the Yankees purchased left-hander Herb Pennock in January 1923 to join the other five top-flight pitchers they had snagged from the grieving Hub. Future Hall of Famer Pennock won 19 and lost 6 in his first season in New York.

The 1923 season is notable for the first appearance in a Yan-kee uniform of Lou Gehrig. In 13 games Lou batted .423, had 6 extra-base hits, and drove in 9 runs. Barrow shipped the kid back to Hartford in the Eastern League to sharpen his batting skills.

On October 10, when the Giants and the Yankees squared off for their third successive World Series, baseball fans in other cit-ies must have loosed a collective moan. New York's dominance of the game was a depressing illustration of the power of money. In time Branch Rickey at St. Louis devised a solution to the in-equitable distribution of wealth by developing his famous farm system. But soon thereafter the rich clubs, especially the Yan-kees, followed suit and established comparable farm systems.

Happily for fans outside New York, they could not see into the future. From 1921 through 1941, fourteen World Series would be played in part or entirely in New York. Fans are luckier today. All clubs are rich and the player pool inadequate. No longer, it seems, can a single organization establish a baseball dynasty. Ma-jor-league expansion does have redeeming features.

After winning it all in 1922, McGraw had not been content to stand pat. He never was. The Giants spent $75,000 for San Francisco outfielder Jimmy O'Connell, $65,000 for Baltimore pitcher Jack Bentley, and far smaller amounts for three future Hall of Famers—first baseman Bill Terry, shortstop Travis Jackson, and outfielder Lewis "Hack" Wilson. The acquisitions helped beef up an already powerful offense. In 1923 the Giants would lead the league in batting and score more runs than any team in the majors except Cleveland. Setting aside the abundance of runs, it is a tribute to McGraw's brilliance that, while working with a pitching staff that compiled the league's third worst ERA, he was able to keep his team in first place every day of the schedule.

Although Ruth had the honor of hitting the first home run at Yankee Stadium in April, he did not get the first World Series home run. The honor went instead to Casey Stengel. In the ninth inning of Game One of the 1923 Series, with the score tied at 4, the left-handed Stengel hit a drive into the limitless power alley in left-center. He is reported to have been an amusing sight, churning around the bases on unresponsive legs. As Casey rounded third, his left shoe came loose and he had to hobble the final sixty feet. A masterful slide brought him in safely under Everett Scott's relay to the plate. Stengel had scored and driven in the winning run in the first World Series game played at Yankee Stadium.

After the Yankees had evened the Series in Game Two at the Polo Grounds by a score of 4 to 2, Stengel resumed his home run heroics in the third game, again at Yankee Stadium. This time he blasted a pitch into the right-field bleachers in the seventh inning to provide the margin of victory in a 1-to-0 thriller. As Stengel crossed the plate after a leisurely trip around the bases, he thumbed his nose at the partisan Yankee crowd, provoking the sometimes pompous Colonel Ruppert to demand that Commissioner Landis censure Casey for ungentlemanly behavior. But Landis felt that the episode was funny and Casey went unreprimanded.

In the end, however, Casey's effort went for naught. The Yankees had too much pitching, too much everything, to be denied the big prize a third time. They took the Series, 4 games to 2, and at last were World Champions, a title that charmed them so much that in future only infrequently would they relinquish it. Babe Ruth set a World Series record by hitting 3 homers, all at the Polo Grounds, a fact not without significance. As expected, the 1923 Series broke all previous records for attendance, drawing more than 300,000 paying fans for the 6 games.

When the 1924 season opened there was every reason to expect that the New York teams would meet in the World Series for the fourth consecutive year. The Giants finished in front, the Yankees did not. Unlike the restless McGraw, Miller Huggins saw no reason to make a change in his 1923 champions except for getting rid of the talented but ungracious Carl Mays, with whom he had been feuding for years.

The 1924 Yankees were the same great team, but they were a year older and they sorely lacked foot speed. Ruth, whose world-famous beer belly was now approaching record proportions, may still have been the fastest man on the Yankee squad. In any case, the power-laden New Yorkers lost out by 2 games to the younger, more eager Washington Senators, managed by twenty-eight-year-old second baseman Stanley "Bucky" Harris. Washington hit only 22 home runs for the season, the lowest total in the majors. But they made their singles and doubles count and they had excellent pitching.

Ruth contributed more than his share in a vain effort to bring the Yankees a fourth pennant. He won the American League batting title with a .378 average and led the majors in home runs with 46. Once again the Triple Crown eluded him. Washington's Goose Goslin beat him out for the RBI title.

Despite the handicap of mediocre pitching, the 1924 Giants sneaked home a game and a half in front of a fast-closing Brooklyn team that boasted excellent pitching. In the end, New York was saved by its hitting. Six regulars batted over .300. The Giants' superb right fielder, Ross Youngs, led the team with a .356 average, his eighth consecutive year above .300. Sadly, it was Youngs's last great season. In 1925 his performance would decline sharply, evidence that Bright's disease, which would kill him two years later, was already running its lethal course.

In addition to leading the majors in batting with a .300 average, the 1924 Giants led the National League in home runs, evidence of their new style of play. Not even the crafty McGraw, however, could continue to produce pennants with home runs and mirrors. The Giants' need for stronger pitching had become desperate. After 1924, McGraw would never win another pennant, and in his final World Series, owing largely to inadequate pitching, he lost a heartbreaker to the Washington Senators, 4 games to 3.

In a perfect world, Brooklyn would have won the National League flag in 1924. They deserved to win. In mid-August the Robins were in fourth place, 12 games behind the Giants. Inexplicably, Wilbert Robinson's ragtag squad, who had spent three seasons in the second division, suddenly came alive. Led by left-fielder Zack Wheat, who was having his greatest season in a Hall of Fame career, and first baseman Jacques Fournier, on his way to the league home-run title, Brooklyn won 24 of 28 and by early September actually moved ahead of New York by half a game. At one point the Robins swept four doubleheaders on successive days and put together a 15-game winning streak.

Pittsburgh chose this time to put on their own stretch drive, which should have spelled double trouble for New York. In fact, it worked against the Robins, who couldn't handle the Pirates in the closing weeks of the season, while the Giants had no problem with them. Brooklyn remained in the race until the final two days, but fell a game and a half short. It would be their single moment of glory until the end of the decade.

The batting career of Zack Wheat, possibly the most popular player ever to wear a Brooklyn uniform, underscores again the difficulty of ascribing causes for the expansion of hitting in the twenties. Wheat came to the majors in 1909 and by 1912 was established as one of the National League's finest hitters. In 1918 he won the batting championship. But through 1919 his lifetime average was exactly .300 and he had never collected more than 177 hits in a season.

In 1920, Wheat entered the golden twilight of his career. From that season until he hung up his spikes in 1927, Zack's smooth left-handed stroke brought him a cumulative .339 average, with three seasons of more than 200 hits. In 1923 and 1924, already thirty-five, the Missouri farmer twice batted .375. In spite of the lure of the right-field wall at Ebbets Field, the 170-pound Wheat was never tempted to imitate Babe Ruth. To the end Zack remained a straightaway hitter, averaging no more than 12 home runs a season.

Can we ascribe to the abolition of the spitball Wheat's surge to superstar status when he was past thirty-five? Probably the case can be made. At all events, the pattern of Wheat's career brings to mind a comment by Casey Stengel, a pretty good hitter himself. Late in life Casey, with undisguised rancor, often referred to the spitball as "the pitch that almost drove me out of baseball when I was twenty-five." The spitter must have been tough on most hitters.

By the mid-1920s a generation that would disdain a .280 hitter as a "sure out" had reached the age of consciousness. They were spoiled, yes, but what bliss they lived in. As John Thorn suggests, "Wouldn't it be nice to have someone hit .400 again, no matter what it means?" There are kinds of inflation that are not all bad.

SIX

...AND
THE
MISSISSIPPI

"You can't tell me nothin' about that ball
park in Saint Looie in July! They got it all
growed out in grass in April, but after July
first . . . hell!—it's paved with concrete."
—NEBRASKA CRANE in Thomas Wolfe's
You Can't Go Home Again

DESPITE ALL THE rumbling and flashing at the Polo Grounds in the
early 1920s, it was actually St. Louis that held sway as batting
capital of the majors. The ascendancy of the Mound City can be
traced in part to the characteristics of its ballpark, which, as was
true in New York, was used by both leagues. The oldest park in
the majors in continuous service, Sportsman's Park had one of
the smallest playing areas of the period. Still, it was something
more than the short right-field fence that endeared the place to
hitters of every stripe—something elusive, ineffable.

Throughout its ninety-one-year history, its several and often
bizarre configurations, Sportsman's Park enjoyed the reputation
of a hitter's park. The average fan probably understands the term
to mean a good background for the batter, fences at a friendly
distance, favorable conditions of light and shadow around home
plate, and no prevailing winds blowing in from center field. For
the player, "hitter's park" may mean all or some of these things

plus innumerable subtleties that no fan would ever dream of. It's enough for the bleacherite to know that at a hitter's park he can expect generation after generation of batters, friendly and hostile, to belt the ball with authority.

Way back in 1887, when the chatterbox St. Louis Browns of the old American Association were atomizing rivals with regularity at the juncture of Grand Avenue and Dodier Street, their lanky left fielder, James "Tip" O'Neill, rolled up a batting average of .492. One of the first Canadians to play in the majors, Tip was never heard to denigrate the summer heat and humidity of the city or threaten to withdraw his smoking shillelagh to the cool of his native Ontario. Like many famous St. Louis batsmen to follow him, Tip must have grasped early on how well the ball carries in the steamy atmosphere of the Mississippi Valley.

Let me be quick to point out that O'Neill and his fans— "kranks," as they were called then—*thought* that Tip had hit .492. They went to their graves believing it. But, of course, some baseball rules of 1887 favored the batter. A base on balls, for example, counted as a hit, and the first called strike did not count. On the other side of the coin, the strike zone was expansive—from the top of the shoulders to the bottom of the knees—and it took five balls to earn a walk.

Anyway, in 1968 Baseball Commissioner William Eckert appointed a Special Records Committee to purify the record book so that all records would reflect approximately the standards of 1968. Armed with the Commissioner's mandate, the committee dutifully whittled away at the records of those who lived in ages more fortunate than their own. They "normalized" O'Neill's 1887 performance to .435.

Although Sportsman's Park has been gone for almost a quarter of a century, at last report the Hoover Boys Club of St. Louis was still playing on a diamond at that location and lodging no complaints about the way the ball carries off aluminum bats. Can it be that particular patches of turf are enchanted, putting hitters at an advantage?

Don't scoff at the idea of ballyard numina. In 1921, when the St. Louis Cardinals abandoned old Robison Field at Vandeventer and Natural Bridge Avenues and moved in with the Browns at Sportsman's Park, *The Sporting News* reported:

Baseball fans in St. Louis have no regrets at the passing of
Cardinal Field as a playing field. Not only were the transportation arrangements inadequate and inconvenient, but
there is a deep-seated conviction in the Mound City that
the old park was a hoodoo. On the other hand Sportsman's Park is connected with some of the Mound City's
greatest baseball successes.

It is a matter of record that from the moment the Cardinals
moved to Sportsman's Park, their luck changed for the better.
What about the Browns? someone asks. They weren't so lucky. I
am not sure. In time they became the Baltimore Orioles.

No less an authority than Babe Ruth early satisfied himself
that Sportsman's Park was a spot that smiled upon hitters. In 1915,
when he had been in the majors scarcely long enough to dribble
tobacco juice down the front of his new Boston uniform, the
rookie pitcher clouted a ball over the pavilion roof in right field,
across Grand Avenue and through the showroom window of an
automobile dealer. Babe added a couple of doubles and drove in
3 of the Red Sox's 4 runs as he pitched his team to victory over
the Browns. After the game he posed for news photographers in
front of the broken showroom window, and it was rumored that
local car dealers scrambled for the remaining rental space on the
east side of Grand Avenue.

While the sultry air of Sportsman's Park may have been a fer-
tile medium for visiting sluggers like Ruth, Napoleon Lajoie, Ty
Cobb, and Joe Jackson, it wasn't doing a great deal for the resident Browns in the early years of the century. Clearly hoping to
inherit some of the mystique of the old Browns of the American
Association, in 1902 the owners of the St. Louis franchise in the
fledgling American League revived the name. The gambit didn't
work. That is to say, the Browns didn't win any pennants. On the
other hand, in those years of spitball despotism, they hit about as
well (or poorly) as the rest of the league. As a matter of fact, a
now-forgotten outfielder named George Stone won a batting
championship there in 1906.

By 1918 the Browns had struggled their way to fourth place,
mostly through the efforts of several young ballplayers discovered by Branch Rickey during his brief tenure as Browns manager. When in 1917 Rickey decamped for the Cardinals' front

office, his Brownie protégés, George Sisler, Hank Severeid, and
Baby Doll Jacobson, continued his campaign to show the club a
way out of the darkness.

In the early years of the century, the Cardinals, playing at
hexed and decrepit Robison Field, fared worse than the Browns.
From 1900 through 1920, the Cards finished in the second division sixteen times, six times in the cellar. Yet, in the latter years
of their ineptitude the club managed to stumble on at least one
talented young ballplayer, Rogers Hornsby. From the minute
Branch Rickey took over as president and general manager, he
set to work to build a winning team around this budding superstar. In 1918, when Cardinal field manager Miller Huggins de-
serted Rickey for New York and the Yankees' bullion vaults, the
general manager was forced to descend into the dugout and don
a third hat. Fortunately for the overextended young lawyer, wealthy
car dealer Sam Breadon bought the Cardinals and relieved Rickey
as club president.

Probably not even the editors of *The Sporting News* were prepared for what happened after July 1, 1920, when the Cardinals
abandoned Robison Field and set up shop at Sportsman's Park.
While it is hard to track a team's batting average through the
middle of a long-ago season, an informal survey of the box scores
for the final three months of the 1920 season suggests that from
July onward the Cardinal batters belabored National League
pitching in earnest. Like other clubs in both leagues, the Cards
may have been responding to the adoption of the clean-ball policy. Or possibly it was exultation at escape from that 120-foot
expanse between home plate and the screen at Robison Field.
(Until 1920 the Cards must have held the all-time record for foul-
ing out to the catcher.) Whatever the reasons, when the dust
settled in October, St. Louis had outhit everyone in the National
League with a mark of .289. It was 19 percentage points better
than the league average and 33 above their own effort for 1919.
The Cards outscored pennant-winning Brooklyn, and, on a paltry
32 home runs, managed to head the league in slugging as well.

Unhappily for the fans, all this heavy hitting produced small
results in the league standings. The potent but often porous Cards
finished in the second division yet again, tied with Chicago for

fifth place. Although things were looking up for the Redbirds in their new home, leader Branch Rickey had lots of work ahead of him.

In his three years as Cardinal general manager, Rickey had already upgraded player personnel significantly. And since the Cards were the most economically depressed club in the majors, he had been forced to accomplish the improvement through shrewd dealing alone. The organization had no cash and, except for Hornsby, who was indispensable, few players to attract attention in the trade market. Yet, somehow Rickey had brought together slugging first baseman Jacques "Jack" Fournier, fleet-footed rookie outfielders Austin McHenry and Cliff Heathcote, hard-hitting third baseman Milton Stock, and rookie pitchers Jesse Haines and Bill Sherdel, who between them would eventually win 354 games for St. Louis.

One of Rickey's first acts after taking over the Cardinals had been to rescue from exile in Washington two of his former Brownie favorites—aging outfielder Burt Shotton and shortstop John "Doc" Lavan, who was indeed an M.D. Both were close to the end of their careers, and it's likely that Lavan later turned out to be a better physician than he was a shortstop. Nevertheless, the pair had earlier demonstrated their loyalty to Rickey, and the "Mahatma" placed loyalty very high on the scale of human virtues. In spite of his reputation as a wily baseball negotiator, Rickey was a man of sensitivity and compassion. It may have been this element in his character that moved him to challenge baseball's infamous color line in 1946.

Among individual achievers on the Cardinals in 1920, Rogers Hornsby stood out. Long recognized as one of the league's best hitters, he had averaged .310 from 1916 through 1919 and showed occasional flashes of power. In those years Hornsby was shifted about in the infield but mostly played short. When Rickey finally assigned Hornsby to second permanently in 1920, Rajah responded by winning his first National League batting title.

In 1920 every one of Rickey's regulars batted over .280 except outfielder "Germany Joe" Schultz, who was platooned with left-handed-hitting Jack Smith. Smith made up for Schultz's dereliction by hitting .332. Jack Fournier and Milt Stock also batted over .300. Rookie outfielder Austin McHenry tied for fourth in the league in homers. Rickey's acumen as a horse trader was beginning to pay dividends.

With this kind of hitting and a starting rotation of Bill Doak, Ferdie Schupp, Haines, and Sherdel, each a 20-game winner at some point in his career, how did the Cardinals come to finish in a tie for fifth place? Among other things, three infielders—Fournier, Hornsby, and Lavan—all led the league in errors at their positions. At third, Stock came within a whisker of making it a complete infield of malefactors. Too many game headlines began, ERRORS OF CARDS COSTLY, and in mid-July *The Sporting News* charged bluntly, "The hard truth is that the Cards have been playing some bad ball."

Some of the club's defensive problems may have stemmed from the notoriously poor quality of the infield at Sportsman's Park. The famous red clay that has made St. Louis a city of brick may not be the best medium for playing fields. By the same token, the hard-surfaced infield may have worked to the advantage of the St. Louis hitters.

Regardless of the Cardinals' failure to finish higher than fifth, their improved competitiveness, and especially the dramatic increase in hitting, seemed to please the fans. In a schedule only fourteen games longer than that in 1919, the club almost doubled its paid attendance. The new image that Rickey had produced, along with some highly successful promotions such as the Knothole Gang, were slowly turning St. Louis from a Browns town into a Cardinal town. The Knothole Gang, a program to admit young boys to Cardinal games free, was underwritten by interested St. Louis businessmen and survived for decades.

Speaking of the Browns, in the memorable summer of 1920, the landlords of Sportsman's Park let no lichens gather on their bats either. They worked over American League pitching for a superheated .308 batting average, 44 percentage points better than their 1919 mark. While no one could hope to match Babe Ruth and the Yankees in power, the Browns did finish second to New York in home runs with 50. They also finished second in slugging average with an impressive .419.

Like their tenants, the Browns suffered an endemic hazard.

Visiting batters found the muggy atmosphere of St. Louis equally accommodating and too often the locals came out on the short end of a glorious slugfest. In *The Sporting News* for September 16, under the head "Batters Play No Favorites in St. Louis Games and Fans Seem to Like It As Pitchers Are Murdered," a St. Louis writer comments:

> Phil DeC. Ball's [Browns owner] intentions were to wreck the fences and bleachers at Sportsman's Park after the season closed in order to make improvements that will give St. Louis one of the finest baseball plants in the land, but by the time he gets home from his trip to Seattle he'll find the ball players have done the job for him unless some real pitching is sent out to stop the bombardments that have been featuring recent games. The way they have been hammering the ball against the frame work of fences and bleachers, the whole works will be battered down and there'll be nothing but debris left for the regular workmen to tackle.

Browns manager Jimmy Burke handled the pitchers as well as could be expected. There wasn't much to handle; it was a two-man staff. Ace right-hander Urban Shocker won 20, and Dixie Davis, late of the Cardinals, 18. No one else won more than 9. The Browns were probably lucky to finish fourth. Their fans, in any case, seemed as pleased with the great hitting as did the Cardinals' supporters. The Browns outdrew their tenants by almost 100,000.

The Brownie attack in 1920 was led by George Sisler, an extraordinary player having an unforgettable season. Like his St. Louis neighbor Rogers Hornsby, Sisler won the batting title. In addition to batting over .400, setting the major-league record for hits, and beating out Ruth in total bases, Sisler scored 137 runs and drove in 122. To keep up the circulation in his legs he stole 42 bases.

Backing up Sisler's assault was the outfield of Tobin, Jacobson, and Ken Williams, who collectively batted .334. They also drove in 256 runs, a remarkable figure at the dawn of the age of slugging.

Because of Rogers Hornsby's aggressive style at the plate, there was a temptation at first for St. Louis writers to compare him with

Babe Ruth. But except for their shared genius for hitting baseballs, two men could scarcely have been less alike. All they had
in common was American citizenship, superhuman vision, and a
penchant for slow horses. No swarm of cheering boys ever mobbed
Rajah as he emerged from a hotel or train station. It must have
taken a brave soul even to ask for his autograph. Hornsby was
aloof, austere in life-style, single-minded, arrogant, quick-tem-
pered, and, above all, tactless. The nation can count itself lucky
that young Rogers fixed upon a career in baseball rather than in
the State Department.

Sports publications of the 1920s often ran articles about
Hornsby—sometimes ostensibly by Hornsby—setting forth his
secrets for success in life, his theories about batting, and his advice on playing winning baseball. These pieces present a picture
of a player with a unique batting stance. A right-handed hitter,
Hornsby stood at the rear of the batter's box, feet close together,
as far from the plate as he could get. It left him with the single
choice of striding into every pitch. It may have looked to pitchers of the time as though Hornsby were conceding the outside
half of the plate. They learned, to their sorrow, that it was illusion. Baseball knew no more zealous guardian of the outside corner. And Hornsby had great power to the opposite field.

By modern standards Hornsby's home-run totals are not nearly
as impressive as his batting average. He long insisted that he never
tried to hit homers but gladly accepted them if they came. On
the other hand, Hornsby confessed that he tried to hit every pitch
as hard as he could. Rajah averaged 31 home runs a season for
his nine best years, and in the 1920s stood second only to Ruth
in lifetime totals. Hornsby was renowned among a generation of
catchers as one of only two hitters who would not shorten their
grip with a two-strike count. The other was Ruth.

In matters of training and conditioning, Hornsby was as un-
compromisingly Spartan as Ruth was self-indulgent. During the
season everything was subordinated to baseball—more precisely,
to batting. (Not a bad fielder, except on pop flies to short right,
Hornsby did not hold skill with the glove in high regard.) He
neither smoked nor drank and was in bed early every night to
ensure that he was rested for the next day's game. Rajah would

not even loosen up by attending an occasional movie lest he weaken his batting eye. He was a loner and seemed to have no capacity for conviviality. Outrageously short-tempered, Hornsby was quicker than Billy Martin is to throw a punch, often at team-mates, once at his manager, Branch Rickey.

In his supreme self-confidence Hornsby, like Ruth, was little afflicted by the superstitions that haunt lesser batters. His one concession to ritual—and it might be argued that this one had a shade of scientific support—was Hornsby's unshakable faith in the efficacy of a beefsteak diet. In this quirk he was a true son of Texas. Not just any sirloin from a hotel dining room would do. On the road he would often search out remote and humble diners, where they served exactly the kind of life-sustaining, hit-producing protein he craved. In Hornsby's strained version of camaraderie, he would sometimes invite younger teammates to join him for steak at a newly discovered eatery in the interest of strengthen-ing their hitting.

In the second quarter of this century, it was commonplace for baseball writers to hail Hornsby as the greatest right-handed batter of all time. It was before the era of Willie Mays, Frank Robinson, and Hank Aaron, but within a period graced by such formidable right-handed swingers as Harry Heilmann, Jimmie Foxx, Joe DiMaggio, Al Simmons, and Hank Greenberg. The business of selecting the best anything of all time is as charged with perils as being a volunteer judge at a Hadassah cooking contest. But rare is the baseball writer who can resist exhibiting his powers of assessment.

What may carry more weight than the judgment of baseball writers is the testimony of contemporaries on the field. Ty Cobb, who played against Hornsby in the California winter league, pro-nounced Hornsby the greatest batter he had ever seen, presum-ably either right-handed or left. George Sisler said that Hornsby had the best sense of the strike zone of any batter in baseball.

In what may be the most fascinating piece of baseball analysis done before the advent of sabermetrics in the 1970s, *Baseball Magazine*'s J. Newton Colver, in a three-part series in 1927, weighed the offensive achievements of every batter of ten years' major-league service, going back to 1876. Under the title, "Who

Was the Greatest Batter of All Time?" Colver cranked in every conceivable measure of batting known to the period, including the parks hitters played in and the opposition faced. He also considered the number of times a player won league honors, such as the batting title or slugging title. The surprise result of Colver's calculations—surprise to me at least—was the naming of Hornsby.

The other St. Louis batting wizard, George Sisler, different in batting style from Hornsby and vastly different in personality, is often described by contemporary writers in superlatives left over from the age of New York Giant hero Christy Mathewson—quiet, modest, manly, honorable, brilliant, gracious, thoughtful, etc. As in the case of Matty, there was a touch of the elitist about Sisler. An exquisite bat handler, the left-handed Sisler acknowledged Ty Cobb as his model. Like Cobb, Sisler possessed some power, but was convinced that his best course was to place the ball rather than to blast it. George's speed on the bases plus his superb fielding made him a more complete player than Hornsby.

In the winter of 1920–21, St. Louis baseball fans watched yellowish ice floes drift past the steamboat landing and in their minds replayed the batting heroics of the previous season. With such hitting, how could their fine lads long be denied a place in the sun? Sisler, Hornsby, Fournier, Jacobson, McHenry, Williams, Tobin, Stock . . . It had to count for something.

In the St. Louis City Series in April, the Cardinals lost to the Browns in a closely contested 7 games. But the Cards brushed it off. On Opening Day they broke from the gate eagerly—and immediately fell on their faces. They lost 7 of their first 8 games. At the end of April they were last, 7 games under .500. By May 8 they had won only 3 games.

On the tenth the Cardinals banged out 15 hits, enough to nose out the Giants, 7 to 6. Hornsby went 4 for 4. But one full month into the season they had won just 5 games. There was no complaint about the hitting. In St. Louis there was never a lack of hitting. Hornsby was tooling along at .471. Almost all the other Cardinal regulars were in the "normal" .300 range. Yes, the Cards were hitting. Unfortunately, so was the opposition.

Bang, bang went the Cardinals' bats. In late May the team

steadied. Slowly they began to rise. The rattling offense was having its effect. Rickey consumed cigars at a record pace and continued to horse trade. On June 18 he talked Brooklyn owner Charlie Ebbets into taking left-handed ace Ferdie Schupp in exchange for Edward "Jeff" Pfeffer, a former 20-game winner who wasn't getting anyone out for the Robins that spring. On this one the Mahatma ate Ebbets's lunch. Schupp had an intractable sore arm and was washed up. Pfeffer went 9 and 3 for the Cards.

Boom, boom went those bats. By the Fourth of July the Cards had hammered their way into the first division. Hornsby was hitting .428. Team home-run production was up more than 60 percent over the 1920 pace. Through the sweltering days of July, the Cardinals contended with the faltering Brooklyn Robins for third place. In first and second place, Pittsburgh and New York were gradually outdistancing the rest of the league.

As August opened Hornsby was still hitting close to .410. Fournier and McHenry were around .350, on their way to what in the 1980s would be called career seasons. Still, the team gained not an inch on the leaders. Rickey paced the dugout. On Sundays he paced at home, close to the telephone, while Burt Shotton ran the team. (Rickey had promised his pious mother never to appear at a ballpark on Sunday and he never did.) The Mahatma fiddled with the lineup. He had fatherly talks with no-control pitchers. Mornings in the clubhouse there were chalkboard talks, just like the old days when he coached football at Ohio Wesleyan. The system must have driven rough-hewn men like Hornsby and Fournier crazy. But it didn't spoil their hitting.

In August the Cardinals cut in the afterburner. On the nineteenth they got 17 hits while beating the Robins, 9 to 4, behind Brooklyn reject Jeff Pfeffer. Hornsby was 4 for 5. The next day the Cards beat the Giants, 10 to 1, on 15 hits. On the twenty-second they beat the Giants again, 6 to 0. On the twenty-third they got 15 hits to pound the Giants a third time, 10 to 7. At long last the Cardinal pitchers were holding the opposition to fewer than 8 runs. Infielders were catching up with ground balls before they stopped rolling. New York writers began to call the Cards the Mound City Maulers.

The Cardinals' bats began to sound like M-1s on a practice

range. At Philadelphia on the last day of August they piled up 23 hits as they clobbered the inoffensive Phillies, 12 to 5. Jack Smith went 5 for 5, Hornsby 3 for 4. At one point Hornsby lined a shot off the forehead of Phillies right-hander Bill Hubbell. The ball bounded high in the air and was caught by third baseman Russ Wrightstone. When the miraculously uninjured Colorado cowboy was helped to his feet by worried teammates, he commented good-naturedly, "Well, fellers, I found a way to get that dude out."

As September opened the Cardinals continued to roll, sweeping a 3-game series against first-place Pittsburgh and just about sealing the Pirates' fate for 1921. In Chicago, they handled the Cubs as easily.

Rickey was pleased but never ready to stand pat. *Puff, puff* went the ubiquitous cigar as he daily juggled lineups. The Cardinals stayed hot. They won 32 of their final 44 games as they roared past Brooklyn and Boston. The way they were playing, they might have overtaken the sinking Pirates had the season lasted another week or ten days. Given three weeks it's possible that the Cardinals could have snatched the pennant from the Giants. As it was they settled for third place, 7 games out and only 3 behind Pittsburgh. In all, St. Louis won 87 games, the highest total in the club's history. Undeniably, the poor start in April had done them in.

As a team the Cardinals batted .308 to match the Browns' performance of 1920, and they slugged for .437. It was enough to lead the league in both categories. Although St. Louis did not lead in home runs—they were nosed out by the last-place Phillies—the Cardinals were the only team to have three batters in double figures, the first to do so since the 1915 Cubs.

In November, when league statisticians finished doing sums with their steel-nib pens, it was announced, to no one's surprise, that Rogers Hornsby had won the National League batting title. Rajah came within 2 homers of becoming the first Triple Crown winner in the majors since the Giants' Heinie Zimmerman turned the trick in 1912. In fact, the home-run title would have given Hornsby the lead in every category of batting except bases on balls. Along with his .397 batting average he had the league's highest slugging percentage at .639, the most hits at 235, doubles at 44, triples at 18, runs at 131, total bases at 378, and runs batted in at 126. Career season? Not for Hornsby. He would soon have St. Louis fans forgetting 1921.

Of the other Cardinals, nine batted over .300, including all regulars except shortstop Doc Lavan. Perhaps Doc had strained his eyes poring over *Gray's Anatomy* on swaying Pullman cars. Before you ask how a guy who batted only .259 dared to show up in the Cardinals' clubhouse, I should point out that in 1921 Lavan drove in 82 runs. Maybe the hits weren't falling regularly for Doc, but when they did there was always someone on base. It was one of the benefits of playing for the Cards.

Brilliant twenty-six-year-old left fielder Austin McHenry, a character straight from an A. E. Housman poem, batted .350 and drove in 102 runs. Sadly, he would be dead of a brain tumor within a year. Big, retread first baseman Jack Fournier hit .343 and more than quintupled his home-run output. Poor Rickey. If one other pitcher on his staff had come close to matching spitballer Bill Doak's performance (15 and 6, 2.59 ERA), the Cardinals might have taken it all.

Meanwhile, the Browns were doing more than their bit to uphold the honor of St. Louis. Like the Cardinals, the squires of Sportsman's Park finished third in their league, thanks to a great stretch drive after half a season spent in the second division. As usual, the problem was lack of pitching depth. Staff ace Urban Shocker won 27, but he couldn't carry the team alone. The rest of the starters specialized in winning games by scores of 13 to 10. Nevertheless, under the lash of new manager Lee Fohl the Browns won more than 80 games for the first time in thirteen years.

Unlike the Cardinals, the Browns permitted their bats to go slack for a time in 1921. They hit only .304, not good enough to lead the league in the newly established hitter's world. Perhaps their fall from grace can be charged to Sisler, who had an off year. Gorgeous George hit a mere .371, to finish fourth in league batting. On the other hand, the Browns' redoubtable outfield batted a collective .350. With his change in batting stance, the unassuming Kenny Williams had by this time become a world-class slugger and tied New York's Bob Meusel for second place in the majors in home runs with 24. It was a familiar St. Louis story. The Browns scored a ton of runs—835, in fact—but their opponents scored more.

In the wake of a strong finish by both St. Louis teams, optimism about 1922 reached new heights as spring approached. With all those veteran sluggers returning, fans reasoned, team performance could only get better. At the Chase Club, on the steamboat *St. Paul,* in the Jefferson Hotel lobby, and other places, there was open talk not of a pennant but *pennants.* In a gesture of confidence in the future, the Italian organ-grinder at the corner of Broadway and Market outfitted his monkey in a spanking new vest of cardinal red and added "Avalon" and "Kitten on the Keys" to his faded repertoire of wartime pop songs. Perhaps anticipating a more significant meeting in October, the Browns and the Cardinals skipped their traditional preseason 7-game City Series and settled for a couple of exhibition games.

Breaking with an old St. Louis tradition, both teams got off to a good start in 1922. The Browns actually broke in front and led the Yankees going into May. For the remainder of the season, St. Louis and New York would duel over first place in the American League. In their league, the Cardinals played better than .500 ball in the early months, but necessarily trailed the streaking Giants As the season entered June, Pittsburgh, the only other contender of the moment, slumped badly. The Cardinals took sole possession of second place.

On July 1 the Cardinals remained 6 games behind the Giants. Despite playing good baseball, St. Louis couldn't narrow the gap. Then Hornsby's always-hot bat really began to blaze. He launched what would grow to a 33-game hitting streak. Rajah was also hitting home runs at a pace that put him ahead of Ruth.

On July 15 the Giants arrived in St. Louis for a 4-game series and dropped 3, the last a 9-to-8, no-holds-barred brawl. On the day after the Giants left, the Cards won a squeaker from Boston, 7 to 6, as Hornsby homered in the bottom of the ninth with 2 on. On the twentieth they beat the Braves again, 5 to 4. Hornsby hit home run number 26. On the twenty-first Jack Fournier assumed the hero's role with a game-winning grand slam. And on the twenty-second St. Louis rallied for 6 runs in the eighth inning to nose out Boston, 9 to 8. The Cards made 15 hits in the game, the Braves 16. Clearly, it was not airtight pitching keeping St. Louis in the race. Nevertheless, on this glorious July day Rickey's squad moved into first place, the first time in the club's history that they had been in front later than the first week in May. The Giants had not faded; the Cardinals had simply run up their backs.

Meanwhile, on the same day back in Philadelphia, the Browns hammered out 20 hits as they steamrollered the Athletics, 10 to 1. As they had since mid-June, the Browns maintained a slender lead over second-place New York. Sisler was batting well over .400. Ken Williams was off on a 29-game hitting streak and in home runs was well ahead of a troubled Babe Ruth. In April, Williams had hit 3 homers in one game against Chicago, the first American Leaguer and the first twentieth-century player to do so. At the end of July he would hit 2 in one inning, the first American Leaguer and first modern player to do that. Offensively, the Browns were sizzling.

As the sun set in St. Louis on July 22 with the Cardinals and Browns both in first place, fans were in a delirium. In back kitchens across the city, *Heimgemacht* flowed like Victoria Falls. *Männerchöre* chanted "Gott mit Uns." St. Louisans even stopped complaining about the heavy industrial smoke that hung over the city in midsummer. For one golden moment it appeared that the millennium might be realized at the intersection of Grand Avenue and Dodier Street.

But even before the good burghers could shake their celebration hangovers, reality set in, and reality was spelled p-i-t-c-h-i-n-g. The Cardinals lost the final game of the Boston series and had to set off on the long Pullman ride that would take them to the chamber of horrors, the Polo Grounds in New York. To compound the difficulties faced by managers Rickey and Fohl, the unprincipled millionaires of New York had once more flipped open their checkbooks. On July 3 Joe Dugan reported to the Yankees. On the thirtieth Hugh McQuillan would don the orange and black of the Giants. When St. Louis civic leaders vigorously protested the unsportsmanlike behavior of both New York clubs, Commissioner Landis responded by establishing the long-delayed trading deadline of June 15 for subsequent seasons.

In New York on the twenty-fifth, the Cardinals lost their

opening game with the Giants, 9 to 8, despite Hornsby's going 3 for 5. Once again they found themselves on the short end of the slugfests, and it was all downhill from there. On the twenty-sixth the Giants beat them 10 to 5, and on the twenty-seventh, 12 to 9. In this one the New Yorkers got 18 hits. Only Jeff Pfeffer seemed able to get anyone out. Bill Doak's spitball had apparently dried off in the summer heat. The Cards salvaged just 1 of 5 games at the Polo Grounds, that one by a score of 4 to 3. They left New York trailing by 3 games and continued to slide.

When the season ended, St. Louis was lucky to have gained a tie for third with Pittsburgh, 7 games behind the triumphant Giants. Though far short of the impossible dream, it was a respectable finish. Rickey had wrought a minimiracle while spending no more than Jake Ruppert's customary pocket change. Cardinal fans had plenty to cheer about. Hornsby had batted .401, hit a record 42 homers, and driven in 152 runs to win the Triple Crown. The team had batted .301. Still, it was not like winning the pennant.

The Browns' story is sadder. Unlike the Cardinals, the Brownies were not destined to achieve glory a few years down the pike. In fact, it would be an agonizing twenty-two seasons before they saw their first and only pennant, made possible in part by the dislocations caused by World War II.

In 1922 the Browns had started the season in front, stumbled a bit in May, righted themselves in June. Toward the end of June they took over first place as the Yankees began to play uneven baseball and a petulant Babe Ruth was getting himself fined or suspended every few weeks. In August the Yankees regained the lead but could put no distance between themselves and the tenacious Browns. The teams were scheduled to meet in St. Louis on September 16 for what looked more and more like the showdown series.

With the Cardinals effectively out of the National League race by mid-September, St. Louis civic hopes rested on the shoulders of Sisler, Williams, Jacobson, Shocker, and crew. Since the Browns were scheduled for a long home stand and the Yankees had to spend the final weeks of the season on the road, the odds favored St. Louis. Regrettably, in this world, palpable bad luck transcends abstract advantage.

On September 13, on the way to one of his greatest seasons and riding a consecutive-game hitting streak one short of Ty Cobb's American League record, George Sisler fell hard while making a play at first and severely injured his right shoulder. For a few hours on that Wednesday night it looked as though he might miss the remainder of the season. But when the Yankees arrived at Sportsman's Park on the sixteenth leading by half a game, Sisler courageously took the field. He could scarcely raise his right arm.

St. Louisans fought for tickets, some of which were being scalped for as much as forty-five dollars. Eventually, 30,000 squeezed into a park intended to seat 17,000. In consequence, that curse of the affluent 1920s—the overflow crowd—threatened to make play impossible.

Browns fans may have hoped for a free-hitting contest, which, even against the powerful Yankees, could operate to their advantage. Instead the game went into the bottom of the ninth with New York holding a shaky 2-to-1 lead. What followed will always be remembered in the history of St. Louis baseball as "the pop-bottle incident."

As Yankee center fielder Lawton "Whitey" Witt chased a fly ball, a bottle flew from the overflow crowd and struck him in the forehead. Unconscious and bleeding, Witt had to be carried from the field on a stretcher. The culprit was never caught, and in St. Louis as well as in New York the episode set off an explosion of public outrage. When the season was over, George Sisler confided to a reporter that the incident had upset the Browns and seemed to take some heart out of the team. In any case, they lost the game, 2 to 1. But Sisler, despite his injury, extended his hitting streak to 40 games. He had tied Cobb.

The Browns may have been disheartened, but they were far from finished. On the following day, behind left-hander Hubert "Shucks" Pruett, who had the reputation of being a Yankee killer, St. Louis won, 5 to 1, putting them again just half a game behind. Still playing in pain, Sisler pushed his hitting streak to 41 games to set a new league record. But he—and perhaps the Browns—paid the price. The aggravated injury would force the irreplaceable first baseman to sit out twelve games in the final two weeks of the season.

Everything came down to the third and final game of the Yankee series. If the Browns won, New York would leave town in second place. As it turned out, the rubber game revealed the critical difference between the teams. The Yankees were much steadier defensively.

On that fateful Monday, an incredible 32,000 prayerful St. Louisans crammed little Sportsman's Park. For seven innings St. Louis right-hander Dixie Davis blanked the explosive New Yorkers and nursed a 2-run lead. In the eighth inning, Browns second baseman Marty McManus threw wild to first, permitting the Yankees to score an unearned run. Unrattled, Davis retired the side without further damage.

In the top of the ninth, with St. Louis still leading 2 to 1, Yankee catcher Wally Schang led off with an infield single that just eluded Davis's grasp. Catcher Hank Severeid's passed ball put Schang on second. Frantic, manager Lee Fohl yanked Davis and brought in Pruett, who had pitched nine innings the day before. When pitch hitter Mike McNally tried to sacrifice, Severeid threw late to third in an effort to cut down Schang. The Yanks had runners on first and third, none out. Shaken, Pruett walked Scott to load the bases. In desperation, Fohl called on his staff ace, Urban Shocker, to save the day.

Shocker got Yankee pitcher Joe Bush to ground to the erratic McManus, who almost threw wild to the plate. Severeid made a miraculous stop to force Schang. One out. Then, as though the game scenario had been written by Sophocles, Whitey Witt appeared at the plate, head swathed in bandages. Witt singled to center to score McNally and Scott, and put the Yankees ahead, 3 to 2. It hardly mattered that Dugan followed by hitting into an inning-ending double play. Game, season, and era—New York Yankees. When the season closed on October 1, the Browns remained 1 game short of glory.

Why did the Browns fail in 1922? They led the American League in runs scored with a substantial 867, outscoring the pennant-winning Yankees by a whopping 109. The Browns also led in batting with .313, in slugging with .455, in triples with 94, and in stolen bases with 132, more than twice the number stolen by the Yankees. The Browns even outhomered New York, 98 to

95. In all, St. Louis collected 1,716 hits, an average of more than 11 a game and just a clutch short of the American League record. Surprisingly, the Browns boasted a statistical edge in pitching as well. St. Louis led the league in earned-run average, strikeouts, and saves, and gave up the fewest walks.

Individual honors too were plentiful. Sisler took the batting championship with an average of .420. He also led the league in runs with 134, hits with 246, triples with 18, and stolen bases with 51. Years later teammate Baby Doll Jacobson commented that everything Sisler hit in 1922 was a line drive.

Left fielder Ken Williams batted .332 and led the league in home runs with 39, breaking Ruth's string of four consecutive titles. Williams also finished first in total bases with 367 and in runs batted in with 155. Like Sisler he could run. He stole 37 bases to finish second in the league. In total, six Browns regulars batted over .300 and had a collective average of .339. Even pitcher Elam Vangilder hit .344 in 43 games.

And yet the Browns lost. How could it be?

Almost obscured by time and the yellowing of records is the fact that New York made 44 fewer errors than St. Louis in 1922 and tied for the major-league lead in fielding average. For that era the Browns were not really a bad fielding team. The Yankees were simply a whole lot better, the sharpest glove men of their time. In the closing weeks of the 1922 season, Babe Ruth alone was credited with saving at least three games with his strong throws from left field.

In the St. Louis experience of 1920–22 there must have been enough parables to occupy a summer Bible school. Never have two teams in one city visited such sustained fury upon opposing pitchers with nary a swatch of championship bunting to show for it. In three seasons the Browns and the Cardinals lashed out 9,873 hits, more than one quarter of them for extra bases. Their collective batting average was .304. Only the 1920 Cardinals posted a season team mark under .300. In a period when major-league teams averaged a modest 52 home runs a year, the St. Louis teams averaged 72. Their combined slugging average was .428.

From 1920 through 1922 Hornsby won three batting championships, Sisler two. In 1922 both batting leaders hit over .400, the only time it has happened. In the same season Hornsby and Sisler set records for hitting in consecutive games.

For the Browns it was downhill after 1922. Over the winter Sisler developed a sinus infection that seriously affected his vision. He missed the entire 1923 season, and the Browns finished in the second division. When Sisler returned in 1924 he added the manager's job to the burdens of making a comeback. He batted an uncharacteristic .305. Inexplicably, Gorgeous George had lost his sharpness in the field as well. Although Sisler remained a .300 hitter for all but one of his remaining six seasons and finished with a lifetime average of .340, it is tempting to wonder what he might have accomplished had illness not impaired his vision.

Sisler's infirmity was not the whole of the bad breaks for the Browns. In July 1924, Ken Williams fractured an ankle while sliding and missed 40 games. In the following year, headed for his greatest season ever, he suffered a near-fatal beaning and missed the last 52 games. At the time of the injury Ken had 25 home runs and 105 RBIs. Although Williams recovered to play several more good seasons, he had become perceptibly ball shy and was never again the same batter.

The Cardinals faced a happier future after their disappointment of 1922. Hornsby, of course, continued to terrorize National League pitchers. In 1923, while missing about a third of the season owing to a mysterious skin disease, he batted .384. The following year, nursing a dislocated thumb through part of the season, he set the modern batting record of .424. In 1925 he batted .403, his third time over the .400 mark. Over six seasons Rajah had averaged an incredible .397.

Throughout the 1920s and 1930s, Branch Rickey's expanding farm system turned out a steady supply of fine young ballplayers: "Sunny Jim" Bottomley, Ray Blades, Chick Hafey, Taylor Douthit, Charley Gelbert, Ernie Orsatti, George Watkins, Pepper Martin, James "Ripper" Collins, and more. The farm system served as an effective counterweight to the fat bankrolls of New York and Chicago and helped the Cardinals to win five pennants in eight years.

To illustrate the kind of talent Rickey was nurturing, on September 16, 1924, at Brooklyn's Ebbets Field, young Bottomley, in his second year in the majors, gave himself a boost toward the Hall of Fame by batting in 12 runs in a nine-inning game. He did it with 2 homers, a double, and 3 singles. It is perilous to speak of records that will never be broken, but Sunny Jim's mark has been on the books for more than sixty-five years and it's not the kind that you can break simply by extending your career. Look at it this way: It's the equivalent of 3 grand slams in one game.

It is said that ancient baseball fans still sun themselves on benches in St. Louis's Forest Park pondering the cosmic inequities of 1922. Shutting out the squeal of children and the chatter of Frisbee players, they hear once more the satisfying crash of ash against horsehide as Tobin, McManus, Sisler, Williams, Jacobson, and Severeid mount an 8-run rally to seal a glorious 15-to-9 victory. What more can you ask of men? they muse. Why must baseball be such a maddeningly balanced game? Why shouldn't the better hitters always win? Like cricket. Maybe our great-grandfathers acted with too much haste in abandoning cricket. At cricket, we might have beaten the Yankees.

SEVEN

FOR PITCHERS, NO BROTHERLY LOVE

> "On a clear day you could see seventh place."
>
> —FRESCO THOMPSON,
> former Phillies infielder

IN HIS RECORD-BREAKING outburst of the early twenties, Babe Ruth not only amassed more home runs than anyone in history, he also hit the ball such distances that the homer became an event in itself, apart from the outcome of the game. The passion for the home run in absolute terms still survives, reflected in the nightly TV ritual of screening each "dinger" hit in the games of the day. And at the ballpark, of course, we have the exploding scoreboard, unmistakably an altar to the home run.

The fervor with which the fans—particularly newcomers to baseball—responded to Ruth and the long ball could not long escape the notice of club owners whose teams had little to offer but a succession of second-division finishes. Prominent among them was Philadelphia's Connie Mack. After Mack had broken up his champion Athletics of 1910–14—some believe in a fit of anger over loss of the 1914 World Series, but, in fact, out of fear of raids by the Federal League—the A's plunged from first place to

last in a single season. There they remained for seven cheer-
less years.

For the long-suffering Philadelphia baseball fan there was little relief to be found across town at Baker Bowl. After a fleeting
moment in the sun in 1915, the Phillies joined the A's in the
nether regions. When America emerged from World War I, Philadelphia was established in the popular mind as a city of losers.

It is frustrating to follow a last-place team, worse when they
are batting .240 and rarely getting the ball out of the infield. But
after 1919, with increasing frequency, something new was featured on the afternoon bill at both Philadelphia ballparks—the
booming homer. In the case of Connie Mack, exploitation of the
home run as a crowd pleaser was somewhat more honorable than
its use by the Phillies, since it was evident by the mid-1920s that
"The Tall Tactician" was earnestly trying to install a winner at
Shibe Park.

In 1921 the Athletics, still trapped in last place, amused their
fans by producing four batters with double figures in home runs.
Their team total of 83 homers placed them second in the league
to the overpowering Yankees. What is curious about the A's surge
in homers is that all their power hitters were right-handed: infielders Jimmy Dykes and Joe Dugan, left fielder Tilly Walker, and
catcher Cy Perkins. The records that exist of Shibe Park's dimensions in 1921 show the left-field foul pole at 380 feet from the
plate. But since construction of bleachers in left field was going
on sometime in 1921, it is possible that the A's were shooting at
a temporary builder's fence for part of the season.

Whatever the distance to the fence, the cellar-dwelling A's
were clearly committed to the new style of batting and the fans
seemed to approve. The 334,000 who paid their way into Shibe
Park in 1921 approximated the number that had turned out for
the A's last pennant winner back in 1914. If Sunday baseball had
been permitted by Pennsylvania law, the club surely would have
drawn 400,000 or more.

In 1922 the distance to the new left-field bleachers was established at a more friendly 334 feet down the line and 384 in the
power alley. Tilly Walker and his cohort demonstrated their appreciation for management's enlightened policy by busting 111

homers, leaving even the Yankees in the dust. Philadelphia became the second American League team after New York to hit more than 100 home runs. But despite the barrage of extra bases, the Athletics won just 12 more games than they had a year earlier and advanced only a notch in the league standings. Still, 425,000 Philadelphians were convinced that the new-model A's were worth the price of a ticket.

Again four A's sluggers finished in double figures—Walker, Dykes, right fielder Frank Welch, and rookie center fielder Edmund "Bing" Miller. The thirty-three-year-old Walker, who had tied Ruth in homers back in 1918, led the team with 37 and this time finished ahead of the Babe. But it was Tilly's swan song. In 1923, he appeared in just 52 games, gradually giving way to younger competitors.

With the virtual retirement of Walker, the Athletics' home-run total in 1923 fell by more than half. The A's were, nevertheless, a better ball club than they had been in nearly a decade. They finished sixth, just 5½ games out of the first division. Connie Mack was still interested in home runs, but now he was using them to win ball games.

To achieve better balance in his batting order, in 1922 Mack had purchased young left-handed first baseman Joe Hauser from Class AA Milwaukee, where the kid was known among the city's German-speaking population as "Unser Choe." Hauser, acclaimed since his first appearance in the American Association as an embryonic Babe Ruth, rewarded Connie with 16 homers in 1923 and 27 the following year. Young Joe seemed on his way to becoming the glamorous local slugger that every club was seeking by the mid-1920s.

Sadly, in the spring of 1925 Hauser suffered a complicated leg fracture in training camp and missed the entire season. At the major-league level Joe never regained his effectiveness, though he did become a superstar in Class AA baseball, where he twice hit more than 60 home runs in a season. His 69 homers in 153 games for Minneapolis in 1933 remain the Class AA (now AAA) record.

Disappointed as Mack may have been at the loss of Hauser, the manager had by 1925 come up with another young power hitter in Al Simmons and, more important, for the first time in a decade, his team was a contender for the pennant. The Athletics finished second, 8½ games behind the champion Washington Senators. A grand total of 859,000 Philadelphians turned out to cheer the rejuvenated A's that year. After 1925 Connie's "White Elephants" were unmistakably on their way to success. And it may be that the noisy sideshow by Tilly Walker, Joe Hauser, Bing Miller, and others in the early twenties was what kept the club solvent, giving the canny Mack time to gather the young talent that would lead the team to victory.

Connie Mack's National League neighbors, the Phillies, were also among the first major-league clubs to establish themselves as a home-run attraction. The project was made easier for them by the character of their home park. Baker Bowl, at the intersection of Broad Street and Lehigh Avenue, had been designed and built back in 1887 by player-entrepreneur Al Reach. It may be too cynical to suggest that because Reach was a left-handed batter the park was laid out with the shortest right-field target in the majors. In any case, the right-field line measured a scant 272 and, unlike the situation at the Polo Grounds, the Philadelphia fence ran at right angles to the foul line. Baker Bowl's "tin wall," faced with a huge Lifebuoy soap ad, was a target cherished by several generations of left-handed sluggers in the National League.

From 1920 through 1923 the Phillies led the National League in home runs. In that stretch the club never finished higher than seventh in the pennant race, and that only once. In 1922 the hapless Phils hit 116 homers, to share with the St. Louis Cardinals the honor of being the first National League teams in the twentieth century to hit more than one hundred. The Phillies had five batters in double figures, an unusual display of balanced power.

While it can't be claimed that Phillies fans turned out in record numbers in 1922, the club did draw a survival-level 232,000. As with the Athletics, Sunday baseball would have improved the attendance figure substantially. In the same season, the Boston Braves, with a record only slightly worse than the seventh-place Phillies but with no chance of developing a home-run hero at measureless Braves Field, drew a dismal 167,000. Of course, Boston too was without Sunday baseball.

The Phillies' long-ball circus of the early 1920s was built around center fielder Fred "Cy" Williams, a gangly left-handed hitter who had been in the league since 1912. Williams, a graduate architect, could not have designed a right-field wall better suited to his talents. Obtained from the Cubs in 1918, Cy was the most notorious pull hitter in the majors. A quarter of a century before Cleveland manager Lou Boudreau designed an exaggerated shift of fielders to the right side to combat Ted Williams, every manager in the National League was doing it to Cy Williams. There was wide agreement that had Cy worked on hitting to the opposite field, he probably would have batted .400. As it turned out, his best season mark was .345 and he finished with a nineteen-year average of .292.

Cy Williams's attitude toward the defensive shift may not have been different from that of Ted Williams in the 1940s: Ted insisted that the fans were paying to see him hit home runs, not singles to left. In any case, once Cy had mastered Babe Ruth's technique of lofting the ball, he turned into a superstar and gave the long-suffering Phillies fans a reason to come to the park. In 1923, at the then-advanced age of thirty-six, Williams hit 41 homers to come within 1 of tying Rogers Hornsby's brand-new National League record. That year Cy also tied the Babe for the major-league lead. Williams would become the first National Leaguer to hit 200 home runs, and by the time he retired in 1930 at the age of forty-three, Cy had the second highest total of home runs by any National league player in history and the third highest in the majors.

Inadvertently, Cy Williams may have helped skinflint Phillies owner William F. Baker chart an unfortunate course for the 1920s. In the new era, it appeared that if you had even one home-run hero in the lineup, you could run a shoestring baseball operation indefinitely. For the remainder of his tenure, Baker made sure that, without compromising his coolie wage scale, the Phils' batting order included one or more muscular left-handed swingers. Dutifully, the Phillies took a firm lease on the second division and contented themselves with wrecking earned-run averages.

EIGHT

FIRESTORM
IN THE
BUSHES

> MANAGER: Dutch, you're a cinch to hit three-
>   fifty this year.
> ROOKIE: Really? What makes you so sure,
>   Skipper?
> MANAGER: I'm sending you back to Joplin.
>   —Traditional

IN THE 1920s, the major leagues served just ten cities, concentrated in the northeast and Great Lakes regions and having a combined population of about 15 million. Two cities—New York and Chicago—accounted for two thirds of that population.

For most Americans of the period, about 95 million of them, baseball meant the minor-league game. Almost every town of any size had a professional team. In such an age, what could be more appropriate than to elect as the first postwar president Warren G. Harding, a man who once owned the minor-league franchise in the small midwestern town of Marion, Ohio.

The roll call of minors in the 1920s, especially at the Class C and D levels, evokes tantalizing images of rural and small-town America: the Cotton States League, the Kitty League (Kentucky and Tennessee), the Sally League (South Atlantic), the Nebraska State League, the Evangeline League, the Mountain States League (Appalachian Mountains, that is), the Texas Trolley League, the

Eastern Shore League, the Three I League (Indiana, Illinois, and Iowa), and more. Life in the minors in the early part of the century enriched American folklore with its tales of rickety wooden ballparks, often called ovals, distinguished by rock-pile infields, patchy grass, and motley outfield billboards; kids and dogs wandering on the field; showerless clubhouses and airless rooming houses; one-armed beaneries; and countless other inconveniences. As they were living the experience, the bushers may have hated it all. But since such recollections are inextricably linked with youth, viewed in retrospect they are likely to acquire a patina of romance.

Unquestionably more endearing than the playing conditions must have been the adulation of local fans and the prospect of attentive girls at every stop around the league. To a small-town waitress a nineteen-year-old Class C slugger may have seemed as glamorous as a big-league star.

Bush leaguers of the 1920s were lucky in one respect. In a nation where almost every town of a thousand or more was connected by rail and the fares were carefully regulated by federal statute, train travel was the norm. Motor buses existed, but were few in number and infrequently used outside the city. Even stuffy day coaches on the railroads must have made road trips more bearable than they would become in the 1930s and beyond, when most minor-league clubs had switched to buses.

Precisely the changes in style of play that occurred in the majors after World War I were soon manifest in the minors. Hitting and slugging surged dramatically, pitching and base stealing declined. From Augusta in the Sally League to Seattle in the powerful Pacific Coast League, from Hutchinson in the Southwest League to Montreal in the International League, batters rendered life an ongoing crisis for pitchers. While newly installed President Harding practiced his putting on the south lawn of the White house in 1921, minor-league hitters raised their averages to unheard-of levels. And emulating national hero Babe Ruth, some bushers were hitting balls into the neighboring county. The modest dimensions of those wooden ovals cried out to be exploited by muscular farm boys swinging home-turned hickory bats.

Something of a climax was reached in a Pacific Coast League

game on May 11, 1923. At Salt Lake City's Bonneville Park, the Vernon Tigers pounded the local Bees, 35 to 11. There were 11 home runs in the game, 5 by Vernon right fielder Pete Schneider. Bear in mind, this was not Charlie Brown and his friends on a Saturday morning. These were two of the best teams in what was arguably the most powerful minor league in the country. Vernon, named for a small industrial enclave lying just south of downtown Los Angeles, had recently taken an unprecedented three straight pennants in the Coast League.

Doubtless Bonneville Park's four-thousand-foot elevation contributed to the salvo of long balls, but the Bees had been playing on the site since 1915 without approaching these numbers. Something more than rarefied air was involved.

By 1924, when .400 hitters were no longer unusual in the majors, the batting inflation in the minors kept pace. In the International League, fifty-six batters hit over .300 and the league itself batted .290. League sluggers racked up 693 home runs. Not to be outdone, the Pacific Coast League batted .298 that year and had seventy-three players over .300. Even taking into account the Coast League's long playing schedule, their total of 930 home runs was imposing, an increase of 35 percent over 1921. More than 190 of those homers belonged to the Salt Lake City Bees, who batted an extraterrestrial .327.

In the mid-1920s, the deeper into the bushes you look, the more showy the batting holiday. At the Class D level in 1924, we find a whole league—the Western Association—just a hair shy of a .300 batting average, paced by the legendary Okmulgee (Oklahoma) Chiefs at .328 for 158 games. To show the rest of Organized Baseball that there was nothing intimidating about the 1,000-homer barrier, the Association boys that year hit 1,147. Okmulgee chipped in with 202.

From this point minor-league batters simply slip the traces. In 1925 the Class B Sally League batted .303 and had six teams over .300. The Western League hit .302 and had five teams over .300. The Class A Southern Association, a good sound league with a twenty-five-year history, had three teams over .300. And on and on.

This level of hitting became so widespread in the minors that it is a wonder any youngster of the time could be persuaded to take the mound. In 1930 the inevitable happened in the American Association. All eight teams in a Class AA league batted over .300 as the Association hit a whopping .307. Eighty-five players, more than half the league roster, batted over .300. Curiously, no one hit .400.

What caused the phenomenal upswing in batting in the minors? As in the case of the majors, we can't be absolutely certain, but significant contributors had to be abolition of the spitball, the general shift from forearm hitting to the full swing, following the example of Babe Ruth, and perhaps a slightly livelier, or at least better-quality, baseball. Not to be overlooked either is a possible cyclical decline in the quality of minor-league pitching.

As in the majors, minor-league press boxes witnessed the inevitable clamor about a souped-up ball, but there is no serious evidence to support a charge of deliberate tampering. Some of the top minors used the major-league ball, which, of course, came from the machines of the A. J. Reach Company in Philadelphia. The P. GoldSmith Sons Official League Ball No. 97, used by the Southern Association and several other leagues in the lower classifications, gained the reputation of being particularly lively. Whether GoldSmith was in part or whole a member of the Spalding corporate empire is difficult to determine. It is certain that GoldSmith regularly advertised its wares in the *Spalding Baseball Guide*. In any case, the Southern Association was not hitting the No. 97 any farther than the boys in the Pacific Coast League were driving balls from the Reach Company bin in Philadelphia.

It would be interesting to know the extent to which the various minors adopted a policy of keeping a clean ball in play. Unquestionably, the bushers were prospering in the 1920s, and perhaps they could afford a bit of extravagance. In any case, so many balls were being hit into the bleachers, there was little likelihood that even Class D teams would ever play nine innings with the same scuffed, discolored baseball.

Barred from using trick pitches, young and inexperienced pitchers in the minors must have found it difficult to confront the go-for-broke batting style of the postwar years. Moreover, a case can be made that, influenced by Ruth's success story, a number of the best young athletes of the era forsook careers as pitchers and took up the business of slugging. Some of the greatest minor-league batters of the 1920s were former pitchers: Oakland's Russell "Buzz" Arlett, Baltimore's Jack Bentley (who never abandoned pitching entirely), Salt Lake City's Paul Strand and Frank "Lefty" O'Doul, San Francisco's Smead Jolley, and Missions' Isaac "Ike" Boone. We can never know how many potentially good pitchers never even gave the position a trial, determined from the beginning to play every day, hit home runs, and improve their bargaining position at contract time.

To understand the minor leagues in the 1920s, we must first be aware of how different their role was from that of today's minors. Seventy years ago the principal function of a minor-league franchise was not the training of young players for service in the majors. It was the business of retailing baseball—for profit. The vast majority of clubs were locally owned and independently operated. Their job was to please the fans and sell tickets, and they could best do that by winning. It follows that their chances for winning were much improved when they held on to their best ballplayers.

It is equally important to understand the popular attitude toward the minor-league player of the era. He was universally accepted as a professional, a man making his living at the business of baseball, just as the big leaguers were. He was not necessarily viewed as an apprentice major leaguer, although we may assume that every youngster who signed his first baseball contract hoped to make it to the bigs one day. A player might continue in the job of baseball for twenty years without ever setting foot on a major-league diamond and still command community respect. It was not unusual for a top minor-league star to earn more than a journeyman big leaguer.

Not infrequently in those days a former major-league star, unable to maintain the pace of the big time, would spend his last active years in one of the top minors. It was particularly true in the Pacific Coast League, where the climate was kind to aging bones and the pay was reputed to be good. I have heard elderly baseball fans who grew up far from the centers of major-league play describe the thrill of watching a former World Series hero in action right in their local park.

After the Giants' great right-hander Joseph "Iron Man"

McGinnity left New York in 1908 with what eventually proved to be Hall of Fame credentials, he pitched for *fifteen* years in the minors, winning an additional 207 games to go with his 247 major-league victories. And when future Hall of Famer Sam Crawford had completed a nineteen-year big-league career with Cincinnati and Detroit, he played another four seasons for Los Angeles in the Pacific Coast League. Over the four years, "Wahoo Sam" batted .330 and in 1919, at the age of thirty-nine, almost won the league batting crown.

A minor-league roster in the 1920s did not, as it does today, comprise a dozen and a half kids learning the business of baseball, some shuttling back and forth to a parent major-league club throughout the season. Lineups were stable from April to September and featured a good share of seasoned professional ballplayers, occasionally one with major-league experience. The stability must have been much appreciated by the fans, whose first wish was to see a pennant flying in their town.

Something that helped make the 1920s a kind of Golden Age for the minors was that the small-town fan gave most of his attention and support to the local team. There was no radio or television to bring a nightly wrap-up of big-league activity, not to speak of a play-by-play account of those distant games. News of the major-league races came exclusively from newspapers. A minor-league fan may well have had a favorite among the major-league clubs, especially if a player from the local team had moved up to achieve fame in the big time. And no doubt small-town fans kept abreast of what Babe Ruth was doing, especially in the early years of the decade, when home-run fever was at its height. But the important action was at the local park.

The prosperity of minor-league clubs of the 1920s was linked in large measure to modifications in the draft agreement with the majors. In 1913 the National Commission, a three-man board that governed the majors, had directed all major-league clubs to divest themselves of ownership in minor-league teams. The action was taken in response to complaints from minor-league officials that major-league shareholders were using their equity as leverage to pry good players from the rosters and, in turn, forcing them to use "on option" players who were not really wanted.

The National Commission's ruling helped make the minors truly independent and ultimately more successful at the turnstiles.

But there remained the troubling question of the draft. Under the National Agreement—the constitution of Organized Baseball—all professional clubs were authorized to draft a limited number of players from teams in a lower classification at a fixed price. The price for players of each classification was specified in the agreement and took no account of the individual player's talent. Despite the fact that minor-league teams in the higher classifications such as A and AA acquired many of their own best players in this way, they resented having then to surrender them to the majors for a predetermined draft price ($5,000 in the case of a Class AA player).

The postwar year of 1919, when everyone in baseball was gearing for a fresh start, must have seemed to minor-league operators an ideal time to deal with the draft issue. Consequently, the National Association of Professional Baseball Leagues, the governing body of the minors, voted at their January meeting to withdraw from the National Agreement and end their contractual relationship with the majors. Minor-league owners were now free to sell their players to any buyer for all that the traffic would bear.

Initially, independence may have seemed exhilarating to minor-league owners, but soon they recognized that there had been advantages in being allied with the big leagues. And so, in 1921, after two years of going it alone, the minors entered into a new National Agreement but one that effectively exempted from the draft five of their leagues, including the three Class AA operations—the International, the Pacific Coast, and the American Association. In return for the exemption, the five leagues gave up their right to draft players from teams in a lower classification.

The new arrangement was to have a significant effect on major-league finances through the 1920s and, I am convinced, no small influence on the quality of play in the minors. In the leagues with draft exemption, outstanding players could be kept from advancing to the majors until the clubs that owned their contracts got the price they demanded. For the freebooters among minor-league owners, the downside of the new National Agreement was that

they had consented to place themselves for twenty-five years under the autocratic (and incorruptible) rule of the newly created
Commissioner of Baseball, Kenesaw Mountain Landis. From the
beginning Landis was opposed to any system that would impede
the progress of young players to the highest classification to which
their talents could carry them. Throughout his tenure the Commissioner kept a sharp eye on all sales and trades.

The Baltimore Orioles' Jack Dunn was the minor-league magnate most often cited as having grown rich from the draft exemption. Holding superstars like Jack Bentley and Lefty Grove from
the market for years helped bring Baltimore seven straight International League pennants, but it worked a hardship on the players. And in the end Dunn was still able to get record prices
for them.

From 1919 to 1925 there was rarely a vacant seat at Oriole
Park as the star-studded Birds turned in team batting averages of
.318 and .313 and hit record-breaking numbers of home runs. In
1925, their 188 homers represented a quarter of the total in a
heavy-hitting league. In those years the Orioles produced the league
batting champion in five out of six seasons. And the titles were
won by five different players. Many of these men should have
been in the big leagues years earlier.

With something close to a monopoly on the rich lode of baseball talent in California, Pacific Coast League owners grew especially haughty, regularly demanding sums of $50,000 and $100,000
for players of unproven major-league ability. In some instances
owners refused to sell at any price, preferring to cash in on the
star as a local gate attraction. When the Philadelphia Athletics
sought brilliant young catcher Mickey Cochrane from the Portland Beavers in late 1924, they found it more expedient to buy
the Portland franchise than to open a deal for Cochrane's contract.

Protected from the draft and playing a schedule of up to 200
games, the Coast League produced the wildest batting numbers
of the decade. From 1922 through 1930 the combined average
of the league's batting champions was .397. Four different title
winners hit over .400.

The Salt Lake City Bees of the early 1920s offer a hint of what could happen to batting records should the majors ever put a team, especially a good team, in mile-high Denver. In the reorganizing year of 1919, when the Coast League batted .266 and most of the rest of Organized Baseball was thrashing about in the .250 range, the Bees hit a hefty .284. Their 80 home runs for the season look modest until you consider that it was twice the total hit by any other team in the league except powerful Los Angeles. The following year Salt Lake City raised the team average to .295. Then, for five years, beginning in 1921, the Bees made life intolerable for Coast League pitchers. They batted .301, .292, .327, .327, and .321. They also launched a cloud of home runs, finishing with 194 in 1924 and 197 in 1925. In 1925 Salt Lake City outhit the league by 33 percentage points. But as fans in St. Louis had learned before them, the Salt Lake faithful discovered that stupendous hitting doesn't automatically translate into victory. The Bees failed to win a pennant during their decade in Salt Lake City, and after the 1925 season the franchise folded. Still, it must have been fun to watch them in those years.

There was the Bees' outfield, for example. In 1924, thirty-six-year-old playing manger Duffy Lewis, a former American League star, hit .392 to snatch the league batting title from his left fielder, Lefty O'Doul, by a few thousandths of a point. Lewis had served twelve years in the majors, where he played left field for the Red Sox alongside Tris Speaker and Harry Hooper, in what was long hailed as the greatest outfield of all time.

O'Doul may have been operating at a disadvantage in the batting duel, since he was doing double duty as a pitcher. When Lefty abandoned the mound for good in 1925, he would crank out an average of 270 hits and 155 RBIs over a three-year stretch against Class AA pitching.

The third man in that 1924 outfield at Salt Lake City was Johnny Frederick, who batted a pallid .353 on 289 hits. Johnny was destined to move on to Brooklyn, where in a career that lasted but six years he won a measure of Flatbush immortality.

In 1925, Lewis supplemented his murderous outfield with a rookie shortstop named Tony Lazzeri, who hit 60 home runs and had 222 RBIs. Can you imagine having a slick-fielding shortstop who hits 60 homers?

As individual performance in the top minors spiraled upward, owners in the draft-exempt leagues pushed their asking prices to record levels. Rich and ambitious teams such as the Giants, the Cubs, and the Yankees had to dig ever deeper into their cash reserves for minor-league talent that they coveted. Poorer major-league clubs were simply priced out of the bidding. Seventy-five thousand dollars became a routine tag on a young hotshot out of Class AA. In 1924 someone told San Francisco's splendid young right fielder Paul Waner that he would probably have to hit .400 before a major-league club would cough up the $100,000 his owners wanted for him. The following season Waner complied with a .401 average and Pittsburgh president Barney Dreyfuss sighed and wrote out the check.

Even slick fielders were fetching record prices. In 1923 the Chicago White Sox paid $100,000 for San Francisco third base-man Willie Kamm, whose strong suit was his glove. It was just three years after the Yankees had paid that amount for Babe Ruth, an established major-league superstar who hit better than anyone in the world and could pitch too. Fortunately for the White Sox, Kamm proved to be a superb big-league infielder and gave years of good service. It is tempting to speculate that had Comiskey's $100,000 been used to beef up the niggardly salaries of his 1919 champions, the money might have served to keep Cicotte, Jackson, Williams, and their infamous fraternity happy—and honest. At all events, as prices for minor-league stars continued to rise, it was only a matter of time before major-league owners would balk at the new arrangement.

The high prices were painful enough even when the big-league operator got value for his dollars, as in the cases of Kamm and Waner. Not all buyers were so lucky. There was, for example, the saga of Paul Strand.

Abandoning an undistinguished career as a pitcher, Strand switched to the outfield and in 1923 while with Salt Lake City won the Pacific Coast League Triple Crown. He batted .394, hit 43 homers, and drove in 187 runs. It was actually a Quintuple Crown, since he also led the league with 325 hits and 180 runs. Admittedly, Strand had 194 games in which to put together these numbers. Still, 325 is a lot of hits.

Back in Philadelphia, Athletics manager and part owner Con-

nie Mack, eager to break out of the American League second division and start building another winner, persuaded his wealthy
partners, the Shibes, to support an offer of $70,000 for Strand's
contract. Mack, one of the most astute judges of baseball flesh in
the game's history, had not made the decision on Strand's numbers alone. He had actually traveled to the West Coast to check
Paul's teeth and withers. Convinced, he delivered the check.

The following spring at Shibe Park, which, of course, is at sea
level, poor Strand had trouble driving the ball beyond the infield.
After 47 games he was hitting .228, and this was a season in which
the entire American League would bat .290. By July the disillu-
sioned Mack had seen enough. He shipped Strand to Toledo for
Bill Lamar, a well-worn journeyman outfielder, who, it turned out,
really could hit big-league pitching.

Comfortably resettled at the Class AA level, Strand found
American Association pitching much to his liking, and in what
remained of the 1924 season he hit .323 and drove in 71 runs. A
couple of years later Paul was back home in the Pacific Coast
League with Portland, still batting up a storm. Meanwhile, $70,000
poorer, Connie Mack must have longed for the days when you
could have a thorough look at a phenom like Strand for the draft
price of $5,000.

In time even the free-spending Jake Ruppert confessed that
he could no longer afford the inflated prices for minor-league
stars. Following the example of Branch Rickey and the Cardinals,
Ruppert established what would become an extensive and highly
successful Yankee farm system.

Baltimore's Jack Bentley typifies the minor-league superstar,
ruthlessly penalized because he was a local draw. The versatile
Bentley was often called the Babe Ruth of the International League.
In 1920, playing in 145 games, 22 of them as a pitcher, Bentley
batted .371 on 231 hits, 71 of them for extra bases. He led the
league in RBIs with an extraordinary 161. When he was not pul-
verizing baseballs, Bentley was mystifying batters, as he went 16
and 3 for a winning percentage of .842. He also led the league in
earned-run average with 2.11. Bentley batted .365 over five seasons before he persuaded Jack Dunn to sell him to the New York
Giants—as a pitcher. He was already twenty-eight years old.

Pitcher-outfielder Buzz Arlett of Oakland in the Pacific Coast

League may have been another casualty of the draft exemption. Arlett spent his first four years at Oakland as a pitcher and won 95 games. When the six-feet-three-inch 230-pounder abandoned pitching for full-time duty in the outfield, he quickly demonstrated that he had Ruthian skills at bat as well as on the mound. A switch hitter, perhaps the greatest in the history of the minors, Arlett had never batted .300 during his years as a pitcher. When at last he joined the good guys, he never again batted under that mark—for fifteen consecutive seasons. For the remainder of his stay with Oakland—eight years—Buzz batted .355. Over this period he also averaged 226 hits, 52 doubles, 10 triples, 30 homers, 138 RBIs, and 18 stolen bases a season. Undeniably the totals are affected by the long schedule in the Coast League, but, in fact, Arlett averaged only 634 at-bats in these years, about what a major leaguer might post for a full season while hitting in the top half of the order. In 1929, the only season in which he played a full schedule, and this included 17 appearances as a pitcher, Buzz clouted 70 doubles, 39 homers, and drove in 189 runs. No matter how you assess it, the big switch hitter was a terror at the plate.

Arlett retired with a lifetime total of 435 minor-league home runs, still the all-time mark for an American minor-league ballplayer. Had he begun his career as an everyday player immediately after Ruth revolutionized the game, say in 1921, Buzz almost certainly would have hit more than 500 homers in minor-league play.

The reason that Arlett was held in the minors for so long is more complex than in Bentley's case. We can assume that the Oakland owners were not eager to part with Arlett, an Oakland icon. Moreover, Buzz was a notoriously poor fielder. The best guess is that no major-league owner was willing to part with a king's ransom to add an assured bad glove to his lineup before testing whether Arlett could hit big-league pitching. There can be little doubt, however, that at the old fixed draft prices, Arlett would have had a shot at the bigs while he was still young. As things turned out, Buzz was thirty-two before he played in his first big-league game and, according to tradition, his weak fielding forced him back to the minors after just one season.

In addition to Arlett and Strand, there were other minor-league superstars who seemed to be programmed by nature to shine at Class AA level and no higher. In his brief stay in the majors, Ike Boone, who would make batting history with the Coast League Missions and the Toronto Maple Leafs of the International League, hit well enough—.319. But, like Arlett's, Ike's glove was largely ornament. For his fourteen seasons in the minors, Boone, a left-handed batter, hit .370 and led four different leagues.

Smead Jolley, a native of Wesson, Arkansas, population 67, had a career remarkably like that of Ike Boone. In some ways Jolley is the quintessential minor-league batting hero of the twenties, a character straight from Ring Lardner. A rangy country lad of sunny disposition and unhurried speech, "Smudge," as he was affectionately known to his teammates, began his professional career as a pitcher. But in his second year as a pro he hit opposing pitching with such ferocity that he was assigned to part-time service in the outfield. In 1924, the first season in which Jolley appeared in more than a hundred games, he hit .383 against pitchers in three different leagues. By the following year he had worked his way up through every level of the minor-league system to Class AA San Francisco, where, still listed as a part-time pitcher, he batted .447 in 38 games. From then on it was doomsday for his brothers of the toeplate.

Beginning in 1927, when big Smead had finally abandoned all pretense of pitching, he rang up three seasons in which he hit a cumulative .396 and won two batting championships. The third year he was nosed out for the title by the redoubtable Ike Boone. Over the three-year period Jolley averaged 290 hits, 38 homers, and 170 RBIs.

Like most minor-league supermen, Jolley eventually had his shot at the big time. He did brief stints with both the White Sox and the Red Sox. Smudge hit well, of course, but apparently not well enough to make up for disabilities in the field. There is a story that in desperation White Sox manager Lew Fonseca (no great glove man himself) tried to convert Jolley into a catcher on the premise that a passed ball was less likely to result in three bases than was a dropped fly. According to Fonseca, he abandoned the experiment when a sporting-goods manufacturer de-

clined to design a catcher's mask that protected the top of the
head as well as the face.

There is also an indestructible baseball legend that big Smudge
once committed 3 errors on a single play at Fenway Park. It is
alleged that he let a sharp single go through the wicket and roll
to the wall, muffed the carom, and then threw behind the runner
going to third. The late Ed Rumill of the *Christian Science Mon-
itor,* who witnessed the play, told me that although it had unfolded pretty much as traditionally described, the official scorer
of the day, a saintly type, charged Jolley with only one miscue
and laid a second on Boston's third baseman, who may well have
deserved it. Anyway, not long after the episode, the big slugger
was once again back in Class AA, where perhaps he felt less pressure. In all, Jolley won six batting championships, his last at the
age of thirty-nine in the Class B Western International League. In
a minor-league career that spanned more than 2,200 games,
Smudge compiled a lifetime batting average of .366.

We must not infer from the careers of men like Jolley and
Arlett that all minor-league superstars who failed to make it in
the majors were men of silver bats and iron gloves. More often
the reason for being returned to the bushes was an inability to
deal effectively with a big-league curveball.

The destruction of the minors ranks as one of the ten worst
calamities to visit baseball in the twentieth century. (For the
record, the other nine, roughly in order of malignancy: the
Designated-Hitter Rule, artificial turf, domed ballparks, night
baseball, major-league expansion, division play, the spitball, the
Black Sox scandal, and the installation of the first ballpark organ.)
At their greatest extent, in the late 1940s, the minors comprised
59 leagues and more than 460 teams. At that point they were
drawing more than 40 million paying customers, a figure that the
majors would not match until years later. At its peak the minor-
league system supported roughly 10,000 professional baseball
players. Then came television and the coaxial cable, which spread
its destructive tentacles into every village in America. By 1960
only 22 minor leagues remained in operation. Attendance was
down 75 percent. One of the most colorful chapters in American
social history was rapidly approaching its close.

In 1925, when the Chicago Cubs' young Charles "Gabby" Hartnett hit 24 home runs in fewer than 400 at-bats, he emancipated catchers from their traditional eighth spot in the batting order. Gabby's 1930 slugging average of .630 is the highest ever recorded by a catcher. NATIONAL BASEBALL LIBRARY, COOPERSTOWN, N.Y.

By the mid-1920s, many major-league clubs sought a home-run hitter as a gate attraction. Sweet-swinging Leon "Goose" Goslin drew the unenviable assignment at Washington's spacious Griffith Stadium. Although Goose's lifetime total of 248 homers is modest by today's standards, he drove in more than 100 runs in eleven of thirteen seasons. NATIONAL BASEBALL LIBRARY, COOPERS-TOWN N.Y.

One of the first young sluggers of the 1920s with no professional experience in the pre-Ruth era, the Philadelphia Athletics' Al Simmons lost no time impressing himself on big-league pitchers. In his first eight seasons he batted .363 and drove in more than 1,000 runs. NATIONAL BASEBALL LIBRARY, COOPERSTOWN, N.Y.

Multimillionaire brewer Jacob Ruppert may have been the first owner to operate a big-league baseball team strictly as a hobby. Ruppert's willingness to spend large sums from his personal fortune to buy star players like Babe Ruth turned the New York Yankees into the most successful sports franchise in history. NATIONAL BASEBALL LIBRARY, COOPERSTOWN, N.Y.

In 1929 this innocuous-looking pair, Philadelphia Phillies Charles "Chuck" Klein (*left*) and Frank "Lefty" O'Doul, out-slugged the legendary power combos of Ruth and Gehrig, Simmons and Foxx. Klein and O'Doul were playing their first season as major-league regu-lars. The following year they upped their combined slug-average ten notches to .650, but the hapless Phillies still lost 102 games and finished last. COURTESY OF *THE SPORTING NEWS*

Outside the Ebbets Field rotunda, Brooklyn fans mill about Sullivan Place, hoping to cadge a stray ticket to an important game between the Robins and the Cubs, ca. 1930. Born half a century before the ascendancy of faded jeans and torn T-shirts, the natty fans in boaters and Panama hats are less likely to be bankers than filing clerks or bricklayers. NATIONAL BASEBALL LIBRARY, COOPERSTOWN, N.Y.

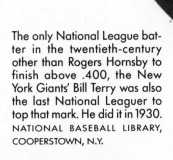

The only National League batter in the twentieth-century other than Rogers Hornsby to finish above .400, the New York Giants' Bill Terry was also the last National Leaguer to top that mark. He did it in 1930.
NATIONAL BASEBALL LIBRARY, COOPERSTOWN, N.Y.

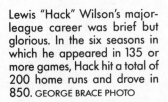

Lewis "Hack" Wilson's major-league career was brief but glorious. In the six seasons in which he appeared in 135 or more games, Hack hit a total of 200 home runs and drove in 850. GEORGE BRACE PHOTO

Reared in a small town, Smead Jolley typified the minor-league superstar of the 1920s. Shown here in the uniform of the San Francisco Seals, the gentle, easygoing "Smudge" batted over .370 seven times and won six minor-league batting titles, the last at age thirty-nine.

Brooklyn's mildly eccentric manager, Wilbert "Uncle Robbie" Robinson, surveys his unpredictable charges from the protection of the Ebbets Field dugout. In the crazy season of 1930, Robbie's ragtag crew almost made off with the pennant in the face of four more-gifted National League clubs. COURTESY OF THE BROOKLYN PUBLIC LIBRARY, BROOKLYN COLLECTION

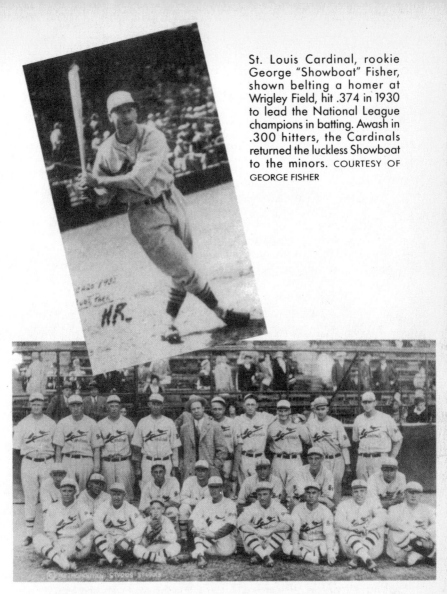

St. Louis Cardinal, rookie George "Showboat" Fisher, shown belting a homer at Wrigley Field, hit .374 in 1930 to lead the National League champions in batting. Awash in .300 hitters, the Cardinals returned the luckless Showboat to the minors. COURTESY OF GEORGE FISHER

In 1930 the St. Louis Cardinals scored a league record 1,004 runs on 1,732 hits as every regular batted over .300. The effort was good enough for a pennant, but the Cards finished an undistinguished third in the league in batting at .314. *Standing, left to right:* Lindsey, Bell, Johnson, Haines, Grimes, Bottomley, Hafey, Fisher, Wilson, Puccinelli. *Middle row, left to right:* Grabowski, Hallahan, Mancuso, Orsatti, Frisch, Gelbert, Blades. *Front row, left to right:* Watkins, Wares (coach), team mascot, Street (manager), High, Adams, Douthit, Smith. NATIONAL BASEBALL LIBRARY, COOPERSTOWN, N.Y.

This aerial shot of Navin Field, Detroit, ca. 1924, shows the recently completed second deck. Despite additional seating, the popular Tigers are coping with an overflow crowd. A low sun in the southwest and lightly leafed trees on National Avenue suggest that the season must be April or early May. The team in the field looks like the Chicago White Sox, so Sunday, April 27, 1924, might be a good guess at the date. Those are temporary bleachers in the right-field corner, good for only a ground-rule double. The distance down the right-field line to the wall and home-run territory is 370 feet. COURTESY OF THE BURTON HISTORICAL COLLECTION, DETROIT PUBLIC LIBRARY

NINE

SOUND
AND FURY ON
MICHIGAN
AVENUE

> "It was murder. You'd go into Detroit for a
> series and find the entire Tiger outfield was
> hitting four hundred."
>
> —WAITE HOYT

THE KIND OF hitting witnessed in St. Louis in the early 1920s had
been a staple in Detroit for decades. Occasionally it had actually
brought the Tigers victory. From 1907 through 1909, under rookie
manager Hughie Jennings, Detroit won three pennants and, of
course, led the American League in batting. Then the pitching
soured and Jennings discovered that hitting alone was not enough.
For the next eleven years Jennings continued to field his customary crushing lineup—the Tigers were first or second in batting
for seven out of ten seasons—but never again was he able to
bring the team home in front. In 1915, for example, though
Hughie's lumber merchants fashioned 100 wins, it was only good
for second place.

Through the years of frustration, Detroit baseball writers
charged Jennings, who practiced law in the off-season, with all
manner of dereliction, but chiefly the mishandling of pitchers.
The fact is Detroit never had much pitching to mishandle. An

unpredictable pitching staff was not the manager's only worry. In his playing days a sure-handed shortstop with the legendary Baltimore Orioles of the 1890s and a future Hall of Famer, Jennings was forced to look on helplessly as his heavy-hitting nine struggled to subdue batted balls, often without success. A weary Detroit correspondent, reporting in 1920 from the Tigers' training camp at Macon, Georgia, wrote, "We see a lot of hitting here, but with Detroit, that's all you get."

As a solution to this grievous imbalance of baseball skills, club president Frank Navin in 1921 fired defensive specialist Jennings and replaced him with Ty Cobb, baseball's most brilliant batter. Mysterious are the ways of baseball owners.

More difficult to understand than Navin's quixotic appointment is Cobb's willingness to take the job. His motive could not have been the extra money. Already one of baseball's highest paid players, Cobb, as a result of shrewd investments, was unquestionably the wealthiest. Perhaps the contentious Georgian was incapable of sidestepping a challenge. In the season past, Cobb's chief batting rival, Tris Speaker, had managed the Cleveland Indians to a world championship while batting .388 and playing the most brilliant center field in baseball. To an overachiever like Cobb, it may have been tempting to try to match Speaker's virtuoso performance. Whatever Cobb's thinking at the time, years later he would describe his decision to manage while still an active player as "the biggest mistake of my life."

Cobb's arrival in Detroit early in 1921 for investiture as manager turned into a civic love feast. There were demonstrations at the railroad depot, bands, parades, receptions, and a testimonial banquet hosted by local business leaders. Most Detroit baseball writers, along with many fans, shared Navin's conviction that The Georgia Peach was just the leader to turn the Bengals from mangy also-rans into sleek champions. Intoxicated with the idea, a few writers went so far as to predict that the Tigers would win it all in 1921.

Cobb took a more cautious view. He promised only that if the club failed to improve on its record for 1920 he would offer his resignation. In was hardly a daring vow. The 1920 Tigers had finished seventh, 37 games out of first place.

The new manager pledged something more. Compared with the rough-hewn ballplayers of his youth, Cobb said, the modern player was vastly more intelligent and better educated. He was amenable to reason and persuasion. This being so, the manager went on, it was his intention to exercise a light touch on the reins. For a man of Cobb's volcanic nature the resolution was absurd. Before three innings had been played in the first intra-squad game, he would lapse into what his DNA commanded him to be—a snarling, vituperative, autocratic, totally hands-on slave driver.

Unluckily for Cobb, he had taken on a rebuilding job at per-haps the worst time in baseball history. Newly exempted from the draft, minor-league owners were pushing player prices through the Van Allen belt. Since Frank Navin, a fugitive accountant, had long ago raised frugality to a minor religion, the rookie manager faced a mammoth challenge.

The Tigers' performance in 1921 may never be matched. The team batted .316, still an American League record. In 154 games they hammered out 1,724 base hits, also a league record. They scored 883 runs, more than the World Champion Cleveland In-dians had produced a year earlier. And they finished sixth, 27 games behind the first-place Yankees. Cobb could have been for-given if, like Casey Stengel, he had admonished his barber: "Shave and a haircut, but be careful not to slit my throat. I might want to do that myself."

The 1921 Tigers had a problem that frustrated several big-league clubs of the period, notably the Browns and the Cardinals: Baseball rules did not permit them to remain at bat in both halves of an inning. Actually, statistics for Detroit's pitching staff in that year don't look as bad as a sixth-place-finish suggests. Even the club's fielding average is respectable for the era, just slightly be-low that of the champion Yanks. Of course, fielding stats are no-torious for concealing deficiencies that may be distressingly evident on the field, especially lack of speed. The thirty-five-year-old Cobb, running on ravaged legs, led the 1921 squad in stolen bases with a humble 22. It represented 23 percent of the team total.

In spite of the team's lowly finish, Detroit fans reveled in the glittering performance at the plate. The Tigers' batting average represented an improvement of 46 percentage points over their very respectable .270 of a season earlier. Slugging average was up a remarkable 74 percentage points to .433, second only to the explosive New York Yankees. Local writers drew an inescapable conclusion: The new manager had imparted some of his own bat magic to the troops.

Cobb's prize batting pupil in 1921 was right fielder Harry Heilmann. From the time of his arrival in the majors in 1916, the ponderous Heilmann had been a fine journeyman batsman, averaging .294 over five seasons and driving home his share of runs. Although Cobb and Heilmann played side by side for years, it was not until the new manager's first training camp that he began to offer Heilmann tips on stance and pitch selection. Suddenly "Slug" became an assassin at the plate. He went on to bat .394 and win the first of his four American League batting titles, beating out his mentor by 5 percentage points. Heilmann also hit 19 home runs, drove in 139 runs, and rolled up a slugging average of .606, second only to Ruth's stratospheric .846.

When Detroit writers pressed Cobb on why he had not offered counsel earlier in Heilmann's career, the tempestuous Georgian fell back on the posture of Southern gentility that he occasionally affected. Until recently, Cobb pointed out, Heilmann had been his teammate and peer. It would have been presumptuous to offer advice to so excellent a player. It might have been ill received, Cobb sniffed, and properly so. Once he had been elevated to manager, however, it was another matter. Implicitly he had become responsible for Heilmann's welfare as well as that of the team.

Heilmann was not the only Detroit hitter to benefit from Cobb's knowledge of the strike zone. Rookie first baseman Luzerne "Lu" Blue batted .308, rookie catcher Johnny Bassler .307, third baseman Bobby Jones .303, backup outfielder Ira Flagstead .305, and veteran second baseman Ralph Young a career high of .299. Even the weak sister in the batting order, aging shortstop Owen "Donie" Bush, a congenital .240 hitter, clubbed the ball at a .280 clip until late August, when Navin sold him to Washington. Cut off from Cobb's tutelage, Bush quickly slipped back to the more familiar level of .214.

Many years later, in his baseball autobiography, *My Life in Baseball: The True Record,* Cobb wrote, "In all modesty, I could teach hitting." The claim can hardly be disputed.

All Detroit performance in 1921 pales before that of the outfield of Cobb, Heilmann, and Bobby Veach. Collectively they batted .374. They scored 348 runs. All three finished in double figures in home runs and triple figures in RBIs. On a modest total of 47 homers they drove in a staggering 368 runs, the third highest total by a regular outfield in baseball history and still the American League standard.

Cobb may have been supportive and congenial in the batting cage, but elsewhere he was as unapproachable as a pit bull. From the outset he established strict rules for deportment, including a prohibition against fraternizing with opposing players, even National Leaguers in a spring exhibition game. He demanded seriousness and hustle every minute a player was on the field. His favorite maxim was, "A tough, aggressive spirit never hurt anyone." Oddly, Cobb's tyranny did not extend beyond the playing field. For instance, he never imposed a curfew on his players, a policy unique in the era.

And then there was the dog. One spring a tattered mongrel invaded the Detroit training camp and attached itself to a couple of the players, who fed it scraps. Conscious that the men were tense under his tyrannical field supervision, Cobb saw the cur as an instrument for relieving stress. He *commanded* every man on the squad to pet the dog at least once a day or answer to the manager for his failure to do so.

There is a story that Cobb became obsessed with the idea that left fielder Bobby Veach was playing below his potential because he lacked competitive fire. The affable Kentuckian infuriated the manager when occasionally he bantered with opposing pitchers and even smiled at them. Cobb's notion was ludicrous on its face. Veach had long been one of the league's finest hitters and had three times won the RBI title.

In any case, Cobb ordered good-natured Harry Heilmann, who batted behind Veach, to ride his teammate from the on-deck circle, to accuse him of being gutless and trying to curry favor with pitchers he feared might come inside on him. Cobb assured Heilmann that once the scheme worked he would confess to Veach and exonerate Harry.

Reluctantly, Heilmann followed orders and soon converted his laid-back teammate to a running state of anger. Whatever the reason, Veach did in fact have an outstanding season, achieving personal highs in home runs and runs batted in, while batting .338. Having gotten the performance he sought from Veach, Cobb forgot his pledge to Heilmann and went back to Georgia without squaring matters. Despite poor Heilmann's repeated efforts to explain the episode, Veach remained unforgiving.

Cobb placed great store by vituperation as a weapon. From the coaching lines he was tireless in his efforts to destabilize opposing players by heaping abuse on them. No subject was off limits: ancestry, personal hygiene, sex habits, dress, food preference—anything that came to hand. His favorite target was Babe Ruth, the man who had displaced him as the biggest drawing card in baseball. Babe was known to be hypersensitive. At the same time he was a veteran big leaguer and had witnessed Cobb's terror tactics for years. In most instances Ruth chose to answer Cobb's tasteless jibes with base hits. In one 5-game series at the Polo Grounds in 1921, the Babe pounded Detroit pitching for 7 home runs as the Yankees swept the series. To make certain that Cobb got the message, Ruth volunteered to pitch one of the games, in which he took particular delight in striking out the seething Detroit manager.

As the 1921 season drew to a close and Detroit's slide grew steeper, Cobb's congenital rage widened. A snarl became his habitual mode of expression. When he went so far as to provoke a fist fight with gentlemanly umpire Billy Evans over an unimportant call at second, the choleric manager was suspended by league president Ban Johnson for what remained of the season.

If the 1921 season was gall and wormwood to Cobb, it seemed not so to Detroit fans. At any rate, they paid their way into tiny Navin Field in record numbers, almost 700,000 at a park that seated a scant 21,000. But who wouldn't turn out to see that crew maul opposing pitchers? By contrast, the Tigers' sixth-place counterpart in the National League—Cincinnati—drew a bit more than 300,000, a more conventional figure for a second-division club of the era. The Reds' respectable .278 batting average was still the lowest team mark in their league, graphic evidence of how the hitter's world had changed in three years.

Despite the pressure of managing, Cobb's performance on the field in 1921 was characteristically brilliant. In 128 games he batted .389 on 197 hits for 302 bases. He achieved a personal high in home runs with 12 and drove in 101 runs for a slugging average of .596. Typically, he struck out only 19 times. For much of the season Cobb had batted above .400, but in the final weeks he tired perceptibly and was denied his thirteenth batting title (one he would never win) by the emergence of his protégé Harry Heilmann.

Publicly Cobb blamed his failures as a rookie manager on shaky pitching. The story is more complicated. While it is true that the Tiger pitching staff failed to sparkle in 1921, Cobb himself may have been the problem. Anyone who has managed or coached a baseball team, from Little League to the majors, quickly learns that pitchers cannot be handled like linebackers. Operatic tenors might be a more appropriate model. Baseball's supreme batsman may have been congenitally incapable of understanding the species.

Among other things, in the course of a game Cobb would frequently call time, trot in from center field, and counsel the pitcher on how to deal with the next batter. Veterans on the staff hated it. They might have minded less had Cobb been signaling pitches from the dugout like bench managers McGraw and Mack, but in all likelihood Cobb would not have grasped that it made a difference. He micromanaged the team to an extent that was unusual in his generation and appeared singularly oblivious to players' feelings. In time the hostility of left-hander Hubert "Dutch" Leonard toward the insensitive Cobb became almost pathological.

Three Detroit starters—Leonard (not to be confused with the younger Emil "Dutch" Leonard, who pitched in the 1940s), Howard Ehmke, and Hooks Dauss were all proven big-league winners. In their combined careers they would put together 526 major-league victories. Even with a staff that ran no deeper than this, three top starters should have been enough to keep the Detroit fence busters out of the second division.

Detroit's manifest disability in 1921 was one that plagued several heavy-hitting outfits of the era. They could not field. The only first-rate fielders on the team were Cobb and two rookies—Blue at first and Bassler behind the plate. The middle of the Tigers' infield remained as unobstructed to batted balls as Australia's Nullarbor Plain. No manager who also played center field could long be unaware of it. Early in September, as the Tigers continued to come out on the short end of high-scoring games, H. G. Salsinger of the *Detroit News* (Cobb's favorite writer, since he wasn't one to criticize the locals lightly) reported to *The Sporting News,* "Detroit is a miserable fielding team. . . . They discount fairly good pitching by poor and stupid fielding."

Determined to put the Tigers into contention in 1922, Cobb bullied Navin into opening the rusty locks on his cash box. The owner parted with about $40,000 in cash and players for two young right-handers from the Portland club of the Pacific Coast League, Herman Pillette and Sylvester Johnson. The rookie pitchers were especially welcome, since over the winter malcontent left-hander Dutch Leonard had decided to quit baseball.

In the off-season Cobb tried hard to obtain veteran shortstop Everett Scott from Boston. He also sought Philadelphia's gifted third baseman Joe Dugan for conversion to a badly needed second baseman. But the Yankees still held seigniorial rights to any scrap of baseball talent loose at Fenway Park. They got Scott, of course, and when Dugan was traded to Boston, the Yankees seized him as well.

While Cobb's frustration must have been great, he patched up the infield as best he could. From Pittsburgh he obtained competent but aging second baseman George Cutshaw on waivers. Then he picked up young shortstop Emory "Topper" Rigney from Fort Worth of the Texas League. It meant that Rigney had to make the jump from Class A to the majors. Cobb was left little choice.

In a grand Detroit tradition, Cobb's outfield represented a surfeit of riches. To supplement the firepower already on line, the Tigers brought up Bob "Fats" Fothergill from Rochester, where he had led the International League in batting with an average of .383. That spring Cobb also had nineteen-year-old Floyd "Babe"

Herman in the rookie corral, but he optioned the kid to Omaha, where Babe blistered Western League pitching for a .416 average.

Despite the nickname, Fothergill was no more than stylishly stout when he first reported to the Tigers. By mid-career, however, seduced by the largess of major-league meal money, he carried upward of 230—some say 250—pounds on his five-foot-ten-inch frame. Fothergill is one of a multitude of colorful figures who peopled the big leagues in the 1920s, and he may rank as the consummate backup outfielder of the period. A right-handed hitter of admirable consistency, he batted .326 over a twelve-year big-league career with Detroit, Chicago and Boston. Not considered a power hitter in his own day, Fothergill nonetheless compiled a lifetime slugging average of .460. In his eight seasons at Detroit, Fats hit .336 and was never below .300. He still ranks fifth on the all-time list of pinch hitters, and his 19 for 53 in 1929 remains one of the best single-season performances ever.

For all his bulk, Fothergill was an aggressive, heads-up fielder. It is well documented that in an exhibition game in Virginia he deliberately ran through a wooden outfield fence in pursuit of a fly ball. And a story from Hall of Fame catcher Mickey Cochrane, a very reliable source, attests to Fat Bob's agility. One day in the late 1920s, as Cochrane recalled, when the Tigers were at Shibe Park and Mickey was catching for the Athletics, the Philadelphia bench, enthusiastically seconded by the local fans, were ragging Fothergill about his size. It was the sort of thing that Fats faced in most enemy parks and he disregarded it. The Athletics' big right-hander George "Moose" Earnshaw decided to join in the fun. He came inside with a high, hard one that singed the stubble on one of Fothergill's several chins. (Cochrane may well have called the pitch and that's why he remembered the incident so vividly.)

Fothergill went down with a crash that must have rocked the cupola over Connie Mack's office. Then, according to Cochrane, Fats carefully dusted off his size-52 uniform and hit the next pitch into Delaware County. Not only was it the longest home run that Fothergill had ever hit at Shibe Park, it may have been the longest that anyone had ever hit there, including Jimmie Foxx. All smiles, Fothergill circled the bases, and as he approached home he executed a forward flip in the manner of Ozzie Smith and landed gracefully on the plate. The home crowd, Cochrane said, was respectfully silent as Fothergill trotted to the Detroit dugout.

A well-established baseball legend holds that Fothergill eventually ate himself to death. While it is impossible to confirm such a conclusion medically, it is a sad fact that the picturesque outfielder died of a stroke in 1938 at the age of forty.

At all events, in the spring of 1922 Cobb needed a Bob Fothergill like he needed a third thumb. He yearned for middle infielders with range and soft hands and pitchers who could throw strikes—low strikes. In the face of these deficiencies, the fiery manager nevertheless psyched himself into believing that the Tigers had a realistic shot at the pennant.

Cobb's optimism, if it can be called that, may have had roots in his view of human achievement. To the end of his life Cobb insisted that he was not a naturally gifted athlete like Babe Ruth, Honus Wagner, or Joe Jackson, that rather he had forced himself to succeed through willpower. Implicit in such a conviction is the expectation that some of the modestly talented ballplayers in his charge could do the same—if they had the guts. Cobb's dogma translated into anguish for a number of his players, since they had little hope of measuring up.

Even while the Tigers were still playing their exhibition schedule, the 1922 season began to look inauspicious. In the ninth inning against a minor-league opponent, with Detroit leading by 9 runs, Cobb seriously injured his right leg trying to go from first to third on a short single. It put him on the disabled list for the first month of the season. Responding to a postgame remonstrance from a Detroit writer, the manager explained that it was the only way he knew how to play baseball, regardless of opponent or score. Unfortunately, he was now thirty-six years old and, as he put it, "easier to hurt, harder to mend."

By the time Cobb was able to hobble back into the lineup, the Tigers were unpropitiously settled in last place, 8 games under .500. Cobb fumed. He ranted. He pounded his fists against any hard object within reach. Hustle, he demanded, let's have more hustle. And after that, even more hustle. Magically, Cobbian fire informed the exhausted Tigers. In spite of the unsteady fielding, the lack of foot speed, and the inconsistent pitching, the team began to right itself. Leading by example as well as fiat, Cobb soon had his own batting average over .360.

The Tigers had opened the month of June by losing 4 straight on the road. Comfortably back at Navin Field on June 6, they vented their frustration on the Athletics in a 14-to-1 blowout. Since that felt so good, they pounded the hapless A's twice more. The victory virus had taken hold. Detroit went on to win 13 of 15, including a run of 8 straight. On the fourteenth they beat league-leading New York to move into the first division. Sweeping the remaining 3 games of the series, the Tigers found themselves in third place just 4½ games behind the Yankees. In New York it was rumored that oddsmakers were demanding a saliva test.

On June 18 the Tigers welcomed Boston to Navin Field with a 15-hit assault, winning 8 to 1. On the following day they beat the Red Sox, 11 to 9, and again made 15 hits. On the twentieth the Tigers administered a third shellacking, 9 to 8, which was to become a typical score for a Detroit game and evidence that they were simply hammering their way to victory. It was a dangerous way to live. As proof, on the twenty-first, although Detroit collected its customary 15 hits, Boston reversed the score and beat them, 9 to 8. Incredibly, in 25 outings during this period, the rampaging Bengals would average just under 14 hits a game.

As July opened, Cobb, Heilmann, and Blue were all batting over .360, with the remainder of the Tiger wrecking crew not far behind. Bobby Veach, in particular, was weighing in with key hits. This winning ugly must have driven a perfectionist like Cobb to the brink of apoplexy. Still, with the personnel he had, there seemed no alternative strategy. Showing the way, Cobb became downright demonic at the plate. On July 25, as his team cuffed the peerless Walter Johnson for 14 hits, Cobb took over the batting lead from George Sisler, who was on the way to one of the greatest seasons any player has ever had. The aging, ailing Cobb was hitting .411.

Early in August, Detroit reeled off its second 8-game winning streak of the season. Hitting safely in 16 consecutive games, Cobb had raised his average to .415, 13 percentage points above rival

Sisler. Still, the Tigers were not gaining on the leaders, St. Louis and New York.

Late in August, despite their self-destructive ways, the Tigers were 5 games back of St. Louis and very much in the pennant race. In fact, they had just won 8 of 9 when calamity struck. At Washington on the twenty-sixth, Harry Heilmann broke his collarbone in a freak accident at first base and was lost for the season. At the time, the right fielder was batting .356 and had 21 homers and 92 RBIs. Moreover, Harry was renowned as one of the strongest finishers in baseball. For a team so dependent on hitting for survival, the loss of Heilmann proved fatal. Detroit went into a flat spin and was lucky to cling to third place. They finished 16 games out of first and 15 behind the second-place Browns. Had the season lasted another week, the Tigers might have slid past Cleveland and Chicago, deep into the second division.

Although Detroit's season had been less than sensational, the Tigers did finish in the first division. Until the injury to Heilmann, they appeared to have an outside shot at the pennant. Except for Cobb, everyone in Detroit was reasonably pleased. Owner Frank Navin must have been delighted. All season the click of his abacus had competed with the crack of Tiger bats as 861,000 paying fans fought their way into Navin Field. Equally important, the Tigers had established themselves as the second-best road attraction in baseball after Babe Ruth and the Yankees.

While Detroit hitters failed to match their 1921 heroics, their performance was still impressive. The team batted .305, 18 percentage points better than the pennant-winning Yankees. Detroit also outscored New York. (In the matter of giving up runs, however, the Yanks were 22 percent more efficient.) Leading his team at bat, Cobb hit .401, his third time over the .400 mark. On just 4 home runs he drove in 99 runs in 137 games.

Led by Cobb's great effort, the five Detroit outfielders combined for an average of .354. Bobby Veach had his usual sterling year, driving home 126 runs. But, then, everyone expected Tiger outfielders to hit a ton.

The big surprise was rookie shortstop Topper Rigney, who batted .300 and drove in 63 runs. Cobb's guidance? Very likely. Another of his rookie pupils, utility infielder Fred Haney, hit a sizzling .352 in 80 games. Detroit's superb catching corps of Johnny Bassler and Larry Woodall combined for a .328 average and 59 RBIs. In fact, only third baseman Bobby Jones, who batted .257, had to be concealed behind the water cooler when visitors called. On the up side, Jones was the most improved fielder on the club. Except for rookie right-hander Herman Pillette, who had a 2.85 ERA and won 19 games, Tiger pitching in 1922 was undistinguished.

Finishing in the money should have been a source of pride for Cobb. It wasn't. His creed was: "I've got to be first—in everything." Anything less than victory tasted of ashes.

In Detroit's 1923 training camp the brightest prospect was— you guessed it—yet another lumbering, hard-hitting outfielder. In his one full season in the minors, twenty-one-year-old Henry "Heinie" Manush batted .376 and more than a third of his 245 hits had gone for extra bases. Manush's arrival gave Cobb six of the strongest-hitting outfielders in baseball, and by the end of May he felt secure enough to peddle the versatile Ira Flagstead to the Red Sox. Even in the gloom of Boston, however, the eccentric ex-lumberjack forgot none of what Cobb had taught him about hitting. Flagstead batted .312.

On the eve of the 1923 season, coming off an injury-plagued spring exhibition schedule, Cobb flew in the face of reason and predicted that his Tigers would win the pennant. If the declaration was intended to raise fan enthusiasm, it worked. Advance ticket orders broke club records. Spearheaded by the auto industry, the economic boom of the 1920s was rapidly gathering force. Detroit workers had more disposable income than ever before and many seemed eager to spend it on baseball.

Despite the optimism of Cobb and the Detroit fans, the 1923 season unfolded very much as the experts predicted. The powerful and smooth-fielding Yankees were scarcely ever out of first place. The Tigers, on the other hand, went into a May swoon and played less than .500 ball well into August. Cobb, whose hair was thinning at the time he became manager, was now almost bald. Cynics in the press box suggested that in frustration the manager had uprooted the remnant himself.

But 1923 was not without positive results. The Tigers finished second, though admittedly a poor second, 16 games behind the winners. In league standings, it was their best showing since the frustrating 1915 season.

For the third time running, Cobb's Tigers showed that they were capable of one burst of good baseball a season. In 1923 it came late. In the final third of the season the Tigers played .630 ball, winning 34 of their last 54 games. In the last two weeks they turned white hot, taking 11 of 13 to beat out Cleveland for second place by half a game. The Tigers' stretch drive might have carried them closer to the Yankees had they not been forced in mid-September to play six doubleheaders in six days, all on the road. They failed to sweep a single one.

Before World War II, consecutive doubleheaders were not uncommon as teams scrambled to make up games postponed in rainy April and May. Since a double bill virtually assured increased attendance for the day, owners probably welcomed them. Oddly, such brutal scheduling did not always work to a team's disadvantage. In 1924, beginning on Labor Day, Brooklyn swept four doubleheaders in four days to begin a drive that almost netted them a pennant.

When official statistics for 1923 were released in December, they revealed a familiar story. For the third consecutive season Detroit had batted .300 or above, as they outhit the World Champion Yankees by 9 percentage points. Once again the Tigers outscored New York. But, as usual, the slugging Yanks were the most niggardly team in the majors in surrendering runs.

Although Cobb had a bit of an off year at .340, Harry Heilmann joined the now-not-so-exclusive .400 club, taking the league batting title with .403. All five Detroit outfielders topped .300 and had a collective average above .350. The infielders logged a modest .288, but Rigney and Pratt were well over .300.

In 1923 Detroit's problem was not hard to pinpoint. The pitchers had the second worst earned-run average in the league. The bright spot was Hooks Dauss, who won 21 games and had a decent 3.62 ERA.

If 1923 meant continued disappointment for Cobb and the team, it produced renewed smiles in the front office. More than 900,000 fans showed up at Navin Field, a home-attendance record second only to the Yankees, who were playing in their new 70,000-capacity park. On the road too Detroit was second only to the new World Champions. Whatever Cobb's shortcomings as a field general, his traveling batting carnival had turned Detroit into one of the two most profitable franchises in baseball.

Over the winter, encouraged by the steady rise in attendance, Navin added a second deck to his ballpark, from first base around to third. The addition increased seating capacity to just under 30,000. On the roof of the new upper deck the owner installed an elevated press box similar to the one fronting the mezzanine at Yankee Stadium. Traditionally, press boxes were located at field level. Navin must have felt that it was time for the prospering Tigers, like their stylish rivals in New York, to go first class.

It must have been uniquely frustrating to managers like Cobb, Rickey, George Gibson and Bill McKechnie of Pittsburgh, even Tris Speaker, to run teams that could score runs by the dozen yet at times had to struggle to stay out of the second division. These men had grown to baseball maturity in an age when a run was as precious as six bits to a homeless man, when a base hit of any kind was cause for celebration on the bench. Now they watched entire outfields on also-ran clubs hit .350 and backup catchers knock in 50 runs a season. In was indeed a whole new ballgame.

It's a pity Cobb didn't have the sense to surrender the reins after 1923. In just three seasons he had raised the moribund Tigers from seventh place to second. He might have gone down in baseball history as a highly irascible leader, handcuffed by unpredictable pitching and shaky fielding, who had done an admirable job with the material at hand.

Had Cobb entertained ideas of quitting in 1923 he would have faced a dilemma. If he stepped down as manager, he would have to leave Detroit. It would be impossible for a man of his temperament to play effectively for a successor, perhaps even help the new man succeed where he had failed. In addition, few men knew more about baseball than Cobb, and perhaps he sensed that the veteran Yankee machine, now at the top of the world, would soon begin to show signs of wear. Detroit, after all, had finished second, and since the Red Sox had no more talent for the Yankees to plunder, 1924 might offer the ideal opportunity to slip past the perennial champs. If such surmise encouraged Cobb to continue as manager, he was at least partly correct.

Training camp in 1924 saw yet another rookie outfielder with a big bat—Absalom "Red" Wingo, younger brother of Cincinnati catcher "Ivy" Wingo. Red couldn't field a lick, of course, but if he hit up to the standards of the Detroit outfield it would scarcely be noticed. With the untested Wingo aboard, Cobb lost no time in banishing the aging but serviceable Bobby Veach to Boston. Starting in fewer than 130 games for the Sox that year, Bobby still led his new club in RBIs with 99.

In addition to Wingo, Cobb had acquired rookie left-hander Earl Whitehill. Whitehill would prove to be the only young quality starter to join the Tigers in the whole decade of the 1920s.

After winning 5 games in the opening week, Detroit went into its customary spring trance and seemed headed for the second division. The slump proved brief, however. Responding to the manager's exhortations, the Tigers held their own through May and in June began to rise. Free from pain and injuries for the first time in years, Cobb hit like a man possessed. Perhaps inspired by the old man's performance, the team turned hot, winning 12 of 15 in July. On the twenty-third they took over the league lead. It was the latest point in the season that a Detroit team had occupied first place since 1916. By August 1, professional gamblers—the most hardheaded judges—acknowledged by a shift in the odds that Cobb's lads could go all the way.

It was not to be. As Cobb may have suspected, the Yankees were not the world beaters of old. But he could hardly have foreseen the emergence of a young Washington club with superb pitching, led by Walter Johnson, still formidable at thirty-seven. Detroit did not collapse so much as slowly fade under pressure from two contenders. The Tigers suffered some bad breaks as well. In August first baseman Lu Blue injured his leg and was lost for the season. Tormented by sinusitis, Harry Heilmann had what was for him an off year. He batted .346 and drove in a modest 113 runs. (Before the appearance of antibiotics, sinusitis crippled a number of baseball's fine hitters, among them Sisler, Jimmie Foxx, and Hal Trosky.)

Despite setbacks, the Tigers were game, and in a last-gasp effort took 7 straight at the tag end of the season, including a gratifying sweep of the Yankees. The defeats cost New York a fourth straight pennant. In all, Detroit won 86 games, their best record since 1916, as they finished a respectable third, 6 games out of first and 4 behind the Yankees.

Paradoxically, in this most successful year of the Cobb era, Detroit's hitting fell off—slightly. The team batted .298. That was still good enough to top the American League. Predictably, the Tigers outscored both Washington and New York. As evidence that Cobb's lads were off their feed, the five outfielders batted a constrained .322. Otherwise commendable, the collective figure veils a shameful fact. Sophomore Manush and freshman Wingo both batted below .300. After the final home game, the humiliated youngsters, one a future Hall of Famer, must have slunk from the park by way of the Cherry Street gate.

For the first time in years, Cobb had played in every one of Detroit's 155 games. In other respects, however, it was an off year for The Peach. He hit .338, and knocked in only 74 runs. On the plus side, his scarred old legs fetched him 23 stolen bases, enough to put him among the league leaders in an age when running had become unfashionable. Cobb also led American League outfielders in fielding percentage, a reflection perhaps of diminishing range rather than sustained skill with the glove.

Had the Tigers not done so well in 1924, Frank Navin might have been emboldened to fire Cobb, putting both the manager and most of the team out of their misery. It was openly reported that as many as fifteen players had been to Navin's office demanding to be traded, an unusual occurrence in a period when baseball owners exercised autocratic powers. Any fate, even playing in Boston, may have seemed preferable to Cobb's despotism.

But Navin dared not move precipitously. Cobb was still enormously popular with the Detroit fans (who didn't have to earn their living under him). Furthermore, the Tigers had just played before more than a million at home, only the second major-league club to accomplish that. They had, in fact, come within 38,000 of outdrawing New York. Six years into the Ruth era, Ty Cobb remained one of baseball's biggest attractions.

By the spring of 1925 a Detroit fan sequestered in the Ant-
arctic could have projected in his imagination the Tigers' season.
The team would hit a ton, outscore everyone in sight—and go
absolutely nowhere. In fact, the Tigers batted .302—their third
.300-plus season in four years—scored more than 900 runs, and
finished fourth, 16½ games out.

Harry Heilmann provided a measure of excitement by winning a neck-and-neck batting-title duel with Cleveland playing
manager Tris Speaker. At age thirty-seven Spoke still swung an
authoritative stick and had led the league through much of the
second half of the season. But in September Heilmann, as was his
custom, came on with a rush. Going into the final day, Speaker at
.389 led Heilmann by a percentage point. The Cleveland manager
decided to stand pat and sit out the last game.

Meanwhile, Detroit had a doubleheader against the Browns at
St. Louis. In the first game Heilmann went 3 for 6, and his teammates, calculating correctly that Slug had the title won, urged
him to sit out the nightcap. But Heilmann, a player with class,
wanted no title he hadn't won standing up. In the second game
he went 3 for 3 to make it 6 for 9 on the day. It brought his
average to .393, a comfortable four percentage points ahead of
Speaker.

As usual, individual batting honors at Detroit were dazzling.
In addition to Heilmann's title performance, Cobb himself hit closer
to his normal level—.378. Red Wingo, playing regularly in left
field, became the proper Detroit outfielder by hitting .370. In
part-time action the steady Fats Fothergill hit .353, and Manush
logged a respectable .303. The three regulars—Cobb, Heilmann,
and Wingo—combined for an eye-popping .382, which may be
the highest average by a regular outfield in this century. Although
Waite Hoyt's later characterization of a Detroit outfield hitting
.400 may have been intended as playful hyperbole, for a period
in 1925 the Detroit regulars actually were batting over or around
the mark. Old reliable, Lu Blue, recovered from torn ligaments,
led a patchwork infield with .306, and drove in 94 runs on a slim
3 homers.

The 1925 season may be best remembered among old-time
Detroit fans for one of the most extraordinary batting feats of the

twentieth century—by Cobb, of course. On May 5, before a game at Sportsman's Park, his team mired in last place (having blown 14 of their first 19 games), Cobb addressed writer H. G. Salsinger of the Detroit *News* in the presence of Sid Keener of the St. Louis *Star* and several other reporters. "Gentlemen," Cobb said, "I would like you to pay particular attention today because for the first time in my career I will be deliberately going for home runs." Unlike the case of Ruth's called shot in the 1932 World Series, there can be no question about Cobb's intention. There were too many witnesses.

In the first inning the master rifled one of Joe Bush's fastballs into the pavilion in right field. Up again in the second, he hit an Elam Vangilder slow curve completely over the pavilion and across Grand Avenue. Demonstrating that all pitchers looked pretty much alike, in the eighth Cobb hit reliever Milton Gaston for a third homer. Sandwiched among the home runs were a double and 2 singles. Cobb went 6 for 6 and set a major-league record for total bases with 16. It remains the American League record though it has been tied.

That's not the end of the story. On the following day Cobb singled his first time up, to run his streak of consecutive hits to 9, counting 2 in the St. Louis opener on May 4. Left-hander Dave Danforth finally got Cobb out on a long fly ball, caught at the foot of the right-field wall. But in the fifth he tagged Danforth for his fourth home run in two days, and in the ninth he added another off left-hander Chet Falk. Five home runs in two games. It is still the record, although it has been tied a number of times, first by Tony Lazzeri of the Yankees eleven years later. Having made his point, Cobb went back to spray hitting. He had only 7 additional home runs for 1925.

Detroit's attendance was down sharply in 1925, attributable perhaps to the team's woeful start. As the Tigers rallied late in August to pull themselves into the first division, fans returned in force and the club realized a profitable 820,000 paid admissions, more than the second-place Giants drew in New York. Still, there were indications that Detroit fans might be tiring of a batting circus that produced no winners.

As the 1926 season approached, even a man of Cobb's iron

will must have acknowledged that he had hold of a tar baby. The situation at Detroit was not going to get better. Like the Cardinals, Browns, Pirates, and others, Cobb's Tigers had demonstrated that you can't club your way to victory. And yet the pitching and defensive talent that Cobb sought seemed unavailable. Even a cursory study of the majors in the 1920s suggests that there was a general shortage of effective pitchers, not so much among top starters as in the second rank. In addition, of course, career relief pitchers were unknown.

Possibly, as Cobb later charged, Navin was unwilling to spend the money needed to produce a winner. The manager never forgave Navin for refusing to buy young Johnny Neun from St. Paul to replace the injured Blue while the Tigers still had a shot at the pennant in 1924.

In December 1925 the battle-worn Cobb turned thirty-nine. He confided to intimates that a summer spent playing golf and rocking on his front porch was mighty tempting. Financially, he would never have a worry. Yet, to quit short of victory was unthinkable.

One month before the 1926 season Cobb had eye surgery for the removal of fleshy growths that had hampered his vision for some time. It makes you wonder what a guy who hit .378 might have batted with unimpaired vision.

For the ailing, harried Cobb, the campaign of 1926 must have been like replaying a nightmare. The spring collapse; the drain on his emotions to drive the team above .500—not accomplished until midsummer; the late-summer rally—as always, too little and too late. The one bright spot was the arrival of young Charlie Gehringer, who would fill that troublesome hole at second base for the next fifteen years and one day be elected to Cooperstown.

When the season ended Cobb was back where he had started— in sixth place. Ironically, the second-division Tigers finished 4 games closer to first than in their second-place effort of 1923. In batting, Cobb's men had now sunk to .291, but in a year that saw everyone slump the Tigers came within 1 percentage point of leading the league.

Slow to recover from the eye surgery, Cobb benched himself late in the spring for lack of hitting. He was batting .335. For most of 1926 he stayed with Manush in center, Fothergill in left, and Heilmann in right. The portly Fothergill found himself in the paradoxical position of being the fastest man in the Detroit outfield.

The ponderous outfield remained true to the grand tradition of Michigan Avenue, however. They batted a combined .370. In a year that saw Heilmann falter and hit only .367, Heinie Manush stepped in manfully and took the batting title with .378. When Harry came back to win a fourth title in 1927, it would mean that 17 of 21 American League batting championships had been taken by Detroit outfielders.

In Cobb's six years as manager the Tigers had hit for a breathtaking .302. The figure includes the efforts of pitchers, bullpen catchers, middle infielders up from the minors for a trial—everyone who waved a stick in support of the Motor City. Seven different Detroit outfielders had hit a collective .352. All the team had to show for an avalanche of base hits, 9,716 of them, or about 10.5 per game, was second-place money—once. Measured in today's terms, it must be reckoned a monumental waste of offense. And yet, if you had been a 1920s teenager, sitting in those steep right-center-field bleachers at Navin Field, watching your heros outduel the Browns, 15 to 14, it might live in your memory as the best of times.

During the 1985 media maelstrom that accompanied Pete Rose's pursuit of Cobb's lifetime record for base hits, the trifling attention given to Cobb himself focused on his prickly personality. There was scant talk of his accomplishments as a player. Many young fans may have been left with the impression that the Georgian had been little more than an ill-tempered singles hitter. In fact, Cobb's lifetime slugging average is a full 100 percentage points higher than Rose's. Cobb was, in fact, one of the most prolific run producers in baseball history.

From that slight crouch, hands spread about five inches apart on the bat handle, the left-handed Cobb drove in 1959 runs during his twenty-four-year career—and he did it on just 118 home runs. He currently stands fourth on the all-time RBI list, just behind Lou Gehrig. In scoring runs he is first with 2,244. He also stole 892 bases. It is worth noting that the three men ahead of

Cobb in lifetime run production averaged 654 home runs in their careers. Finally, there is the not insignificant fact of Cobb's lifetime batting average—.367, still tops in the history of the major leagues.

Not even the close scrutiny of today's computer-assisted comparisons can dull the luster of Cobb's achievements. Sabermetrician Bill James, who tends to be mildly skeptical of batting records set before World War II, ranks Cobb the top center fielder in history for career value. Pete Palmer also ranks The Peach first among center fielders.

As imposing as Cobb's batting record is, there is the temptation to ask, "What if?" Suppose the great star had sensibly declined the managership in 1921 and played out his final years with nothing more on his mind than four or five plate appearances a game followed by an evening spent calculating profits from his Coca-Cola stock. In an era when the batting averages of many other players were soaring 50 to 75 percentage points over their pre–World War I levels, what might a man have done who had batted .420 when the spitball was at its zenith? A man who at the high noon of the so-called dead-ball era consistently outhit his league by about 100 percentage points? What he did achieve while under the pressure of managing is impressive enough. For the six seasons Cobb batted .365 and drove in an average of 88 runs.

Early in November 1926, Cobb announced his retirement both as a manager and a player. He explained to reporters that he saw little hope of a Detroit pennant in the immediate future and that he was "just plain tired." What Cobb said was true. What he left unsaid was that he had been forced out. In the spring, left-hander Dutch Leonard, always a brooding and vindictive character, had gone to Ban Johnson and accused his former manager of conspiring with Tris Speaker to fix a game back in 1919. In evidence he produced some vaguely worded letters from Cobb that at the very least raised suspicions that the story might be true.

Johnson's reaction was wholly inappropriate but in character. He went to Navin with the letters and the two agreed to pay Leonard $20,000 hush money. Then the American League president waited until the season was over before informing the other

club owners and the Commissioner. Cobb and Speaker were suspended pending a ruling by Landis's office. There was a wonderful historic inevitability in Ty Cobb's being betrayed by a pitcher,
a left-hander at that.

When the flamboyant Landis had milked the episode for its
drama and publicity, going so far as to entertain gratuitous testimony from several of the outlawed Black Sox, he ruled that neither Cobb nor Speaker was guilty of fixing games, but at worst of
indiscretion of a type common before 1920—betting on ball games.
He rescinded the releases and restored the two to their club rosters. The Commissioner, however, lacked authority to restore them
as managers. The story doesn't end there.

An enraged Cobb vowed to sue Organized Baseball into obliv-
ion, and he had the means to hire the lawyers to do just that. He
also had political clout in Washington, where baseball's exemption from antitrust laws was under running scrutiny. But on the
heels of his exoneration, Cobb found himself flooded with offers
from other clubs, who were willing to pay him big money just to
appear in their uniform. It had to be gratifying to the old warrior
to learn that even in the presence of Babe Ruth he was still considered dynamite at the gate.

The Giants wanted Cobb, Washington wanted him, Cleveland
wanted him, even the Baltimore Orioles of the International League
wanted him. By far the most persistent suitor was Connie Mack,
who traveled to Georgia to talk with the aggrieved superstar. In
time the attention and flattery from so many quarters disarmed
Cobb and he abandoned plans to sue baseball. The chance to play
ball again must have seemed vastly more appealing than the prospect of expensive litigation conducted in unventilated court-
rooms. Cobb accepted Mack's offer of about $70,000, which made
The Peach once again the highest-paid player in baseball, higher
than Babe Ruth.

It is not clear what Mack was up to. By 1927 the Philadelphia
manager was well along toward building another champion on a
foundation of bright young stars like Al Simmons, Mickey Cochrane, and Jimmie Foxx. Suddenly, Connie began to collect fading
superstars. In addition to Cobb, over a couple of seasons Mack
had signed Zack Wheat, Jack Quinn, and Eddie Collins, and would

later add Tris Speaker. They represented a combined age of 204 years. Possibly Mack sought to lend his club a touch of nostalgic appeal until he could actually bring it home in front.

If Mack's signing of Cobb was essentially a public-relations gesture, he got more than expected for his $70,000. In 1927 Cobb played like—well, like Ty Cobb. Never questioning Mack's decisions he drove his forty-year-old body through a punishing 134 games, the most he had played in three seasons. In the outfield he recklessly pursued everything hit in his direction. On the base paths he never failed to seek the extra base. If he caught a pitcher napping, he did not hesitate to steal home. Cobb batted .357, drove in 93 runs, and scored 104. He stole 22 bases to tie for third place with Johnny Neun, who was fourteen years his junior. When the season closed, Mack pronounced Cobb "The easiest player I ever managed."

Cobb's performance in 1927 would have made the perfect finale to an incomparable baseball career. He had handsomely restored his reputation following the Dutch Leonard episode. Yet, the relentless Peach was not ready to call it quits. He told his manager that he would be ready in 1928. Mack was frank. He could not afford another $70,000, perhaps only about half that. Cobb signed anyway. He surely didn't need the money.

Why would a forty-one-year-old multimillionaire leave his family and the comfort of his Georgia estate to spend the summer on the hot diamonds of the American League, doing battle with players on average ten to twenty years his junior? Possibly he saw a chance to play once more on a championship team, since the A's were clearly headed for the top. It's a rational motive, but not compelling enough to move a man like Cobb to work for half pay. It had to be something more powerful. It has been said that the three most addictive thrills known to man are—in reverse order—hitting baseballs, flying high performance aircraft, and consorting with spirited women. No man willingly abandons any of the three. Ty Cobb simply had to play baseball.

When the 1928 season opened, not even Cobb's iron will could prevail against encroaching age. He appeared in fewer than 100 games, customarily sitting out one game of a doubleheader. He batted only .323, his lowest average in twenty-two years. He produced only 93 runs, stole just 5 bases. When pitchers could hold Ty Cobb to less than 1 hit in every 3 at-bats, it was time for him to lay down his thick-handled bat forever.

But even in retirement Cobb could not be long without the feel of an ash stick in his hands. I once read an eyewitness account of Cobb conducting a batting clinic at Seattle's Sick Stadium shortly after World War II. Those present stood in awed silence as The Georgia Peach, then in his early sixties, lashed line drives to all fields.

Sometime in the early 1920s, before one of those Donnybrooks between the Tigers and the Yankees, the unfailingly warmhearted and generous Babe Ruth, responding to a denunciation of Cobb by a New York baseball writer, said, "Yeah, I guess you're right. Cobb is a prick. But he sure can hit. God Almighty, that man can hit."

TEN

THE HEYDAY OF MURDERERS' ROW

"Bottom of the seventh. Stand by for five
o'clock lightning."
—Bleacherite Folk Saying

SOMEWHERE THERE MAY be an octogenarian ex-pitcher or two who
wake trembling in the night, having dreamed that once again they
were facing the 1927 New York Yankees—Murderers' Row. The
recurring nightmare would not be surprising, not even after two
thirds of a century. In fact, Murderers' Row may be significantly
more intimidating now than they were in the sunshine of 1927,
even to those who actually confronted them across a no-man's
land of sixty feet six inches. The passing years have endowed the
Yankee batting order of that season with the aura of elite shock
troops: Caesar's Tenth Legion, Napoleon's Imperial Guards,
Cromwell's Ironsides. In 1969 the Baseball Writers Association
presumably put the question beyond debate by voting the 1927
Yanks the greatest baseball team of all time.

Even today's skeptical baseball analysts are likely to concede
that the 1927 Yankees were a tolerably tough outfit. They won
110 games, leaving an excellent Philadelphia Athletics team in
second place, 19 games back. In the World Series that year, Mur-

derers' Row swept aside a strong Pittsburgh team in 4 straight. The Yankees' storied batting order of Earle Combs, Mark Koenig, Babe Ruth, Lou Gehrig, Bob Meusel, Tony Lazzeri, and Joe Dugan hit a collective .330, highlighted by 144 home runs. The team itself hit .307. And the team's slugging average of .489 remains the major-league record. In the grand Yankee tradition, fielding too was excellent and the pitching sound. That winter, New Year's Eve celebrants at Fifty-second Street speakeasies joked that the last-place Red Sox had finished so far behind, it was Thanksgiving before Boston learned who had won the pennant.

Just two seasons earlier no fan or writer watching the Yankees stumble to a dismal seventh-place finish would have imagined that, with a few prudent adjustments, the club could be turned into the greatest team of all time. In the spring of 1925 Ruth had suffered a serious abdominal abscess, unsympathetically tagged by baseball reporters "the bellyache heard round the world." This medical event seemed to cause the great Yankee machine to start throwing nuts and bolts. The 1925 Yanks finished 28½ games out of first place.

Ruth's tummy rumbles may have dominated the headlines, but he was not the only Yankee player out of shape. There was consensus among New York writers that a majority of the high-flying Yankees, including prominent members of the pitching staff, had long trained on Prohibition Scotch. The 1925 staff, essentially the same men who would shine in 1927, recorded an earned-run average of 4.33. Shunning the fashion of the hour among Yankee pitchers, abstemious left-hander Herb Pennock, who that year led the American League in innings pitched, posted an ERA of 2.96. It's a clue to how ineffectual his staff mates must have been.

It wasn't as though the Yankee batting order had misplaced its legendary power. They tied St. Louis for the league lead in home runs with 110. Instead, the Yanks forgot how to hit singles. The 1925 team batted a shameful .275, 17 percentage points below the league average. But, then, who wants to stand on first base in the hot sun while fighting a hangover?

Perhaps the fall from grace of famous young athletes in 1925 is not to be wondered at. The Jazz Age was just reaching for high C. Five years into the Noble Experiment, as Prohibition was known among its adherents, New York City sheltered an estimated 32,000 speakeasies. The speakeasies had displaced a modest 1,500 licensed saloons of the pre-Prohibition era. In Chicago, mob boss Johnny Torrio, like the ancient Roman dictator Sulla, retired at the height of his power so that he could enjoy the $30 million he had made during five years of brewing bootleg beer. One of the reigning pop tunes was "Ain't We Got Fun," and in August, Babe Ruth, who had an ear for that kind of lyric, drew a historic $5,000 fine and an indefinite suspension from an irate Miller Huggins. The manager charged that the home-run king's off-field gambols were undermining the quality of his play and hurting the team. To hearten what was left of the nation's clean-livers, in Hollywood of all places, director Cecil B. de Mille made ready to shoot his quasi-religious screen epic, *King of Kings.*

After the Yankees' seventh-place finish, a worried Jacob Ruppert, who never suffered failure gladly, reacted as a rich man might. He began to wave his checkbook at the problem. As it turned out, the solution cost him little cash. The Yankees were potentially a strong club, and beyond tightening training rules and changing one or two faces in the lineup there was not a great deal to be made right.

The most important step in the rebuilding job had been taken unconsciously in 1923, when the Yankees were on the threshold of their first World Championship. Yankee scout Paul Krichell signed sophomore Lou Gehrig right off the Columbia University campus. But since veteran Wally Pipp still looked like one of the best first basemen in the American League, manager Huggins was letting Gehrig grow to baseball adulthood on option to Hartford of the Eastern League—to the chagrin of Eastern League pitchers.

As insurance against the precipitous slowing down of the aging Whitey Witt in center field, in early 1924 the Yankees had purchased Earle Combs from Louisville of the American Association, where the Kentucky Greyhound batted .380. Unluckily, Combs suffered a serious ankle break in spring training and spent most of his rookie year on the bench. In the dark season of 1925, however, Combs brought a ray of sunshine to management when his Bible-reading, teetotaling life-style helped him to outhit his capering teammates by 67 percentage points.

Beyond matters of training and conditioning, the Yankees' problems were fairly easy to identify. The team was showing its age, especially up the middle, where it can hurt most. The acquisition of Combs, of course, had strengthened center field. At shortstop, Everett Scott, though still relatively young, gave evidence that he might have burned himself out by playing in more than 1,250 consecutive games. And at second, Aaron Ward, not quite thirty, was manifestly past his peak both at bat and in the field.

If the youngish Scott and Ward were over the hill, the Yankee front office must have viewed catcher Wally Schang, at thirty-five, as nearing senility. But in shunting off the catcher to the St. Louis Browns, Miller Huggins made one the biggest errors of his managerial career. In 1926 Wally caught more than 100 games for the Browns and batted .330 as he went on to play six more creditable seasons in the majors. Indeed, in 1946, at age fifty-seven, Schang was still catching for Marion in the Class D Ohio State League, President Warren Harding's old club.

The Schang deal helped create the one prominent gap in Murderers' Row because early in 1926 young Bernard "Benny" Bengough, counted on to handle most of the Yankee catching for the future, suffered a shoulder separation. The injury was to keep Bengough inactive for most of the season and, in fact, lessen his effectiveness for the remainder of his career. Yankee general manager Ed Barrow hastily resurrected Tharon "Pat" Collins, who had served several undistinguished years as backup catcher for the Browns before slipping back to the minors. Collins worked out better than anyone had reason to hope. When Pat donned the pinstripes his bat miraculously came to life. Still, he was no Wally Schang.

Before the 1926 season opened, a couple of flourishes of Colonel Ruppert's pen fetched shortstop Mark Koenig from St. Paul of the American Association, and, from Salt Lake City, Tony Lazzeri, a second shortstop, to be sure, but a versatile athlete who could handle a number of positions. Huggins acknowledged that Koenig's glove was not likely to cause fans to forget Honus Wagner, but the youngster was aggressive in the field—and he could hit. As for Lazzeri, the slender San Franciscan with the powerful wrists had just hit those 60 homers and put the Coast League RBI record permanently out of reach.

With new faces in the middle infield, plus Combs and Gehrig, who had to be counted veterans of a sort, Yankee fortunes in 1926 experienced a dramatic turnaround. By the end of June it looked as though New York might run away with the pennant race. Then, in midseason, the reconstructed and presumably re-formed Yanks began to lurch and stagger. In the end, it was a mutual throat-cutting among five challengers—Cleveland, Philadelphia, Washington, Chicago, and Detroit—that permitted the New Yorkers to limp home in front, 3 games ahead of their pursuers.

Totally out of character for a Yankee team, it was unsteadiness in the field, particularly the erratic play of new shortstop Koenig, that almost did them in during the latter half of the season. In the World Series, too, the defensive uncertainties that had put the pennant at hazard continued to plague New York. Critical errors by Koenig and Meusel in Game Seven helped Rogers Hornsby's St. Louis Cardinals to their first World Championship. This was the game in which old "Pete" Alexander struck out Tony Lazzeri in the seventh inning with the bases loaded and the Yanks trailing by 1 run. Pete had 2 wins and a save in the Series plus an ERA of 1.33.

The 1926 season was the wacky one in which everyone in the majors except Babe Ruth and Heinie Manush seemed to forget how to hit. National League fans witnessed the unheard-of spectacle of a catcher winning the batting championship. Cincinnati's Eugene "Bubbles" Hargrave came out of nowhere to win with a modest .353 average. Hargrave had only 326 at-bats, and under today's rules the title would have gone to Pittsburgh rookie Paul Waner, who batted .336 but played in 144 games.

In both leagues collective batting averages took a precipitous drop—.012 percentage points in the National League, .011 in the American. Equally surprising, home runs were down 31 percent in the National League, 20 percent in the American. It is tempting to point the finger at the newly introduced cushioned-cork-center ball, but the truth is that we really do not know why hitting was off in 1926. Even the manufacturer's own *Reach Guide* for

1927 expresses astonishment at the sudden decline. If the cushioned-cork center played a role in the unexpected downturn,
batters quickly adjusted to the change. In the very next season
hitters launched a comeback. By 1929 the two leagues would be
hitting a record number of cushioned-cork centers over the fence.

In 1926 Babe Ruth once again showed himself immune to
forces that affect ordinary men. After his disastrous season in 1925,
when he batted .290 and hit 25 home runs in 98 games, Babe
had a lot to make up for. In the new season he hit .372 to finish
second to batting champion Heinie Manush. In home runs no one
in either league came remotely close to Ruth's 47. Hack Wilson
led the National League with 21.

Built around Ruth's talents, the Yankees of 1920–24 were a
splendid team, the first offensive powerhouse of the twentieth
century. What moved the Yankee club into the realm of legend
in the late 1920s, however, was the addition to the lineup of Lou
Gehrig. For nine seasons Gehrig would team with Ruth to form
the most powerful two-man attack in the history of the game.

In his generation Gehrig was baseball's chief exemplar of the
Protestant work ethic, just as Ruth was the game's model syba-
rite. Had Lou taken up, let's say, banking, instead of baseball, he
would have been at his desk at the dot of eight every morning,
made few bad loans, and been odds-on choice to retire as board
chairman. Gehrig played in 2,164 major-league games, 2,130 of
them consecutively, and you can bet the farm that there was not
a single inning in which he was not bearing down. What young
fans are least likely to guess about Lou Gehrig is that when it
came to hustle he was in a class with Pete Rose. In 1978, SABR
researcher Raymond J. Gonzalez unearthed the long-forgotten fact
that Gehrig, who was built like a slab of granite, stole home 15
times in his career. All-time base-stealing champion Lou Brock
never did it a single time. I like the comment attributed to veteran catcher Hank Gowdy, "the old Sarge": "Gehrig never learned
that a ballplayer couldn't be good every day."

Allowing for the changed conditions of the game, I still blink
when I review Gehrig's batting record, especially the category of
runs batted in. In his thirteen full seasons Lou drove in 1,907
runs, an average of 147 per season. He did this while batting

immediately behind two of history's greatest base-cleaners, Babe Ruth and Joe DiMaggio. The current lifetime RBI leader, the much longer-lived Hank Aaron, in his thirteen best RBI years—and they are not consecutive—averaged 118.

How did Gehrig amass such numbers? To begin, Lou was a timely hitter, as evidenced by his 23 grand slams, still the major-league record. For a hard swinger, he was an outstanding contact hitter. His lifetime average of .340 ties him with George Sisler for ninth on the all-time batters' list. In eight of Gehrig's thirteen full seasons he had 200 or more hits. It ties him for third on the all-time list with Willie Keeler and Paul Waner and puts him behind Ty Cobb, who had nine 200-hit seasons, and leader Pete Rose, who had ten. Unlike Gehrig, the other four were classic straight-away hitters.

For a guy who hit 493 home runs, Gehrig was never easy to strike out. In 1934, when he hit 49 home runs and won the Triple Crown, he fanned just 31 times in 579 at-bats. Lou's swing was not a thing of beauty. It seemed to originate in the neighborhood of his left hip pocket. Yet extra-base hits kept popping off the sweet spot of his bat.

The leadoff man for Murderers' Row was center fielder Earle Combs. A left-handed hitter, Combs batted from a decided crouch. In the 1920s he was viewed as the ideal leadoff batter, but he is not in the category of a Rickey Henderson or a Vince Coleman. Combs, a good contact hitter, rarely stole a base despite his much-heralded foot speed. In his most active years he averaged about 65 walks and 63 RBIs. Earle did put his speed to good use in the outfield and was an excellent ball hawk, but he had a weak arm. Providentially, he played between the two best throwers in base-ball, Meusel and Ruth.

The 1927 season, when Combs batted .356, was by far his best. Remarkably, he finished third in the league that year in total bases, not far behind slugging teammates Ruth and Gehrig. In 1970 Combs was, I suspect, a sentimental choice by the Veterans Committee for the Hall of Fame.

Shortstop Mark Koenig, who followed Combs in the order, was converted to a switch hitter after coming to the Yankees, although he hit much better from the left side. From either side,

he rarely failed to make contact. He could bunt and move runners along, but had no power at all. Koenig had his best seasons
at bat during his four years with the Yankees and retired with a
ten-year average of .279.

Hitting in the third spot, Ruth had another of his great years,
finally bettering his own single-season home-run record of 59. He
also batted .356, drove in 164 runs, and drew 138 walks. Babe
was not eligible for the Most Valuable Player Award that year
because under the rules then in force a player could receive the
honor only once in a career. In any case, the selection could not
have been difficult. MVP Lou Gehrig batted .373 on 218 hits, 117
of them for extra bases—52 doubles, 18 triples, and 47 home
runs. It is hardly surprising that this barrage drove in 175 runs.

If an American League pitcher of 1927 somehow survived the
awesome tandem of Ruth and Gehrig, he still had serious work
ahead of him. Batting behind cleanup hitter Gehrig was the
sphinx-like Bob Meusel. Except for the Yankees' disastrous season of 1925, when Meusel was the surprise league leader in home
runs and RBIs, Long Bob never quite fulfilled the promise he had
shown when he broke in at the Polo Grounds. Although he was
a good contact hitter, Meusel was not selective. He was known
around the league as likely to jump on the first pitch. In 1927
Meusel hit for his highest average, .337. He also drove in 103
runs.

In the sixth spot in the order Huggins usually penciled in
second baseman Tony Lazzeri, one of the first major leaguers to
be identified as a wrist hitter. Slight of frame, Lazzeri had arrived
from the West with a reputation as a tremendous power hitter,
although it is likely that the Yankees wanted him mostly for his
steady glove. Like Meusel, the right-handed-hitting Lazzeri must
have felt his heart sink when he first sighted the steppelike left-
center field at Yankee Stadium. Worse, the park had been built at
sea level. Always the good soldier, Tony concealed whatever misgivings he might have felt and responded with 18 home runs and
114 RBIs in his rookie year. Defying the sophomore jinx, he hit
another 18 homers in 1927, to finish third in the league behind
Ruth and Gehrig. And again Tony drove in more than 100 runs.

In his own generation, Lazzeri's lifetime batting average of

.292 may have been viewed as pedestrian, but in seven of his twelve full seasons he drove in more than 100 runs. Early in his career Tony showed a tendency to chase bad balls. As his steadily diminishing strikeout totals suggest, he eventually brought the habit under control. Lazzeri, an epileptic, was reserved in speech and manner. Unlike the taciturn Meusel, however, he projected no air of chilliness. Tony enjoyed great popularity with the fans and the writers both in New York and around the league. In that less sensitive age, some New York baseball writers seemed to think that by frequently referring to Lazzeri in print as a wop or a dago they were demonstrating affection for him. Curious reasoning.

Third baseman Joe Dugan, a pretty fair hitter in his youth, was playing his last regular season. From seventh place in the order he batted .269 and hit but 2 home runs. Jumping Joe's Yankee pinstripes can't have frightened many pitchers that year.

Rounding out the legendary batting order, the catching corps of Pat Collins and Johnny Grabowski combined for a .276 batting average and 61 RBIs, not bad for catchers even in that prodigal age of base hits.

On close inspection, it's apparent that if you could get by Ruth and Gehrig, Murderers' Row was less than awesome. Unhappily for pitchers, that was a big if.

One of the most fascinating aspects of the story of Murderers' Row is that in the spring of 1927, no one, including the New York writers, suspected how great they were. Not even the professional oddsmakers picked the American League champions to repeat. The universal favorite to win the pennant was Connie Mack's rebuilt Philadelphia Athletics.

Fred Lieb of the *New York Post,* who had covered the Yankees for years, declared that unsteady pitching would keep the New Yorkers from repeating. Lieb's is a curious reservation when we look back and see that the Yankees were starting Waite Hoyt and Herb Pennock, both now in the Hall of Fame, and Urban Shocker, who may belong there. As the season opened, these three had already compiled 435 major-league wins among them. At the close, they would be first, second, and fourth in winning percentage in the American League. Add to this trio the veteran left-hander Walter "Dutch" Ruether, obtained from Washington late in 1926, and you are talking about a starting rotation with 559 big-league wins to their credit on Opening Day.

In support of the writers' apprehensions about Yankee pitching, in 1926 the New York staff had finished no better than fifth in the league in earned-run average. And, of course, no one could have foreseen the emergence in the new season of thirty-year-old Yankee rookie Wilcy Moore as baseball's top relief pitcher. At any rate, it is reassuring that the press corps did not share the fans' simple-minded faith in the efficacy of slugging.

Bewitched by the 1927 Yanks' record slugging average of .489, their 552 extra-base hits, and 975 runs scored, generations of fans have cherished the illusion that beginning on Opening Day, Murderers' Row battered a helpless American League into submission. Not so. Like any truly great team, the Yankees won as much on good pitching and sound defense as they did on hitting. Despite the preseason apprehensions of the writers, the pitching staff finished with a 3.20 ERA, almost 1 run better than the league's average and the second-best mark compiled in the two decades before World War II. The first team to improve upon it would be the 1942 Yankees.

Although the Yankees opened the season auspiciously by beating the favored Athletics three times and continuing to play good baseball through April and May, there was little reason to suspect that they would run away with the race. Philadelphia and Chicago remained in close pursuit. Significantly, the Yanks were both winning and losing an unexpected number of close, low-scoring ball games. On the weekend of May 21, when Lindbergh was making his historic nonstop flight to Paris, the Yankee sluggers sleepwalked through a series in Cleveland, in which 3 games were decided by 1-run margins. Finally, on the day after Memorial Day, in the second of back-to-back doubleheaders against Philadelphia at Shibe Park, the middle of the Yankee batting order began to justify their traditional title of Murderers' Row.

The New Yorkers pounded the powerful Athletics, 10 to 3 and 18 to 5, and brightened the afternoon with 6 home runs. Ruth hit 1 in each game. In the first game Gehrig missed hitting for the cycle by the breadth of a single, and the normally innocuous Pat Collins became only the second man to clear the roof of Connie Mack's three-year-old double-deck grandstand in left field. In the second game Ruth hit a ball that went across Twentieth Street, which ran behind the right-field wall, cleared the first row of houses on the east side of the street, and presumably landed in the backyard of someone who lived on Nineteenth.

To prove to the Philadelphia fans that they were a sound club and not just a bunch of wallbangers, the Yankees on the following day made it 3 straight over the A's with a ninth-inning 2-to-1 victory. It was only May and New York had already won 8 and lost only 2 against the team that was favored to take the pennant. Yet, despite their mastery of the Athletics, the Yanks found themselves at the Memorial Day marker only a game and a half ahead of the surprising Chicago White Sox.

In June, what had been an unusually cool and wet spring—hence the abundance of doubleheaders—turned into high summer. The sudden and favorable change in the weather breathed life into Murderer's Row. Between June 1 and 23, the Yankees won 20 out of 24. The starting lineup was batting well over .350.

On July 4, the traditional midpoint of the season, Murderers' Row showed what the second half of the season would be like for their opponents. The Washington Senators, having just moved into second place ahead of the rapidly fading White Sox, arrived in New York for a holiday doubleheader. The Yankees demolished them, 12 to 1 and 21 to 1, to open an 11½-game lead. Gehrig hit home runs in each game, the second a bases-load shot of record distance. From this point, the season turned into the rout of legend. With the pennant race virtually decided, popular attention shifted to the home-run duel between Gehrig, who had 28, and Ruth, who had 26.

Looking back on Ruth's greatest home-run season, when he finished 13 ahead of Gehrig and 42 ahead of Tony Lazzeri, who was third in the league, it may seem surprising that anyone entertained the idea that the Babe might be headed. But for most of the season Ruth and Gehrig were neck and neck, with Gehrig leading the Babe as late as August 20. Then Ruth demonstrated why he was Sultan of Swat. In September he hit a fantastic 17 home runs. Gehrig managed only 6 for the month. Babe's 17 remained the major-league mark for home runs in a single month until Detroit's Rudy York hit 18 in August 1937, a month with thirty-one days.

In contrast to the popular hysteria that accompanied Ruth's slugging in 1920, press and public reaction to his record-setting sixtieth home run on September 30 was surprisingly restrained. Today, when there are so many automobiles and so much beer to be sold, television marketing managers would make such an event rival the fall of kings. Not so the press of 1927.

The Yankees were facing Washington left-hander Jonathan "Tom" Zachary before a scant 10,000 noisy fans at Yankee Stadium. A day earlier about 7,500 had watched the Babe sock homers number 58 and 59. Although the Yankees would draw 1.2 million at home for the season, crowds were small in the final weeks, when the New Yorkers had pulled 19 games ahead of the second-place Athletics. Despite Zachary's pains to give the Bambino nothing good to swing at, the big guy was having a perfect day, with an intentional walk and 2 singles. But through seven innings Ruth had looked in vain for a pitch he could drive.

In the eighth, with a man on and the score tied at 2, Ruth in pure frustration picked a low curve off his shoe tops and golfed it into the right-field bleachers for number 60. According to reporters, the loyal 10,000 present made the noise of 20,000 and at the conclusion of the game many rushed onto the field to congratulate the Babe personally. The men in the press box inserted suitable encomiums in their game accounts and that was about it. (A few papers outside New York printed a small box announcing that Ruth had tied Lazzeri's Pacific Coast League record.) There was some celebrating that evening at the city's more fashionable speakeasies because writers and fans had been tracking the Babe's progress closely, especially after he got hot in September. Yet in the end, it was his own record that the Babe had broken and the excitement quickly subsided. It was not the same as in 1920. Then Ruth had outhomered fourteen major-league clubs.

It was during the 1927 season that the Yankees considerably reinforced a tradition that began when Ruth and Meusel first came to New York in the early 1920s. With the Yankees trailing going into the late innings, Ruth and his mates were often able to pull the game out with a sudden burst of long balls, especially if the opposing pitcher had begun to tire. Since games in New York started at three-thirty, these booming late-inning rallies often came at about five o'clock, hence the metaphor "five o'clock lightning." In 1927, with Ruth, Gehrig, Meusel, and Lazzeri batting in succession, five o'clock lightning struck often.

Since the Yankees had clinched the pennant on September 13, it meant that they had more than three weeks to cool their heels and possibly grow stale while the National League settled a four-team dogfight among Pittsburgh, St. Louis, New York, and Chicago. As it turned out, the National League race was not settled until the next-to-last day. Throughout the 1920s the National League never boasted a club as powerful as the Yankees or the Athletics at their best, but the senior league was in general better-balanced and offered a good pennant fight almost every year. When the National League season ended on October 2, the Pittsburgh Pirates had crawled home a game and a half in front of a bleeding pack.

As much as anything, Murderers' Row mythology has fed on the Yankee sweep of Pittsburgh in the 1927 World Series. We can set aside immediately the cherished delusion that the Pirates, a team that batted .305 during the season, experienced psychological collapse after watching New York take batting practice on the day before the Series opened in Pittsburgh. According to legend, as the Yankee behemoths powdered batting-practice pitches to distant corners of Forbes Field, Pirate center fielder Lloyd "Little Poison" Waner, five feet seven inches tall, observed to his brother Paul, who at five feet eight and a half inches was "Big Poison," "Gee, they're pretty big dudes, aren't they." It was precisely the kind of comment that a little guy might make under the circumstances, his envy but thinly veiled. Lloyd's mistake was that he said it within earshot of a New York reporter, Ken Smith of the *Daily Mirror*. The rest, as they say, is folklore.

Nor was the Series itself the bloodbath that generations of Yankee fans want desperately to believe it was. There were only 2 home runs in the 4 games, both by Ruth. Two games were decided by 1-run margins and the clincher was won on a wild pitch. Thanks to strong New York pitching, the Series was over so fast that nine Yankees never got into the lineup. What is fact is that Murderers' Row swept a strong Pittsburgh team and demonstrated convincingly that there was no one in baseball to challenge them. Ruth's home-run record apart, the Yankees' fabled batting order had turned 1927 into one of the dullest seasons of the decade.

The Yankees opened 1928 as though it were a continuation of the World Series. They won 39 of their first 48 games, and by the Fourth of July led the potent Athletics by 12. But 1928 was not 1927. For one thing, there were injuries. Lazzeri, Meusel, Bengough, and Pennock were all out for substantial periods. Urban Shocker, who had won 18 games in 1927, fell ill and died during the season without having registered a single decision. Reliever Wilcy Moore, the bullpen phenomenon of a year earlier, was generally ineffectual. Although Gehrig batted .374, he was hitting everything on a line, and his home-run total dipped by 20. The aging of third baseman Joe Dugan forced patching and filling in the infield.

Gamely, the Yankees played through the disabilities, but what they did not count on was the resurgence of Philadelphia in the second half of the season. Connie Mack's youth corps had finally gotten its act together. In July the Athletics posted a record of 25 and 8. They kept the pressure on through the dog days of summer. On September 8 the hungry A's passed the faltering Yankees and moved into first place.

On the following day, a Sunday, the New Yorkers showed what they were made of. With a reported 85,000 fans crowding every corner of Yankee Stadium, the home team beat the Athletics twice, 5 to 0 and 7 to 3, to regain the lead. It was the day that pitcher Urban Shocker died of a kidney ailment at a Denver hospital. The crippled and saddened Yankees hobbled through the final three weeks of the season to win by 2½ games.

Along with the lively pennant race, American League fans in 1928 were treated to the closest batting duel of the decade when Washington left fielder Goose Goslin squared off against Heinie Manush, who had been traded to the St. Louis Browns from Detroit by Cobb's successor, George Moriarty. For several weeks in

September Goose and Heinie were so close that unofficial record-keepers like the Associated Press were not sure who was in front. By chance the league schedule brought the combatants head to head in the final game at Sportsman's Park, with Goslin unofficially leading Manush, .379 to .377.

Going into the ninth, Goslin was 1 for 4 and was due up at least once more. Manush, 2 for 4, had taken his last turn unless the Senators should tie the score. Goose calculated in his head—a perilous practice—that if he skipped the turn, he would win the title. Postseason computation proved that he was correct in this assumption. But the margin would have been .000279, a virtual tie at .378 apiece.

Goslin's Washington teammates were less sure of their arithmetic and pressed him to stand up and win the title like a man, the way Heilmann would have done it. There was the added pressure of Manush watching from left field. In *The Glory of Their Times,* the irrepressible Goose tells a story of getting cold feet while already in the batter's box and trying to get himself thrown out of the game. In that event, the turn at bat would not count. According to Goslin, umpire Bill Guthrie loftily rejected the ploy and told Goose that no matter what outrage he committed, he would have to stand in and hit. The ebullient slugger came through with what he described as a lucky single and the batting title was his—by a margin of .00164. In fact, neither Goslin nor Manush could have known for sure who won until mid-December, when the official averages were released.

The 1928 World Series was in reality what the 1927 Series has become in legend—butchery. In 4 games Murderers' Row blew away a strong St. Louis team, but a team badly lacerated from a typical National League pennant rumble. The Yanks outscored the Cardinals almost 3 to 1. Unlike the Pirates of 1927, the young Cards had some home-run power. First baseman Jim Bottomley had tied for the National League lead with 31 and center fielder Chick Hafey had finished third with 27. In all, St. Louis had four regulars in double figures in homers. The Cards' weak spot was an aging pitching staff.

St. Louis never even got a chance to show its wares as Ruth and Gehrig buried them in an unprecedented display of power.

Babe got 10 hits in 4 games for an incredible .625 average and hit 3 homers, all in the last game. After fourteen years of big-league service and countless dissipations, the Babe still bestrode baseball like a colossus. His performance in the 1928 World Series was so extraordinary that Bob "Believe It or Not" Ripley made it the subject of a column.

Lou Gehrig batted a more charitable .545. But he had 4 homers and 9 RBIs for a slugging average of 1.727, a performance that deserved a Ripley column of its own. Except for Cedric Durst, subbing for the injured Earle Combs, no one else on the Yankee side hit higher than .250. More graphically than at any time before, the 1928 World Series illustrated that as long as the Yankees had Ruth and Gehrig hitting back to back, the team must be reckoned a power. The two supermen were together for another six years.

After what the Cardinals had done to the Yankees in 1926, the rout of 1928 must have been sweet revenge. New York's chief tormentor in 1926, Grover Cleveland Alexander, this time registered an ERA of 19.80. The forty-one-year-old Aleck lasted a total of five innings in 2 games. Within two years the famous right-hander would be gone from baseball.

While no team had an offensive weapon to rival Ruth and Gehrig, there were some formidable batting orders on the loose in 1927 and 1928. We can begin with the Pittsburgh Pirates, unfairly remembered only for their humiliating loss to the Yankees. The Bucs were a hard-hitting outfit. It was a Pittsburgh tradition. From 1922 through 1930 Pittsburgh teams averaged .300 at bat, six times finishing above the mark. If you calculate the performance of just the Pirate regulars through those years, the figure is obviously much higher. In the same period Pittsburgh clubs scored an average of 834 runs.

Like several other teams of the 1920s—Cleveland and Detroit immediately come to mind—the Pirates could crush their opponents with singles and doubles. Their 1925 World Champions, for example, hit only 77 home runs but scored 912 runs and boasted four regulars with more than 100 RBIs. Of the 1925 lineup, only second baseman Graham "Eddie" Moore batted under .300.

In 547 at-bats, Eddie came within a measly single of joining the others. He batted .298.

The 1927 Pirates, despite the humiliating World Series loss to the Yankees, were no patsies at the plate either. Over the course of the season they averaged more than 10½ hits a game. And had they not played at spacious Forbes Field, the team would surely have improved on its season home run total of 54. Even Murderers' Row couldn't manage a home run in the games they played at Forbes Field.

Pirate third baseman Harold "Pie" Traynor is an interesting figure of the era. Hailed before his retirement as the greatest fielding third baseman of all time (an inflated assessment of an excellent player), Traynor was surely one of the finest contact hitters of his generation. Only Cleveland's Joe Sewell was harder to strike out. A fairly big man, Traynor hit just 58 home runs in a seventeen-year career. Forbes Field had a lot to do with that, of course, but, like everyone else, Pie played 77 games a year on the road.

The right-handed Traynor was notorious for his impatience at the plate, and during his most active years averaged fewer than 35 walks. It's clear that Pie was eager to lay wood on the ball, something he did often enough to put together seven seasons of 100 or more RBIs. In 1928, for example, he drove in 124 runs with the help of just 3 homers. He also scored 91 runs that year and struck out a barely discernible 10 times. But the antsy Traynor drew only 28 walks. Had he been more selective at the plate, Pie's impressive .320 lifetime batting average might have been several points higher.

Another tough out in the Pirate order was outfielder Hazen "Kiki" Cuyler. One of the fastest men in baseball, Cuyler may have been the most graceful fielder of his time as well. His play has sometimes been compared to that of Joe DiMaggio, who came along a decade later. Like DiMaggio, Cuyler had a strong and accurate throwing arm.

Over an eighteen-year career with Pittsburgh, Chicago, Cincinnati, and Brooklyn, the right-handed-hitting Cuyler batted .321. Even while playing at Forbes Field he showed that he could hit with power. In 1925, with the help of 26 triples and 17 homers, Cuyler put together 366 total bases, still a Pittsburgh club record.

Not even Ralph Kiner, with five seasons of 40 or more homers, was ever able to match it.

Halfway through the 1927 season, with his team fighting to stay in first place, Pittsburgh manager Owen "Donie" Bush, a hypersensitive runt with a .250 lifetime batting average, benched Cuyler indefinitely for insubordination. As players will do, the outfielder had complained about where he was hitting in the batting order. Kiki never appeared in another game for Pittsburgh and was forced to sit out the World Series, when the team sorely needed his bat and glove. The Pirates, remember, lost 2 1-run games. At the insistence of the obdurate Bush, the Pittsburgh front office virtually gave Cuyler away to the Chicago Cubs. Kiki was only twenty-eight years old. Over the next seven seasons he would bat .328 for Chicago and help them to two pennants.

In 1928 the Pirates led the majors in batting with .309 and outscored everyone except the Yankees. But playing without Cuyler they finished fourth. It's tempting to conclude that it was divine retribution.

Perhaps the best remembered star of the 1927 Pirates is Paul Waner, although he is in large measure a player of the 1930s. Paul was the consummate line-drive hitter, a batter who effectively used the whole field. In his first five seasons at Pittsburgh, he batted .359 and averaged 211 hits. At 150 pounds, Big Poison could not compete with the Ruths and Gehrigs in home runs, but consistently about one third of his hits went for extra bases. In 1927, his second year in the majors, Waner batted .380 to win the National League batting championship and also drove in 131 runs. He was named Most Valuable Player.

Paul Waner is one of a group of old-timers around whose names has gathered a wealth of merry tales concerning drinking. Waner may well have been an after-hours celebrant—many players were—but I find it difficult to believe that he played drunk, not with the kind of record he compiled. One story has Big Poison seeing three baseballs on every pitch and building a Hall of Fame career by swinging at the middle one. Another says that Waner attended a revival meeting in St. Louis and was so moved that he took the pledge—and promptly suffered the first slump of his career.

One afternoon at Ebbets Field, a story goes, Waner was being horse-collared by a member of the imposing Dodger pitching staff. In the ninth inning Paul came up with the bases loaded and the Pirates trailing by a couple of runs and tripled off the right-center-field wall. As Waner slid into third, it is said, Brooklyn manager Wilbert Robinson took a few steps out of the dugout and screamed, "Damn you, Waner, why'd you have to sober up with men on?"

The 1927 Pirates were one of the strongest, finest teams of the 1920s. Someone had to take on Murderers' Row in the World Series. The Pirates drew the short straw.

Along with the Yankees and the Pirates, the 1927 Athletics could age a pitcher prematurely. They had a team average of .303 and just one regular under .300. Only slightly less intimidating were the perennially potent Tigers, the Cardinals, the Indians, and the Senators. But in 1927 one of the strongest lineups by far plied its trade just across the Harlem River from Yankee Stadium, where John McGraw had put together a junior Murderers' Row of his own.

McGraw's club had six regulars batting over .300 and was the second of his teams to hit more than 100 home runs. Beginning in 1924 the Giants had three times led the league in homers. Less than a decade into the Ruth era, McGraw, the erstwhile high priest of scientific baseball, was deeply committed to the power game.

Since the bruising Giants of 1927 failed to win the pennant, they may be best remembered among trivia buffs for their infield of future Hall of Famers: Bill Terry at first, Hornsby at second, Fred Lindstrom at third, and Travis Jackson at short. This crew batted .328 and drove in 402 runs. It seemed at times, however, that Little Napoleon would have surrendered his famous infield for a future Hall of Fame pitcher—if one had been on the market.

In the autumn of 1926 McGraw had realized at last his wish to bring Rogers Hornsby to the Polo Grounds. Hornsby had just brought St. Louis its first pennant and World Championship, but at the close of the 1926 Series Rajah accused Cardinal owner Sam Breadon of being a tightwad (an understatement, actually) and was summarily put on the trading block. Concurrently, in New York, McGraw staged an Olympic-grade shouting match with his brilliant young second baseman, Frank Frisch. To salve bruised Hibernian egos in both cities, the clubs swapped second basemen.

The trade was a mistake for the Giants. Although, as expected, Hornsby hit well at the Polo Grounds (.361, 26 HRs, 125 RBIs), Frisch was several years younger than Rajah, a superior fielder, and in better physical condition. Besides, Frisch's offensive stats for 1927—.337, 10 homers, 48 stolen bases—were not exactly shabby. Finally, there was the question of how long the autocratic McGraw would tolerate Hornsby's undiplomatic tongue. Perhaps even Little Napoleon might have swallowed his pride in return for 125 RBIs, but unfortunately the terrible-tempered Rajah also insulted the Giants' principal owner, Charlie Stoneham. By January 1928 Hornsby was on his way to the Boston Braves for two players of vastly inferior quality.

Had McGraw not given up on young Hack Wilson two years earlier, he might have fielded a lineup in 1927 not significantly less powerful than the Yankees. In the autumn of 1923 McGraw had purchased Hack from Portsmouth in the Virginia League, and the kid made the adjustment from Class B to major-league pitching in grand style. In his rookie year with the Giants, Hack batted .295 and hit with power. Nevertheless, McGraw optioned Wilson to Toledo, presumably to polish his fielding, and, through an alleged clerical error, failed to protect the Giants' rights. The Cubs quickly claimed the stubby slugger. It was rumored among New York baseball writers that McGraw's oversight was deliberate, that he had wanted to let Wilson go because he could not cope with young Hack's nocturnal antics. Many years later, in an interview with baseball historian Walter Langford, Carl Hubbell confirmed the truth of the rumor.

Despite the sacrifice of Wilson, who tied for the National League lead in home runs in 1927, McGraw still had the superlative Edd Roush in center field and also got an outstanding performance from ancient and much-traveled George Harper, hurriedly acquired from the Phillies to replace the fatally ill Ross Youngs. Moreover, on the bench the manager had Mel Ott, an eighteen-year-old future Hall of Famer. In the best of worlds, McGraw might have been able to balance his Hall of Fame infield with a Hall of Fame outfield, consisting of Youngs, Roush, Wilson, and Ott.

But the Hall of Fame was not to be established for ten years, and besides, McGraw was interested in the pennant, not individual glory for his players. Already in failing health, baseball's most successful manager wanted desperately to add one more championship to his record. As Cobb had done in Detroit, McGraw was trying to win it all with a lineup of overpowering hitters, although the Giants were doubtless a sounder club than any Cobb had ever fielded.

Despite the deficiencies in pitching, the heavy-hitting Giants made a good run at the pennant in 1927. After a listless first half, McGraw's men came to life in July. In mid-June, to shore up his pitching, McGraw had obtained right-hander Larry Benton from the Boston Braves. Benton was immediately effective, and late in August the Giants found themselves in a four-team shootout against Pittsburgh, St. Louis, and Chicago.

With 10 games left in the season the Giants took 3 out of 4 from front-running Pittsburgh to close to within a game and a half of the lead. And New York had a big break in the schedule, 4 games against the hapless Phillies and a couple with sixth-place Brooklyn. For one electrifying moment there was promise of a fourth Nickel World Series in seven years. In the end, however, Pittsburgh had too much class to fold. The Pirates took 6 of their final 7 games—all on the road. Concurrently, the relaxed Brooklyn Robins, following a familiar Ebbets Field scenario, were more than happy to play spoiler against the hated New Yorkers. They also had the pitching to do it. When the closing bell rang, the frustrated McGraw found himself in third place, 2 games out.

Since Benton won 13 games for New York in half a season and compiled the league's best winning percentage, it is possible that the Giants might have copped the pennant had McGraw acted sooner. Ironically, back in 1922, Little Napoleon had twenty-four-year-old Benton under contract but let him slip away in the deal for Hugh McQuillan. In a double irony, McGraw ended up shipping the disappointing McQuillan back to Boston in partial exchange for the kid he should have held on to. In his last years McGraw's genius occasionally slipped a gear.

A World Series between the Yankees and the Giants in 1927 should have proved more exciting than the one that was played. The likelihood of a McGraw-led team being swept, even by Mur-

derers' Row, was remote. And the prospect of Ruth's playing another Series at the Polo Grounds in his greatest home-run year
was a press agent's dream. Unluckily for New Yorkers, it was not
to be.

If McGraw's 1927 effort proved too little and too late, the
outlook for 1928 was excellent. He had his imposing lineup of
young sluggers and in Benton a strong fourth starter. Teenager
Mel Ott was ready to take over right field, which he would hold
for the next eighteen years. From San Francisco, McGraw summoned carefree ex-pitcher Lefty O'Doul, now a certified slugger.
In 1927 O'Doul had clipped Coast League pitching for .378 and
33 home runs.

With prospects running high for a pennant in 1928, McGraw
shot himself in the foot. First there was the loss of Hornsby. Perhaps that can't be blamed on McGraw, who was only a minority
stockholder. Still, with a pennant in prospect, it is hard to believe
that Charlie Stoneham's feelings could not have been soothed short
of surrendering the league's most powerful hitter.

Worse than the Hornsby deal, two weeks before the opening
of spring training McGraw traded his top winner, spitballer Burleigh Grimes, to Pittsburgh for right-hander Vic Aldridge. It must
rank as the worst deal of the 1920s. Again, it may have been out
of McGraw's hands. Half a century later Carl Hubbell revealed
that Grimes had vowed never to pitch another game for the
grumpy manager. Yet, why couldn't a rich club like the Giants
have tried a fat raise to persuade Grimes that the situation wasn't
so bad? It had been done before. The Yankees would never have
lost Grimes.

Aldridge held out until early summer and wound up winning
just 4 games, after which he retired from baseball. Grimes, on the
other hand, appeared in 48 games for the Pirates, pitched 331
innings, and won 25 to tie with Larry Benton for the league's
most wins. Burleigh had a 2.99 ERA. In fact, after leaving New
York, "Ol' Stubblebeard" won another 88 National League games
and pitched on three pennant winners.

As things turned out, McGraw's rotund young knuckleballer
Fred Fitzsimmons unexpectedly blossomed into a 20-game winner in 1928, and at the end of July the Giants snagged left-hander

Carl Hubbell from Beaumont in the Texas League. In the final
two months of the season, the young screwballer would win 10
games for the Giants. With improved pitching to complement the
league's roughest crew of hitters—118 homers—the Giants put
on a stretch drive to rival that of 1927. Yet, once again McGraw
and his team finished 2 games short of the prize. Seldom has it
been possible to say with such conviction that a club had traded
away the pennant.

The 1928 season must have represented the ultimate disappointment for McGraw, who had known many. On September 27,
the streaking Giants had pulled to within half a game of the league-
leading Cardinals. On that day third-place Chicago arrived in New
York for a 4-game series, opening with a doubleheader. If New
York could take both games they would at least tie for the lead
regardless of how the Cards did in Boston. To overtake St. Louis
with just 3 games remaining, all at home, was certain to give the
Giants a boost psychologically. And with St. Louis scheduled to
finish the season with a single game at New York on September
30, the Giants appeared masters of their own destiny.

In the first game, with Chicago leading 3 to 2 in the bottom
of the sixth, New York put men on second and third with no one
out. Giant catcher Shanty Hogan tapped to the box and left fielder
Andy Reese, the runner on third, was hung up. Inexplicably, Cub
third baseman Clyde Beck tried to catch Reese from behind.
Meanwhile, Gabby Hartnett, Chicago's bulky catcher, stood astride
the base line waiting for a throw that never came. In trying to
get around Hartnett, Reese tripped over the catcher's out-
stretched leg and fell heavily, his hand just a foot short of home
plate. Beck tagged out the prostrate Reese. "With a clear baseline," James Harrison of *The New York Times* reported, "he would
have scored easily with the tying run." Despite Hartnett's patent
violation of the rules, plate umpire Bill Klem called the runner
out, leaving the Giants a run short. It was the worst call Klem
ever made in a forty-year career.

An outraged McGraw rushed the plate to claim interference
with the base runner. In baseball's oldest tradition, Klem denied
the appeal and refused to reverse his appallingly bad call. McGraw,
by now hysterical, had to be restrained by coaches and players

from assaulting the umpire. Finally, the trembling, tired old man was led back to the dugout, where he listlessly watched the Giants fail to score and announced that he was playing the game under protest. On the following day, in the second oldest tradition in baseball, league president John Heydler disallowed New York's protest, since it involved a judgment call by an umpire. *The New York Times* wryly pointed out that never in the league's fifty-two-year history had a president reversed an umpire's call, regardless of how mistaken.

The Giants eked out a 2-to-0 victory in the second game that day, but in Boston the Cardinals scored 7 times in the fifteenth inning to win and increase their lead to 1 game. The pathetic scene at home plate on September 27 proved to be John McGraw's last hurrah. The unnerved Giants blew their remaining games and finished 2 games back.

For three more seasons an increasingly bitter and desperate McGraw directed power-laden lineups with diminishing results. Finally, in June 1932, his team languishing in sixth place, poor health forced Little Napoleon to abdicate. In the following season young Bill Terry, McGraw's successor, took a Giant team with not half the power and talent of the 1928 squad to a World Championship.

ELEVEN

TRAMPLED
BY WHITE
ELEPHANTS

"In baseball there's no such thing as a safe lead."

—JOE MCCARTHY

THE 1929 SEASON was marked by transition. The great batters who had been active both before and since Ruth revolutionized the game—Cobb, Speaker, Hornsby, Sisler, Heilmann, Cy Williams, Eddie Collins, Roush, Wheat, even Ruth himself—had either racked their bats for good or were well into the bell lap of their careers. The newer generation, on the other hand, which included Simmons, Gehrig, Goslin, Bottomley, Terry, Wilson, Hartnett, and Paul Waner, were reaching for new heights. The cushioned-cork-center malaise, or whatever it was that had mildly afflicted batters in 1926, was no longer in evidence and slugging recovered to such an extent that 1929 may have witnessed more unofficial tests of the ball than any other year of the decade. Perhaps it was renewed suspicions about the baseball's innards that prompted American League president E. S. Barnard to declare at the winter meetings in New York in December that the official ball of 1929 was the finest used "in the history of the game."

Just as American League batters had shown the way for the National Leaguers early in the decade, the senior league set the pace at the close. In 1929, National Leaguers raised their average

13 percentage points to .294 to reenter the hitter's environment both leagues had enjoyed in the early years of the decade. Three teams—Pittsburgh, Chicago, and Philadelphia—finished comfortably over .300, and for the first time a major league hit more than 700 home runs. Although American League batters added only 3 percentage points to move from an already robust .281 to .284, they increased their home-run total by almost 20 percent.

Among players who appeared in 75 or more games, forty-two National Leaguers hit over .300. So did thirty-six in the American League. Ten National League regulars batted over .350. The surprise is that in this year of renewal no one hit .400, although the Phillies' Lefty O'Doul came within a bunt single of doing just that.

The National League's 10 percentage-point advantage in batting average is hard to account for, since the two leagues had hit an identical .281 in 1928. Perhaps a statistical analyst might devise a formula to explain it, involving barometric pressure at game time, pH of soil samples from selected pitching mounds, muscle-to-fat ratio of National League first basemen, and similar data. What is most likely to strike the eye of the nontechnician examining the records, however, is that the American League had better pitching. In earned-run average they led the senior league 4.24 to 4.81, a margin of almost half a run. That's a lot. Of course, it may not have come as a surprise to anyone when you consider that the Phillies surrendered more than 1,000 runs, the Robins and the Braves more than 875 each. By actual count the National League expended 55,980 shiny white baseballs in 1929, almost eight dozen a game, a fact calculated to bring joy to the heart of any batter.

If you inspect the list of American League starters in 1929, a dozen or more names immediately stand out, men of substantial careers and winning lifetime records. In addition to the stars of Philadelphia's staff, Lefty Grove, George Earnshaw, and Rube Walberg—the most effective in the majors by a significant margin—there are George Pipgras, Waite Hoyt, and Herb Pennock of the Yankees; Wesley Ferrell and Willis Hudlin of Cleveland; Alvin "General" Crowder and George Blaeholder of St. Louis; pioneer relief specialist Fred "Firpo" Marberry and Irving "Bump" Hadley of Washington; George Uhle (reputed father of the slider) and

Earl Whitehill of Detroit; and Ted Lyons and Urban "Red" Faber of Chicago. Even the hapless Boston Red Sox boasted a couple of quality starters in Charles "Red" Ruffing and "Deacon Danny" MacFayden. Eight of these men—Grove, Hoyt, Pennock, Uhle, Whitehill, Lyons, Faber, and Ruffing—would win 200 or more games in their careers. Grove, in fact, would win 300. And Wes Ferrell, on his way to six 20-victory seasons and 193 wins, certainly belongs with the group. Six would eventually make it to the Hall of Fame.

Ruffing's is an interesting case. He lost 22 games for last-place Boston in 1929 after having lost 25 a year earlier. Yet when Red later had the good fortune to be traded to the New York Yankees, he went on to compile 273 wins in a 22-year career that took him past World War II and eventually to Cooperstown.

The list of National League starters for 1929 contains its distinguished names as well: Charlie Root, Guy Bush, and Art Nehf of Chicago; Burleigh Grimes, Ray Kremer, and Larry French of Pittsburgh; Carl Hubbell, Fred Fitzsimmons, and Carl Mays of New York; Jesse Haines and Pete Alexander of St. Louis; Arthur "Dazzy" Vance of Brooklyn; Eppa Rixey and Adolfo Luque of Cincinnati. What is significant about this group, however, is that most are men at or very close to the end of their careers. Perhaps what can be said of 1929 is that the American League not only had more top-quality starters but also younger ones. And while it is harder to demonstrate, I suspect that the junior league also enjoyed an advantage in the age and quality of its second-line pitchers. A fundamental truth of baseball, and it may apply especially in the 1920s, is that a tired pitcher gives up the most base hits. It's a safe assumption that in the general absence of relievers, starters of this era were pushed beyond their limits on many afternoons. And they were facing the new menace of Babe Ruth and his imitators, who could "take them out of the park" on one pitch.

National League fans of 1929 should have suspected that something was in the wind when five weeks into the season Phillies shortstop Bernard "Barney" Friberg was batting .410—and he wasn't even leading the league. What was in the wind was Spalding cushioned-cork-center baseballs. At the winter meeting National League president Heydler would report to the owners that a record 754 had cleared the fences for home runs, perilously close to 100 per team. Heydler reassured the magnates that his umpires were deglossing the baseballs more vigorously than ever in an effort to reduce the carnage. Moreover, he announced, two clubs had increased the height of outfield barriers. Heydler was protesting prosperity. Most fans loved the home runs.

In the most fascinating medical note of the year, recently inaugurated President Herbert Hoover announced on July 3 that because of a stiff wrist he was forced to suspend shaking hands with well-wishing citizens. By the time the Chief's wrist was limber enough to resume pressing the flesh, the bottom had fallen out of the stock market, and there were no takers.

In the same week that the president's wrist stiffened, Transcontinental Air Transport announced the nation's first coast-to-coast air-passenger service. It took two days from New York to Glendale, California, and cost $351.94 one way. In hindsight, the event may be viewed as the first grim step in the direction of major-league expansion.

In the National League there was a new bully on the block. After a decade of mediocrity, the Chicago Cubs reclaimed the respectability owing to the franchise that had won the very first league pennant race back in 1876. They achieved it through an unfailing medium—money.

The Cubs' owner, chewing-gum magnate William Wrigley, Jr., was a mirror image of the Yankees' Jacob Ruppert. Like his friend Ruppert, Wrigley was a millionaire industrialist with an obsession to field a winner, and like Ruppert he sported an open checkbook and a passion for power hitters. Wrigley had taken control of the Cubs in 1921 and subsequently written a lot of checks. His wisest investment by far was to hire William Veeck, Sr., to be president and general manager of the club. Veeck, in turn, may have earned his salary in the single act of hiring as field manager in 1926 Joseph V. McCarthy, a man who had never played an inning of major-league baseball. Today, lack of big-league playing experience is common among managers. In 1926 it was rare.

Backed by Wrigley's dollars, Veeck and McCarthy had in three years put together a wrecking crew that would restore the Cubs to their ancient glory. It included Rogers Hornsby, Hack Wilson, Kiki Cuyler, Riggs Stephenson, Gabby Hartnett, and Charlie Grimm, four of them future Hall of Famers. Having learned his trade in the fiercely competitive American Association, McCarthy took special pains to leaven this explosive offense with sound if unspectacular pitching and the best defense in the league.

But the National League of 1929 was tough turf. In mid-July the Cubs found themselves still slugging it out with powerful clubs in Pittsburgh, St. Louis, and New York. On July 23, McCarthy's team trailed league-leading Pittsburgh by a game and a half. Then the Cubs racked up 9 straight wins to make their record for the month 24 out of 32. That pace proved too much for the contenders. By August 15, the Pirates, Cards, and Giants were ready to say uncle. When the season closed on October 6, Chicago was 10½ games ahead. McCarthy had won more easily than any National League manager of the decade.

The Cubs' victory was timely. The city of Chicago sorely needed some image burnishing. Two months before the season opened, on Saint Valentine's Day to be exact, mobster George "Bugs" Moran and six of his torpedoes had been rubbed out in a Near North Side garage—allegedly by the rival Capone gang. The event made headlines worldwide and helped establish Chicago in the popular mind as the crime center of America.

In May, Capone (a loyal Cub fan) drew a year in jail after being picked up in Philadelphia for illegal possession of a handgun. "Scarface Al" told reporters he actually looked forward to his first time in stir. There he could get a night's sleep without having to keep one eye open.

McCarthy's Cubs batted .303 and hit 140 home runs. Four regulars had more than 100 RBIs apiece. The team scored 982 runs, the most by a major-league team of the twentieth century to that point. It was a record that would last but a single season. Chicago's regulars batted .321 and might have bettered that mark had their slugging catcher Gabby Hartnett not injured his right shoulder so severely in spring training that he caught in only one game and had just 22 at-bats.

Playing a major role in the Cubs' fireworks was the much-traveled Rogers Hornsby. At the close of the 1928 season, Wrigley had shelled out an estimated $250,000 in cash and players for Hornsby. And so Rajah donned his fourth uniform in as many seasons, evidence that his tongue as well as his bat had lost none of its sting. Wrigley got his money's worth. Hornsby played in every one of the Cubs' 156 games, hit .380 on 229 hits, poled 39 home runs, and drove in 149. He also had one of his best seasons in the field, leading the league's second basemen in double plays.

No official record was kept of the number of teammates, writers, and fans Hornsby alienated, but we may be sure they were many. Stories of his arrogance abound. Asked by an awed reporter if he ever experienced batting slumps, the surprised Rajah answered, "Why, yes. I had one this season."

"Really?" the reporter responded. "How long did it last?"

"Oh," the notoriously humorless Hornsby replied, "I must have gone to the plate at least six times without a hit."

In addition to being handsomely supported by Hornsby, Chicago pitchers were well served by the outfield of Kiki Cuyler, Hack Wilson, and Riggs Stephenson. They batted a collective .355, and averaged 23 home runs and 123 RBIs. The major punch came from Wilson, who hit 39 homers and drove in 159 runs. In RBIs he led the majors and was merely flexing his muscles for what he would do the following season.

Though Wrigley stood prepared to pay for whatever talent was needed, Veeck and McCarthy had, in fact, acquired this punishing outfield on the cheap. Cuyler was a gift from Pittsburgh's Donie Bush. Wilson, abandoned by the Giants, had cost little. And the Cubs had sent two long-since-forgotten players to Class AA Indianapolis for Riggs Stephenson. Before going to the minors in 1925, Stephenson had spent five seasons with Cleveland as a utility infielder. Stephenson batted .340 for the Indians but could not persuade Speaker to trust him with a regular spot. Finally, at Speaker's recommendation, the failed infielder voluntarily went back to the minors to learn outfielding. By June of 1926 Veeck and McCarthy were sufficiently impressed with Stephenson's progress to deal for his contract.

"Old Hoss," as Stephenson was known to Chicago fans, responded to the vote of confidence with eight consecutive .300-

plus seasons. Only in 1929, however, did the steady right-handed contact hitter show a flash of power. In addition to batting .362, he hit 17 homers and drove in 110 runs. In a major-league career of thirteen seasons, Stephenson batted .336. He also averaged .6 RBIs per game, an impressive lifetime achievement for a sixth-place batter.

It is curious that in an outfield that included the speedy and graceful Cuyler, Joe McCarthy chose to play stumpy Hack Wilson in center. Wilson stood five feet six inches tall and weighed 195 pounds. He wore a size 18 collar. Hack's massive chest and torso were mounted on stubby legs and almost dainty size-5 feet. Somehow this anomalous figure added up to a natural batting machine. Wilson may have driven baseballs farther than any five-feet-six-inch man who ever lived, and in his best years he hit for a high average as well. Had he been more patient at the plate, a batter of Wilson's power was certain to have drawn a lot more walks and improved on his .307 lifetime batting average.

If legend can be supported, Hack was baseball's reigning authority on bootleg bourbon. Stories of his after-hours escapades are plentiful, some doubtless apocryphal. "I never played drunk," Hack once asserted to reporters. "Hung over maybe, but never drunk." I believe him. As with Paul Waner and other reputed topers of the 1920s, it's inconceivable that men encumbered with a skinful of hootch could perform so brilliantly. The effect of alcohol on coordination is too well documented. On the other hand, I have no trouble with the idea that a man can hit well while fighting a hangover. There's the imperishable example of Babe Ruth. In any case, the sight of Hack's fire-hydrant outline in the batter's box, especially with men on base, must have moved more than one National League pitcher to long for a shot of bourbon himself.

Wilson's reputation as a fielder is enigmatic. There is something close to consensus among fans who remember watching him play that at best Hack was unpredictable with the glove. And yet not only McCarthy but John McGraw as well entrusted Wilson with the security of center field over a period of seven seasons.

The 1929 season produced nothing resembling a pennant race

in either league. As had been true for several years, the story in
the American League was all New York and Philadelphia. Heavily
favored in 1928, the young Athletics had come up short in a
surprisingly close race. In the new season, however, Philadelphia's youth, power, and excellent pitching proved inexorable.
On May 14 the White Elephants pulled ahead of New York and
were never seriously challenged thereafter. The Athletics essentially reversed the story of 1927, winning 104 games and leaving
a formidable Yankee team in second place, 18 games back.

In the early 1920s Ruth and the Yankees had battled for the
pennant with teams unlike themselves in talent and offensive
strategy—Chicago, Cleveland, St. Louis. At the end of the decade,
the ruffians of Murderers' Row at last confronted a club that played
ball they way they did. The Athletics were outstanding defensively and they could hit the long ball.

Up to 1929, word in the New York press box was that the
mere sight of triple-tiered Yankee Stadium was enough to unset-
tle Mr. Mack's kids. It's doubtful that the young A's actually choked,
though it is true that in both 1927 and 1928 they seemed to have
trouble winning the big ones, especially at Yankee Stadium. In
1928, of course, after overtaking the staggering Yanks, they had
blown that crucial September 9 doubleheader in New York. In
the new season, however, Philadelphia was all confidence as they
took 14 of 22 from New York, including 7 of 11 at Yankee Stadium.

Since the Athletics of 1929–31 have long been assessed as
one of the greatest teams in baseball history, it is worth taking a
look at the lineup that the patient Connie Mack had been putting
together since the early twenties. Many baseball writers of the
time were convinced that what had finally turned things around
for the Athletics was the manager's long-delayed decision to play
young Jimmie Foxx permanently at first base. The powerfully built,
moon-faced teenager was multitalented. A ferocious hitter, he was
also a good fielder at several positions. "Double X" had a great
arm and could even pitch if necessary. It may be that Jimmie's
versatility was at the root of Mack's indecision. For almost four
seasons the manager had shuffled the kid from catcher to third
to first and back, trying to "fit him into the lineup," if you can

imagine having to ponder where to put a Jimmie Foxx in your lineup.

In Mack's defense it should be noted that, like Al Simmons, Foxx was a right-handed power hitter and Mack may have been taking advantage of Jimmie's adaptability in the field to free up first base for some much-needed left-handed muscle that would not fit elsewhere. Possibly that is why the veteran manager stayed so long with ailing left-handed slugger Joe Hauser at first. After 1928, however, Mack was forced to give up on Hauser and first base became Foxx's by default.

The Athletics' new first baseman responded with a .354 batting average, 33 home runs, and 117 RBIs. Essentially a player of the 1930s, Foxx was just getting warmed up. In a few years his name would become as synonymous with raw power as Ruth's was in the early twenties. In fact, of all the sluggers of the 1920s and 1930s, including Lou Gehrig, Jimmie comes closest to the Babe's bruising style of hitting.

In a spirit of press-box waggery, the mild-mannered slugger was tagged with egregious nicknames like "The Beast." It was said that he had not been scouted but trapped. Foxx had the forearms and biceps of a blacksmith, and when he began cutting the sleeves from his uniforms, presumably to give him greater freedom of movement, the sight was rumored to cause American League pitchers to tremble. Yankee left-hander Vernon "Goofy" Gomez once deadpanned that he gave up wearing glasses on the mound so that he wouldn't see Foxx so distinctly. Years after Gomez's retirement in 1943, he insisted to reporters that some of the shots Foxx hit off him in the 1930s were still airborne.

Batting just ahead of Foxx was the ebullient Al Simmons, who in 1929 turned in the kind of heroic performance that Athletics fans had come to expect from him—.365 batting average, 34 home runs, and a league-leading 157 RBIs. The combination of Simmons and Foxx had developed into a counterweight to Ruth and Gehrig. Yet, as formidable as the A's power tandem was, it was no match for the Yankee pair. In any case, Simmons and Foxx were not carrying the Athletics alone. They were strongly supported by catcher Mickey Cochrane, outfielders Bing Miller and George "Mule" Haas, and third baseman Jimmy Dykes, a lineup

that batted .338 and hit 111 homers. Add to this brand of power
the best pitching in baseball and it is not hard to understand how
the 1929 A's buried the stalwart Yankees along with the rest of
the American League.

Al Simmons, born Alois Szymanski in one of Milwaukee's south-
side Polish wards, was one of the greatest hitters of his generation and a solid, all-round ballplayer. Reporting to the Athletics
in 1924 after just two seasons in the minors, Simmons was among
the first of the young sluggers to come of baseball age after the
Babe Ruth revolution.

Simmons had broken into Connie Mack's starting lineup almost as soon as he appeared at the Athletics' training camp. He
went on to record eleven straight .300-plus seasons at bat. In that
stretch he ripped league pitching for a .356 average and never
failed to drive in at least 100 runs. Simmons won two batting
titles and came very close to two others. He retired after twenty
seasons with a .334 batting average and a lifetime total of 307
home runs.

Simmons's career illustrates the reformed thinking of the 1920s
regarding a natural style of batting. The powerful right-handed
swinger groped with his left foot for the outside line of the batter's box as he laced extra-base hits to all fields. Because the awk-
ward stance was universally known as hitting with your foot in
the bucket, Simmons quickly picked up the nickname "Bucketfoot Al." Had Simmons entered professional baseball before World
War I, managers and coaches would have been on the kid early
to bat "normally." By the early 1920s, Connie Mack, McGraw,
Rickey, and other wise heads had learned not to tamper with
success. Simmons's inelegant stance may have continued to of-
fend baseball stylists in the press box, but young Al got the job
done.

Actually, Bucketfoot Al's upper body was well positioned to
deal with the outside pitch, as many an American League pitcher
learned the hard way. Simmons's thirty-eight-inch bat probably
helped too in guarding the outside corner. It is the longest known
to have been used in major-league competition. Simmons was
also fast and had a good arm. He was regarded by contemporaries
as one of the best defensive outfielders in baseball.

Mickey Cochrane, acknowledged one of the finest catchers in baseball history, batted third in the Athletics' potent batting order, just ahead of Simmons and Foxx. This was turning the world upside down. By long-established custom, catchers had been slotted eighth, right before their battery mates. It was true even for men like Larry Woodall, Earl Smith, Wally Schang, and Bubbles Hargrave, who could be counted on for a respectable share of base hits. But Cochrane and his contemporaries, Gabby Hartnett of the Cubs and Bill Dickey of the Yankees, were ushering in a new age, when some of the most skillful receivers in the game would hold their own with outfielders in hitting.

The slender left-handed-swinging Cochrane was not in a class with Simmons and Foxx when it came to power. Still, Mickey was good for between 10 and 20 homers a season. And he was fast on the bases. In 1929 Cochrane batted .331 and produced 201 runs. He also caught 135 games. Mickey's .320 lifetime average is the highest among catchers of this century.

The examples of Cochrane, Hartnett, and Dickey in the 1920s must have encouraged baseball scouts to rethink their criteria for catchers. Such performers would always be rare, of course, but here was evidence that they did exist. There was always the outside chance that the high-school diamond in the next town might shelter a Yogi Berra, a Johnny Bench, a Roy Campanella, or a Carlton Fisk.

Of the remainder of Connie Mack's high-flying batting order only second baseman and leadoff man Max Bishop had an off-season in 1929. He hit just .232, 84 percentage points below his 1928 average and his lowest mark ever. As sabermetrics has taught us, however, batting average can be an illusionary measure of a player's offensive worth. "Camera Eye," as Bishop was nicknamed, led the majors in walks with 128, 56 more than the menacing Babe Ruth, and had an on-base percentage close to .400.

In center field, Haas, very much the journeyman outfielder, enjoyed a career season in 1929. He hit .313 and drove in 82 runs from his second spot in the order. Right fielder Bing Miller, one of Connie Mack's charter sluggers of the early twenties, weighed in with a .335 average and 93 RBIs. Playing with the dash of a rookie, the thirty-five-year-old Miller put together a 28-

game hitting streak in June. Another A's old-timer, Jimmy Dykes, "The Round Man," skillfully backed up three infield positions and came through with 13 homers and 79 RBIs in 119 games. Shortstop Joe Boley and third baseman Sammy Hale, paid principally to keep balls from getting through the left side, managed to contribute almost 100 RBIs between them. Not Murderers' Row, to be sure, but the A's of 1929 commanded respect.

Joe McCarthy's Cubs entered the World Series against Philadelphia's formidable lineup with well-founded confidence. The Cubs were easily the equal of the Athletics in power. Among gamblers, however, the A's remained a slight favorite on the strength of their pitching.

In the Series the Cubs got off to a bad start. In Game One at Chicago on October 8, Connie Mack opened with aging right-hander Howard Ehmke, who had pitched only 55 innings during the season and won a modest 7 games. Since Mack's two aces, Earnshaw and Grove, were fully rested, the manager's decision was a stunner. A few observers speculated that the choice was motivated by sentiment because the thirty-five-year-old Ehmke was unlikely to have another chance to pitch in a World Series. Mack was too tough a competitor for that. As proof that he knew exactly what he was doing, in September the calculating Mack had sent Ehmke to scout the Cubs. At the same time, Chicago had little reason to collect a "book" on the little-used Ehmke.

Throughout the Series, Mack remained reluctant to start his left-handers, Grove and Walberg, against a Chicago lineup top-heavy with right-handed sluggers. It is evident that Mack had become convinced weeks before the Series that Ehmke's experience and his side-arm delivery might be just the combination to thwart the home-run swing of Hornsby, Wilson, and the rest—and he was right. Ehmke set a World Series record by striking out 13 of McCarthy's bruisers as he beat Cubs ace Charlie Root, 3 to 1. Connie was one up and he had yet to tap his top starters.

In Game Two, Earnshaw and Grove pitched four and a half innings apiece to win easily, 9 to 3. Once again 13 Cubs fanned. But back in Philadelphia on October 11, Chicago's crafty right-hander, Guy Bush, obviated a third consecutive American League sweep by beating Earnshaw, 3 to 1. Pitching on one day's rest, the burly Earnshaw had limited the Cubs to 6 hits and struck out 10. Bush was a tad better. Still determined not to start Grove or his other lefty, Walberg, Mack was forced to go with forty-six-year-old Jack Quinn in Game Four.

The Cubs got to Quinn for 2 runs in the fourth inning. In the sixth Chicago shelled the ancient spitballer from the mound to lead, 7 to 0, and in the seventh they collected an additional run off reliever Ed Rommel. Meanwhile, Charlie Root had held Simmons, Foxx, and company to 3 scratch hits while facing just twenty batters in six innings. With an 8-run lead and Root in command, Chicago seemed a cinch to tie the Series and be assured of returning to Wrigley Field. What followed ranks as one of the most infamous half-innings in World Series history.

Al Simmons leads off the Philadelphia seventh with a home run over the left-field roof for the Athletics' first run. He returns to the dugout, mumbling, "What a waste of a home run." Foxx singles to right. Bing Miller follows with a lazy liner to center, which drops for a single when Wilson for the second time in the afternoon loses a ball in the sun. Dykes singles sharply to left, scoring Foxx with run number 2 and moving Miller to second. No alarm on the Chicago bench. The Cubs still lead by 6.

But then Boley pokes a ground single through the right side of the infield, scoring Miller and sending Dykes to third. The Cubs may have a 5-run cushion, but Root hasn't retired a batter yet. With A's pitcher Eddie Rommel due up, Mack will surely pinch-hit. No breathing spell for Charlie.

Defying percentage, Connie sends up aging "Tioga George" Burns, a right-handed batter, to hit for Rommel against right-hander Root. Burns obligingly pops up. Great sigh of relief from the Chicago bench. A double play will rescue the Cubs, and standing in is patient-but-weak-hitting Max Bishop. Alas, Bishop spurns the form charts and singles up the middle to score Dykes and cut the Cubs' lead by half. Now it is time to worry.

McCarthy brings in former New York Giant ace left-hander, Art Nehf, to pitch to lefty swinger Mule Haas. Nehf has scarcely had time to warm up but he gets the job done. Haas lifts a high fly to center. But what's this? Hack Wilson is charging in, vainly searching the sky for the ball. It sails over his head and rolls to the wall. Haas has an inside-the-park, 3-run homer.

Chicago should be out of the inning with, at most, the loss of a couple of runs. On a cloudy day they might have been. Instead, their 8-run lead has been reduced to one. A shaken Nehf walks Cochrane as right-handed reliever John "Sheriff" Blake furiously warms up for the unenviable task of pitching to Simmons. Al doesn't homer off Blake to tie the score in storybook fashion. That might have been more bearable. Instead, he bounces a freak single over the head of third baseman Norm McMillan to send Cochrane to second.

Even now all is not lost. Blake manages to keep Jimmie Foxx in the park, but Double X hits his second single of the inning to score Cochrane with the tying run.

In the stands Philadelphia fans learn that hysteria is the threshold to exhaustion. According to legend, in the visitors' clubhouse, the Cubs' trainer, Andy "Doc" Lotshaw, frantically administered sal volatile to starter Root, who had been listening to the game on the radio.

Desperate, McCarthy turns to his 22-game winner, Perce "Pat" Malone, to close the door. Malone quickly reveals the state of his nerves by plunking Bing Miller in the ribs to load the bases. It remains for Jimmy Dykes to deliver the coup de grâce. He doubles off the left-field wall and the A's lead by 2. No one in the city of Philadelphia is really paying attention as Boley and Burns strike out to end the inning. The Athletics' 10 runs have established a World Series record that will be tied in the distant future but not broken.

Now Mack is ready to bring in Grove. The big left-hander fans 4 as he retires the Cubs in order in the eighth and ninth. When shortstop Elwood "Woody" English stares helplessly at a called third strike in the ninth, Chicago sets a Series record for strikeouts.

As though by design, the day following the tumultuous fourth game was Sunday. Under Pennsylvania law there could be no baseball. For the teams it was time for soul-searching and resting of pitchers, for fans an opportunity for gradual reentry into the real world. Later, in the dark days of December, you could find glassy-eyed fans in Chicago speakeasies who would tell you that the teams never bothered with a fifth game. Actually, they did. The Commissioner, a stickler for details, insisted on it. In fact, President Herbert Hoover, still in his pre-Depression honeymoon period, his right hand well shielded from adoring citizens, made the mistake of showing up at Game Five. He was rudely booed by thirsty Philadelphians, who raucously demanded an end to Prohibition, especially on beer.

Even with a 3-games-to-1 advantage, Mack was reluctant to start his ace Lefty Grove against McCarthy's right-handed artillery. On Monday the old man went a second time with Howard Ehmke. Facing elimination, McCarthy bet all his chips on Malone. Showing plenty of moxie, Big Pat made ready to pitch on one day's rest.

For eight innings Malone held the bumptious Athletics scoreless, yielding a couple of scratch singles. In the ninth, with the Cubs clinging feverishly to a 2-run lead, it looked as though Sunday's prayers in a thousand Chicago churches might be answered. Then with 1 out Bishop singled, and before you could say Cornelius McGillicuddy, Mule Haas had homered over the right-field wall to tie the score.

McCarthy had no one warming up in the bullpen. Malone tightened his belt and got the dangerous Cochrane for the second out. For a fleeting moment it seemed possible that big Pat's courage would be rewarded. But Simmons doubled off the scoreboard in left to put the winning run in scoring position. A weary McCarthy signaled Malone to put Foxx on and set up a play at three bases.

The Cub manager still had no one ready to relieve the starter. This situation may strike the modern fan as inexcusable. Keep in mind, however, that in the 1920s baseball was played with starters. As well endowed with pitching as most managers of the time, McCarthy had a staff of five starters and little else. He was surely correct in assuming that Malone offered the best hope of getting the third out. In any case, Bing Miller ended McCarthy's decision-making for the year by doubling off the scoreboard to drive in Simmons.

In addition to losing the Series, the Cubs had set a record

they would be eager to forget. In 5 games, 50 Chicago batters struck out. It remained the record for a Series of any length until 1958, when 56 Milwaukee Braves whiffed in 7 games. Chicago still holds the record for a 5-game Series.

A former catcher, Connie Mack had correctly guessed that Chicago's right-handed sluggers would be trying to kill the ball. In luring the Cubs into the trap, he had handled his pitchers brilliantly. Chicago's lone home run came from first baseman Charlie Grimm, the only left-handed hitter in the lineup. In the crowning irony of a bizarre Series, sun-sensitive Hack Wilson led both clubs in batting with a .471 average but drove in not a single run. Mack, the man who had once declared that "pitching is seventy-five percent of baseball," knew what he was talking about.

Had it not been for Hack Wilson's losing those fly balls, Rogers Hornsby would doubtless have been the Series goat. Rajah, baseball's toughest out, struck out an unprecedented 8 times.

Chicago owner Wrigley was said to be inconsolable over the loss of the Series. Had he been an acquisitive operator like Sam Breadon in St. Louis, Wrigley might have taken solace from the 1.5 million paying customers the Cubs drew in the regular season. But, like his wealthy New York counterpart, Jake Ruppert, the chewing-gum magnate viewed baseball from the perspective of what was called a sportsman, a term that no longer carries its faintly aristocratic 1920s meaning. To Wrigley's generation, a true sportsman gave no thought to profiting materially from his activities on turf or diamond, nor would he accept a victory that had not been won in an absolutely fair manner. Wrigley and Ruppert could afford to be sporting; they were among the few owners of the period not dependent upon profits from baseball for their livelihood.

In a season characterized by a bull market in offense, distribution of batting honors did not follow the book. For the first time since 1919, Harry Heilmann failed to win the American League batting championship in an odd-numbered year. You could tell that Slug was thirty-five years old and just a year short of retirement. He had slumped to .344. The league title went instead to Cleveland's good-hit, no-field first baseman, Lew Fonseca. Fonseca had managed to stave off a late-season charge by Al Simmons and

win with a modest .369, the league's lowest winning mark since
Ty Cobb tagged spitballs for the same average in 1915. Through
most of his twelve-year big-league career, Fonseca was essentially
a utility infielder. Only four times did he appear in more than
100 games a season and never in as many as 150. Four years after
his moment in the sun, Fonseca retired to become a highly successful baseball executive.

You might expect that team-batting honors would go to Connie Mack's hard-hitting White Elephants or possibly the Yankees.
They didn't. The terror of American League pitchers in 1929 was
sixth-place Detroit, 36 games distant from the pennant winners.
True, the Tigers batted only .299, a touch below their accustomed level. On the other hand, they atoned for the shortcoming
by finishing first in runs, hits, total bases, doubles, triples, and
slugging average. Their 110 homers, just 12 fewer than Philadelphia's, were good enough for third place in the league. It hardly
seems necessary to record that Detroit pitchers were first in
yielding runs and walks and had a 4.96 earned-run average, the
league's worst by a margin of .53. Predictably, the Tigers made
the league's most errors. Ty Cobb was long gone from Navin Field,
but little else had changed.

In one category of offense, things went according to form:
Ruth led the majors with 46 home runs. Babe also batted .345
and drove in 154 runs. The Sultan of Swat remained detached
from the statistical ups and downs of league batting. His performance was affected by nothing except the vagaries of his own
training schedule, and he had been on good behavior for four
consecutive seasons.

Long estranged from his first wife, Babe had been taken in
tow by a well-educated, tough-minded actress named Claire
Hodgson, who seemed the only person able to keep the carefree
slugger on a short leash. Ruth had also hired a personal trainer
named Artie McGovern. McGovern, who spent winters toiling to
keep his portly charge in reasonably good physical condition, was
acknowledged to have one of the nation's toughest jobs. Though
the aging slugger was still without peer in poling home runs, a
reformed Ruth seemed somehow not as much fun as the untram-
meled Babe of the early twenties.

On August 11 at Cleveland's League Park, Babe had collected his five-hundredth major-league home run. Just ten years earlier, at the start of the 1919 season, he had had only twenty to his credit. Ruth's ten-year achievement is unparalleled.

In October, *Scientific American* calculated that although the thirty-four-year-old Ruth was still hitting lots of home runs each season, he was no longer getting record distances. That the magazine would view such an analysis as newsworthy is testimony to Ruth's gargantuan reputation. Six years later, the learned editors may have raised a collective eyebrow when a spavined and grossly fat Babe hit his very last big-league homer—number 714—completely over the right-field roof at Pittsburgh's Forbes Field and into Schenley Park, the first batter ever to do so. It was his third home run and fourth hit of the game. In his twenty-two-year major-league career, Babe spent a scant five weeks in the National League, but in true Ruth fashion he succeeded in leaving his mark in the league record books.

Although he no longer reigned in the imperial isolation of his early years, Babe Ruth remained the Sultan of Swat and his janissaries continued to multiply. As evidence, in the National League, no fewer than eight batters matched the 29 home runs with which Ruth had electrified the country just ten years earlier. Among them twenty-year-old Mel Ott hit 42 home runs for the New York Giants, underscoring the continued inclination of youth to follow the Babe's example regardless of protest from baseball reactionaries. In fact, 30 to 40 had become the established range for premier home-run hitters and that would never again change except during the personnel displacements caused by World War II.

The American League witnessed a baseball milestone on April 18 in New York when the Yankees became the first major-league club to field a team with numbered uniforms. Apparently in deference to popular superstition, no Yankee took the field that afternoon wearing the number 13. Other clubs, notably Cleveland, have laid claim to being the first to experiment in numbering uniforms, but the evidence is at best shaky. About the Yankees, on the other hand, there can be no doubt. In 1929 they inaugurated the practice that, in time, all of Organized Baseball would follow.

The long-standing objection to numbering the players had been that it would cut into the sale of scorecards. Since that source of income was not likely of great consequence to Jake Ruppert, it is not surprising that the Yankees were first to commit to numbered uniforms. Beginning with the Washington Senators, other big-league clubs gradually adopted the practice. So far as is known, the innovation did not affect scorecard sales.

With that unfailing instinct for showmanship that characterized every step of his career, Babe Ruth hit a home run the first time he came to the plate wearing a big number 3 on his back. John Drebinger of *The New York Times* was on pretty safe ground when he wrote: "It is now expected he [Ruth] will make '3' as famous as the '77' Red Grange wore at Illinois."

While the Athletics may have failed to lead their league in offense, it stands to reason that the Cubs, with their .303 team average and 140 homers, should have cornered National League honors. Nope. Nor did the star-studded New York Giants. Nor even the battering Pirates or Cardinals with their lineups of .300 hitters. National League, indeed major-league, batting supremacy in 1929 was claimed by the Athletics' threadbare neighbors, the fifth-place Phillies.

Fifth place must have made the Phillies feel light-headed. They had not finished that high since 1917. As late as mid-August, manager Burt Shotton's prehensile gladiators languished in the familiar surroundings of the league cellar. Without warning Brooklyn, Cincinnati and Boston wilted in the heat of late summer, permitting the hammering Phils to pass them. The Phillies batted .309 and clubbed 153 home runs, setting a National League record and falling just 5 short of the major-league record, then held by the 1927 Yankees. The Phils also led the majors in hits and total bases (nosing out Detroit in both categories). Finally, they set a new National League mark for slugging with .467, the second highest in major-league history to that point. Maybe it proves that in the short haul, raw hitting can get the job done. Philadelphia pitchers finished with an ERA of 6.13.

Whenever Shotton played the versatile Barney Friberg at short and Virgil "Spud" Davis behind the plate—about half the games—National League pitchers were looking at eight .300 hitters in the

Philadelphia batting order. That season the Phillies had four men
with 200 or more hits, a feat that has been matched only by the
1937 Tigers. Four Phils batted in 115 or more runs.

Philadelphia's young right fielder, Charles "Chuck" Klein, set
a new National League home-run record of 43, bettering Hornsby's 1922 mark by 1. Under today's rules, the twenty-three-year-
old Klein, who had made the jump from Class B Fort Wayne at
the end of July in the previous season, probably could have been
classified a rookie. In his first full year in the majors, Klein batted
.356 and produced 228 runs. He also compiled 405 total bases,
only the sixth time a major leaguer had topped 400. It was not
enough to give him the league lead. Rogers Hornsby had 409.
Even Klein's hefty 145 RBIs placed him fourth behind Wilson,
Ott, and Hornsby. In fact, the only category in which Chuck led
the league was home runs. It was that kind of year.

Some baseball writers believed that it was young Klein's spectacular slugging in 1929 that drove Phillies owner Baker to turn
baseball purist. The owner ordered a twenty-foot screen added
to the forty-foot tin barrier in right field at Baker Bowl. "Home
runs," Baker pontificated, "have become too cheap in the Philadelphia ballpark." It was not opponents' homers that bothered
Baker, one reporter observed. It was the fear that if Klein began
to match Babe Ruth's totals, he would ask for a Ruthian salary.

There is no record that Klein protested Baker's graceless gesture. Chuck just continued to dent the new screen with line drives
that might otherwise have been home runs.

Exiled to Baker Bowl by the irascible McGraw, Phillies left
fielder Lefty O'Doul won the batting championship with a hefty
.398. To this honor he added 32 home runs and 397 total bases.
Lefty's 254 hits in 154 games set a National League record, which
would be tied by Bill Terry the following year but has not been
approached since.

O'Doul's batting championship could only have intensified the
post-Series miseries of Chicago owner William Wrigley, Jr. A California resident, Wrigley had long paid particular attention to what
went on in the Pacific Coast League. In 1925, on his own initia-
tive, Wrigley paid Salt Lake City owner Bill Lane $15,000 for the
happy-go-lucky O'Doul, and Lefty dutifully reported to the Cubs'

training camp on Catalina Island in the spring of 1926. New Chicago manager Joe McCarthy must not have been impressed by what he saw of O'Doul, either on or off the field. Without regard to Wrigley's judgment or the amount of the investment, McCarthy quickly optioned O'Doul to the Hollywood club and, as McGraw had done with Hack Wilson, conveniently let the slugger slip through the option net. Thereafter, whenever Lefty mauled Cubs pitching—which was often—Wrigley would hold his head and groan, "Oh, no, not O'Doul again . . . my O'Doul."

O'Doul was thirty-two before he won a regular job as a big leaguer. From that point he batted .357 in his too-brief career. In two of his four full seasons he won the batting championship. Had he at an earlier age shaken the delusion that he was a pitcher, as Sisler, Speaker, Gehrig, Goslin, Paul Waner, and others had done before him, he might have made it to the majors early enough to command serious attention. I can't help wondering what O'Doul might have accomplished if in his early twenties he had come under the tutelage of a batting genius and martinet like Ty Cobb. On the other hand, it is possible that there never was enough seriousness of purpose in Lefty in spite of the talent. Like Hack Wilson, O'Doul was a bottled-in-bond creature of the 1920s and probably could not have existed in another period of the game.

Lefty finished out his major-league career with the Giants before returning to the Pacific Coast League to manage. He played a minor but memorable role in New York's triumph in the 1933 World Series. Lefty's rally-sparking pinch hit in Game Two made him enormously popular among the city's kids. As a very young boy I got to talk to him a few times outside the clubhouse at the Polo Grounds, and although I don't recall the Kelly green suits he is reputed to have worn, I carry an indelible recollection of a tall smiling figure. I can attest that O'Doul was unfailingly gracious with kids. Not all ballplayers were.

O'Doul went on to a long and successful career as a minor-league manager with the San Francisco Seals, and among other things helped popularize baseball in Japan, where he was held in great affection until his death in 1969.

At the age of fifty-nine, while managing the Seals, Lefty put himself in to pinch-hit in a game against Vancouver. Later he revealed that it was intended as a gag, but, in fact, there was enough Tabasco in the old swing to fetch him a triple to left-center. I don't know what epitaph appears on O'Doul's grave marker at South San Francisco's Holy Cross Cemetery, but at the very least it should read, "He could hit."

Foreshadowing the many changes that would overtake the major-league scene within a season or two, on September 26, Miller Huggins, the most successful manager of the decade, died unexpectedly of erysipelas following a brief illness. He was barely fifty. Though in retrospect it seems patently unfair, there were some at the time, including Huggins's widow, who charged that the tiny manager's life had been shortened by the strain of having to manage Babe Ruth.

Outside the ballpark, 1929 was marked by economic dislocations that would soon affect every aspect of the national life, including professional baseball. On October 24—Black Thursday—General Electric common stock fell seventeen points in less than an hour, emblematic of the panic selling that undermined most other blue-chip issues. When the bell sounded signaling the close of trading on the floor of the New York Stock Exchange, the ticker was running four hours behind. Some of those present must have had an inkling that the world would never be quite the same again. Fortunately for the players of the major leagues' first-division clubs, who shared in the World Series receipts, the Commissioner's office had not had time to cut the checks, and so none of that money could have gone into the market. Even a fourth-place share would be a welcome nest egg in the troubled times ahead.

TWELVE

THE
CRESCENDO
OF 1930

"It's gotta end sometime. Come November
there'll be snow on the field."
—UNIDENTIFIED PHILLIES PITCHER

WHEN CHICAGO CUBS ace right-hander Guy Bush rolled out of bed
at the Chase Hotel in St. Louis on April 15, 1930, he had no
reason to suspect that the season beginning that afternoon would
be appreciably different from his previous six. The dark-visaged
Mississippian, with his exaggerated sideburns, was thought by some
baseball writers to resemble a riverboat faro dealer—and to pitch
like one too. Boasting a wicked curve and excellent control, Bush
was thoroughly at home on the corners of the plate.

One of the league's workhorses, "The Mississippi Mudcat" had
labored 271 innings in 1929 and finished the season with a record of 18 and 7. Coupled with his performance in 1928, this
raised his two-year win-loss record to a glittering 33 and 13. Bush
had also won the single game that the Cubs had salvaged in the
World Series against Philadelphia. And in a league that collectively surrendered an average of 4.71 earned runs in 1929, his
3.66 bordered on distinguished. No one would have blamed the
cagey right-hander for entertaining thoughts that the hard-hitting
Cubs could help him to 25 victories in 1930.

On September 28, 225 innings later, a weary Guy Bush peeled

off his sodden flannels in the Wrigley Field clubhouse. Despite
having been blasted from the mound in the second inning of the
season's finale, he remained among the top ten pitchers in the
National League with a record of 15 and 10. No one on the pennant-winning Cardinals, for example, had won more. Yet Bush
faced a winter of earnest reflection in the pine woods of his native northeastern Mississippi on the import of his season's earned-
run average of 6.20. In all probability he would not be alone.
Three Phillies pitchers posted ERAs in excess of 7.50. The 1930
season turned out to be one such as no pitcher had ever seen.

For reasons that may never be fully understood, National League
batters in 1930 generated 7,025 runs, still the record for an eight-
team league, 6,046 of them earned—that too a record at the time.
They did this on a record 13,260 hits and compiled 19,572 total
bases, yet another record.

In tavern discussions, 1930 is sometimes identified as "the
year that everyone in the National League hit three hundred." It
wasn't quite that, but not far from it. Collectively, the National
Leaguers batted .303, a twentieth-century major-league record,
and an advance of 9 percentage points over their average for
1929. They hit a record 892 home runs. Of players who appeared
in seventy-five or more games, fifty-four batted over .300, *thirteen* of them over .350. The New York Giants set a modern major-league team record by batting .319, one of six clubs over .300,
and some trivia buff has calculated that the league's regular outfielders averaged .330, 16 home runs, and 107 RBIs. In the course
of the season, twenty-seven major-league batting records were
established.

The experience of Brooklyn slugger Babe Herman illustrates
what a National Leaguer was up against in trying to distinguish
himself that year. Babe hit .393, collected 241 hits—including 48
doubles, 11 triples, and 35 homers, for a slugging average of .678—
scored 143 runs, and drove in 130. Yet he failed to lead the league
in any category. Herman should have suspected early on what lay
ahead. Five weeks into the season he was hitting .424 and ranked
only fifth among batting leaders.

In mid-season John McGraw, whose own hitters were giving
pitchers an unparalleled drubbing, called for immediate reduc-

tion of the pitching distance to 58 feet. Since compassion was not prominent among McGraw's virtues, his startling public proposal focused new attention on the plight of the pitcher. No action was taken on the veteran manager's recommendation.

American League batters lagged behind the National and finished at .288, which could scarcely be described as impotence. The league's first division, of course, more than held their own with the National Leaguers. Philadelphia, Washington, New York, and Cleveland batted a combined .303 and averaged almost 950 runs.

Why the record outburst in 1930? We don't know. It's worth considering, however, that National League pitching talent, thin in 1929, was thinner in 1930—and a year older. Only two National Leaguers won 20 games—Pat Malone and Ray Kremer—and each won exactly 20. Five American Leaguers topped 20, led by Grove with 28. In the course of the season, only two rookie pitchers of top quality reached the majors, both in the American League: Cleveland's Mel Harder and New York's Lefty Gomez. Gomez pitched a scant 60 innings.

When it came to setting records, the fans of 1930 were not to be outdone by the players. Putting the October stock-market crash behind them, Americans showed up at the ballparks in unprecedented numbers. For the first time in history, major-league baseball drew more than 10 million. The National League enjoyed its most profitable season ever. Relaxing in the bleachers, some of the newly impoverished stockbrokers must have congratulated themselves on not having jumped from skyscraper windows. This was not a season to miss.

In assessing the record attendance, we must bear in mind that the Depression didn't descend suddenly on the Friday after the market crash. It was, in fact, slow in developing. Through the spring and early summer of 1930 there were a few bank failures, a discernible slowdown in business, and increasing unemployment. None of this appeared to affect the fortunes of Organized Baseball.

National League fans had more to cheer than the record hitting. That season witnessed one of the most exciting pennant races of the era, with four clubs—St. Louis, Chicago, New York, and Brooklyn—remaining serious contenders well into September. Even the fifth-place Pirates caught fire in late summer and threatened the leaders. It's hard not to believe that the unprecedented hitting contributed to the closeness of the pennant race. When you review the inflated scores in many of the important games of September, it is apparent that the team with something resembling balanced pitching was bound to carry the day. That team was St. Louis.

In the first half of the season in both leagues, form charts had to be trashed. The defending-champion Athletics ran into savage resistance not only from New York, from whom they expected it, but from Washington and Cleveland as well. On May 11, for example, the A's great pitching staff was worked over by the upstart Indians, 25 to 7. On the sixteenth the singles-hitting Washington Senators raked Connie Mack's staff for 16 runs, and from the twenty-first through the twenty-fifth, in a brawling 7-game home-and-home series against the Yankees, Philadelphia pitchers surrendered an alarming 52 runs. The Athletics closed out the tempestuous month against Washington, yielding 20 runs in a 3-game series which they swept. This is not to say that there were no 1-to-0 or 2-to-1 games being played in the spring of 1930. But if baseball's finest pitching staff could be handled so rudely, it was destined to be a hitter's year.

In the National League the situation was worse. (Or, from the standpoint of the hitters, better.) On successive days in early May, the champion Cubs blew two extra-inning games to Brooklyn by identical scores of 11 to 10. Twenty-four hours later, they were lucky to stagger past the Phillies, 16 to 11. All this was before the Cubs had suffered any of the injuries that would cloud their season.

In a 4-game series at Pittsburgh, Giant pitchers gave up 30 runs, 29 of them in 3 games. Somehow the New Yorkers managed to come away with 3 victories. National League pitchers must have been surviving on nerve alone.

Just as Philadelphia was expected to repeat in the American League, Chicago was the preseason favorite in the National. From the start of the season, however, the Cubs played in bad luck. On May 28 veteran right-hander Harold Carlson died of undisclosed causes. Carlson had been 11 and 5 in 1929 and was 4 and 2 at the time of his death. McCarthy was never able to make up the shortfall in pitching.

Two days after Carlson's death, Rogers Hornsby, the league's Most Valuable Player for 1929, broke an ankle sliding. He was already suffering from a bone spur in his right heel. The double affliction sidelined Rajah for the season, and, in fact, he never was able to play a full season thereafter. Hornsby's replacement, Clarence "Footsie" Blair, batted .273 and hit just 6 home runs.

Fortunately for the Cubs, they had regained the services of Gabby Hartnett, not only the league's finest receiver but also baseball's first slugging catcher. As early as 1925, Hartnett had hit 24 home runs to finish second in the league. In 1930 he would hit 37. In his best years Hartnett also hit for a high average—.339 in 1930—and in a 20-year career batted .297.

Gabby was blessed with one of the greatest arms ever hung on a catcher, and there are baseball historians today who consider him the best all-round receiver the game has produced. Every inch an extrovert, Hartnett once drew a reprimand from Commissioner Landis for agreeing to pose for a pregame news photo with gangster Al Capone.

Even without Hornsby, the 1930 Cubs were imposing at the plate. They batted .309 and set a new major-league home-run record with 171, 13 more than hit by the 1927 Yankees. Chicago's season slugging average of .481 is still the National League record.

As in 1929, a significant share of the Cubs' power came from Hack Wilson. Following his fielding misfortunes in the World Series, Hack may have felt driven to redeem himself in the way he knew best—with his bat. In any case, his 1930 performance is majestic. He batted .356 on 208 hits, including 56 home runs, still the league record. Wilson's 190 RBIs for the season look as unassailable as Lou Gehrig's consecutive-game playing streak. In all, Hack produced 280 runs. He also drew 105 walks, his best mark ever.

Things just seemed to go Wilson's way in 1930. On May 26 the United States Supreme Court ruled in a unanimous decision that ordinary citizens buying and consuming alcoholic drinks were not breaking the law of Prohibition. Only purveyors were in violation. A wit in the Wrigley Field press box claimed that Hack's sigh of relief could be heard in Sheboygan, Wisconsin.

As the Cubs' .309 season batting average suggests, Joe McCarthy got outstanding offensive performances from others besides Hartnett and Wilson. Right fielder Kiki Cuyler batted .355, drove in 134 runs, and stole 37 bases, almost a lost art by 1930. Riggs Stephenson, who missed part of the season with injuries, led the team in batting with .367. Shortstop Woody English hit .335 and had the teams' highest on-base average.

Scoring runs was definitely not Chicago's problem. They came within 2 of sending 1,000 runners across the plate that season. But faced with the loss of Carlson, McCarthy found it difficult to work out a four-man rotation that could get consistent results. Most troubling of all, following the injury to Hornsby, the manager was forced to back and fill with his infield. He never found a combination that he could field with confidence. Despite the adversity, from June onward the astute McCarthy contrived to keep the Cubs at or near the top.

The surprise of 1930 was Brooklyn. After five straight sixth-place finishes, the eccentric Wilbert Robinson, in his seventeenth year as manager of baseball's premier clown act, unexpectedly found himself with enough hitting and pitching to be taken seriously. In the early weeks of 1930 the Robins seemed destined to spend the season in the birdlime of last place. Then they blinked, flexed their palsied wings, and headed north. By the end of May, Robbie's flock had flown to the top of the league, where, except for one brief interruption, they would stay until late summer.

Brooklyn's metamorphosis was triggered in part by the immortal Babe Herman, who was having an even better year than he had in 1929, when he hammered National League pitchers to the tune of .381. In fact, things had turned so upbeat at Ebbets Field that a few Brooklyn writers persuaded themselves that Babe's fielding was improved. Herman's teammates first baseman Adelphia "Del" Bissonette, shortstop Glenn Wright, and center fielder Johnny Frederick were also enjoying career seasons.

If there is a single player to whom the Robins' resurgence can seriously be ascribed, it is rookie catcher Alfonso "Al" Lopez, who would go on to catch a career total of 1,918 major-league games, a record that stood for forty-one years. From the minute he first strapped on shin guards at Ebbets Field, Lopez was the complete big-league catcher. And since it was 1930, the kid also had a productive year at bat, his best in fact. Al hit .309 and drove in 57 runs.

The enigma of 1930 was the New York Giants. On paper they appeared to have enough of everything to win. To begin, there was their record team batting average and their 143 home runs, a figure that represented no fewer than six regulars in double figures. The Giants also boasted the league's best defensive lineup, perhaps the best in baseball, plus at least three quality starters: Hubbell, Fitzsimmons, and left-hander Bill Walker, the league's ERA leader of 1929. Yet, the malaise that had afflicted the club for three years endured. John McGraw's interminable petulance and wrong-headedness must have been more than young ballplayers could handle.

The great rags-to-riches story of the twenties is that of Branch Rickey's Cardinals. The general manager's innovative farm system was working so well that each year St. Louis had a predictable supply of baseball talent moving up to the parent club. Rickey was not developing a flood of superstars, but rather solid all-round performers, players thoroughly grounded in baseball fundamentals during their minor-league apprenticeship. By the end of the 1930s, spurred by the Cardinals' success, every major-league club would have some sort of farm system.

In one of their wisest moves ever, the Cardinals had named as manager for 1930 forty-eight-year-old Charles "Gabby" Street, another product of the Cardinal farm system. Early in the century Street served a few years as a catcher with the Senators and the Reds, but the bulk of his career he spent in the minors, as both a player and a manager. The even-tempered Alabamian was baseball's most confirmed optimist and an ideal mentor for rookies not quite sure of their talents. Gabby may be best remembered in baseball lore as the man who caught a ball dropped from the top of the Washington monument.

Measured by the standards of Babe Ruth and his heavy-muscled heirs, the Cardinals of 1930 were underpowered. They boasted no 155-mm howitzers, just hub-to-hub 75-mm field pieces. With the exception of utility infielder Andy High, who saw limited service, every position player on the St. Louis squad batted over .300. Their long-ball hitters, Chick Hafey and Jim Bottomley, were as likely to dent the fence with a clothesline double or triple as to clear it with a high fly.

Day after day Street was able to pencil in a lineup of eight .300 hitters. There was, in effect, no soft spot in the order except that of the pitcher. Indicative of the balance achieved by the Cardinals in 1930, only center fielder Taylor Douthit made more than 200 hits, and he just barely, on a team that amassed 1,732. Second baseman Frank Frisch led the club in RBIs with a modest 114. Thanks to this superbly balanced offense, the Cardinals became the first National League team to score more than 1,000 runs. St. Louis was no slouch in the field either. Led by a keystone combination of Frisch and flashy young shortstop Charley Gelbert, the Cards turned 176 double plays to lead the majors with plenty to spare.

The only significant setback St. Louis suffered during the season was the loss of outfielder Chick Hafey for five weeks in June and July because of recurring vision problems. The club announced to the press that in spite of acquiring new glasses Hafey was "unable to distinguish objects with one eye and the other is below normal." The season of 1930 may have been the only one in baseball history in which a batter could experience serious eye problems while batting .336 and hitting 26 homers.

To offset the lone bad break the Cards lucked out when Commissioner Landis caught Rickey in a cover-up scheme and forced him to keep rookie catcher August "Gus" Mancuso with the parent club or lose rights to him. Late in the season, when regular catcher Jimmie Wilson was injured, Mancuso took over with the skill and confidence of a veteran. Young Gus also batted .366 and drove in 59 runs in just 227 at-bats. There was something close to consensus among baseball writers that without Mancuso St. Louis could not have won.

Except for a two-day foray to the top of the league in May, the Cardinals poked along in fourth place for the first three months. They scored lots of runs, of course, but it was a year when you often had to put double digits on the board just to stay in the game. About half the time the Cards' opponents put up more.

On the eve of the June trading deadline, St. Louis closed a deal that propelled them into the pennant race. From the Boston Braves they acquired the grizzled, indestructible spitballer Burleigh Grimes. In the final three months of the season, Grimes would win 13 games, a number of them vital to the Cards' survival.

Spitballers, incidentally, were doing very nicely in this eleventh year of dispensation. Survivors Grimes, Faber, Quinn, and Clarence Mitchell, with an average age of forty-one, posted a collective win-loss record of 44 and 34. In ERA they were .63 percentage points better than the major-league mark of 4.81. Even in 1930, it seems, the wet one was tough to hit.

The National League race, hot through midsummer, turned incandescent as September approached. The four-team melee, involving Chicago, New York, Brooklyn, and St. Louis, is perhaps best viewed from the perspective of the underdog Robins, a sentimental favorite with many uncommitted fans. As August opened, Brooklyn split a hard-fought 4-game series against the Giants at Ebbets Field to retain the lead they had held for all but a day or two since mid-May. Despite the Robins' tissue-thin margin over second-place Chicago, the odds-makers' choice, the Brooklyn boys were confident as they began a western road trip at Pittsburgh on August 6. There they swept a 2-game series from the good-hit, no-pitch Pirates.

In the opener of a 5-game series at St. Louis on the eighth, Brooklyn sluggers buried knuckleballer Jesse Haines and the fourth-place Cardinals, 11 to 5. The Robins were hotter than the record heat wave that had been punishing the entire country and had killed as many as seventy-two people in Chicago on a single day.

Unexpectedly, on August 8 the heat broke. It may have been a bad celestial sign for Robbie's heroes in this year when their destiny was written in the stars. On that comfortable Saturday afternoon, St. Louis's sometimes erratic left-hander "Wild Bill" Hallahan held Brooklyn's big bats in check to win a squeaker, 4 to 3. The Cardinals' victory would launch them on the most memorable stretch drive of the decade. Having played barely .500 ball through two thirds of a season, the Redbirds now turned ugly and swept the remainder of the series to drop the Robins to second place behind Chicago. Maybe with the departure of the 100-degree weather, Chick Hafey's new glasses had stopped misting over.

To make matters worse for Brooklyn, their next stop was Wrigley Field, where Hack Wilson and his Neanderthal buddies were waiting with forty-ounce bats. In Chicago, the Robins lost 3 of 4, but two of them were tough 1-run, extra-inning struggles, in the second of which they had ruffled Guy Bush's sideburns with a 15-run attack.

In Pittsburgh on the sixteenth, Brooklyn split a doubleheader to make their record for the trip to that point 5 and 8. Although they had been winged by western birdshot, the Robins remained airworthy. Back at Brooklyn's Grand Army Plaza, fans consoled one another with assurances that Uncle Robbie still had the league's best pitching.

The next day was Sunday, dictating a travel caper designed to deal with Pennsylvania's Blue Law. Right after the second game on Saturday, the Pirates and Robins caught a sleeper for New York so that they could play Sunday afternoon's game at Ebbets Field. Although officially it was counted a home game for Pittsburgh, that didn't matter. The cheers of the Brooklyn crowd and the taste of Harry Stevens's hot dogs helped blunt the effect of the long train ride. Dazzy Vance shut out the Pirates, 6 to 0.

Before nightfall the teams were on another sleeper back to Pittsburgh to complete the 5-game series with a second doubleheader. Brooklyn lost both games and dropped to third place. Things weren't looking so good. Still, the Robins were headed for Cincinnati, where the Reds, starved for pitching, had not poked their noses above seventh place since early May. Robbie's troupers had earned the breather.

An aged fan in Borough Hall Park told a reporter from the Brooklyn *Eagle* that what happened in Cincinnati could be summed up in a word—"moidduh." The Reds swept the 5 games, limiting the Robins to a total of 6 runs in the series. Brooklyn was now deep in third place, 6 games behind the first-place Cubs and 3 behind the hated Giants. The Flatbush Faithful, a communal lump welling in their throats, began to question the impossible dream.

Out there in the hinterlands their front-running Robins had nosed into what looked like a fatal plunge. Worse, before the team could reach the nurturing confines of Ebbets Field, they were scheduled for a stop at the malevolent Polo Grounds.

Although Robbie's hitters had slipped into a mild trance on the road trip, Brooklyn's pitching held up admirably. (In this season, of course, *batting slump* is figurative language. The Robins would finish at .304.) In New York both Dazzy Vance and left-hander James "Jumbo" Elliott conquered the powerful Giants to halt the Robins' skid. Their victims were classy southpaws Bill Walker and Carl Hubbell, probably the league's two best pitchers after Vance himself. Nevertheless, Brooklyn retreated from the Polo Grounds with no better than a split in 4 games.

On the final day of August, Robbie's hitters showed signs of emerging from their late-summer catalepsy. Babe Herman was up to .389. He and his mates celebrated their homecoming by bashing the Phillies, 14 to 3. While Brooklyn's record of 11 wins and 18 losses for August was not the kind of which champions are customarily made, it was, after all, 1930. As long as your guys had bats in their hands, anything could happen. But it was not to happen immediately.

Meanwhile, outside the ballpark, the Depression had begun to bare its fangs. In New York's Bowery, St. Peter's Mission trebled the volume of bread and coffee it daily dispensed to the jobless and was still running out before everyone was fed. If an incentive was needed, this scene alone should have stirred pennant contenders to pull out all the stops.

September opened as inauspiciously for Brooklyn as it did for the republic. Before the Robins could have their uniforms laundered, the inscrutable schedule makers dispatched the weary squad to Boston for a Labor Day doubleheader, the fifth twin bill in three weeks. Thanks only to heroic relief pitching by Hollis "Sloppy" Thurston, Brooklyn managed to salvage the second game. On Tuesday Robbie led with his ace, Dazzy Vance, only to have his hitters blanked by Boston's Ed Brandt, 1 of only 4 games the Boston left-hander would win all season.

Brooklyn batters seemed in the grip of something beyond the ordinary slump, something preternatural. As the team headed home, rumor swept the Borough that volunteer sorcerers from Green-point, Canarsie, and Bensonhurst were closing ranks to lift the spell from their heroes and turn the double whammy on the opposition. It worked.

On September 6 at Ebbets Field, Herman, Bissonette, Wright, and company clobbered the Phillies, 22 to 8, before a welcome-home crowd. In their hearts 17,000 faithful rhapsodized, "If only we could play the Phillies every day."

In a single game on Sunday, behind Dazzy Vance, the Robins beat the Giants, 5 to 2. Then, on a mini road trip to Baker Bowl, they blew away the Phillies in a doubleheader, scoring 19 runs in the 2 games. On the ninth, after more than four weeks on the road, the Robins began an honest-to-goodness home stand.

Prophetically, the first visitors to Ebbets Field were the league-leading Chicago Cubs. Brooklyn swept the 3 games. Rookie right-hander Ray Phelps, along with "The Cuban Fox," Adolfo Luque, and Dazzy Vance, came close to shutting out the slugging Cubs for the series. Chicago's lone run came on a solo homer by Hack Wilson in the seventh inning of game three. As Vance struck out his thirteenth Cub in the series finale, happy fans skimmed thousands of straw hats onto the field in a time-honored autumnal ritual. Brooklyn was for real.

Sparked by Babe Herman, now hitting close to .400, the Robins followed the annihilation of Chicago by blowing aside Cincinnati in 4 games to avenge the humiliation of August and run their winning streak to 11. When the sun set over Bay Ridge on September 15, Brooklyn was back in first place, ½ game ahead of St. Louis and 1½ ahead of the Cubs. With the temperature at a record high for the date, exuberant Brooklynites who sought sleep at all that night did so in the parks or on fire escapes.

Meanwhile, the floundering Giants had slipped to fourth place, 5½ games behind the leaders. The proud and arrogant New Yorkers seemed out of the race. Yet, there remained the outside possibility that the ailing McGraw might be forced into a much-needed vacation and turn the team over to coach Dave Bancroft. Freed from Little Napoleon's harsh leadership, the power-laden Giants could conceivably spring to life and trample everyone in sight. "Watching the National League race," John Kieran observed in his *New York Times* column, "is too much of a strain on the eyes."

With only 13 games remaining on the Robins' schedule, 10 against second-division clubs, a delirium that would not see its equal until September 1941 seized the Borough. The Brooklyn front office announced that they were accepting orders for World Series tickets. "There isn't a chance in the world of taking this away from Brooklyn," crowed club secretary and part owner Steve McKeever. But first the Robins had to dispatch the uppity second-place Cardinals.

Knocking off the Cardinals, who arrived in Brooklyn on the sixteenth, didn't seem to be all that much of a challenge. Since beginning their eastern road trip a week earlier, the Redbirds no longer looked like the ball of fire they had been back at Sportsman's Park. At the Polo Grounds they were lucky to gain a split in 4 games. In fact, with a break or two the dispirited Giants might have swept the series. Earlier the Cards had dropped a game in Boston to make their road record 4 and 3. Hardly world-beaters in the view of Brooklyn fans.

It underscores the unique character of baseball that in a season that would see more than 7,000 runs scored in 614 games, and in a month when important contests were being won and lost by scores like 19 to 14, 19 to 16, and 13 to 11, the pivotal meeting in the pennant race should prove to be a 1-to-0, extra-inning cliffhanger.

Before a capacity-plus crowd of 30,000 believers, Robbie, as expected, tapped Dazzy Vance to pitch the series opener. For nine innings the fireballer held Gabby Street's run-mongers scoreless, scattering 5 hits, walking none, and striking out 11. Cardinal lefty Wild Bill Hallahan, disregarding the implication of his nickname, was a trifle better—or luckier. Hallahan did not give up a hit until the eighth, and at the end of the inning had faced the minimum 24 batters.

In the ninth Brooklyn blew an opportunity to win. Catcher Al Lopez led off with a clean single and advanced to second when Vance was safe on a fielder's choice. A successful sacrifice would put men on second and third with 1 out and the heart of the batting order coming up. In attempting to bunt, center fielder

Eddie Moore popped up to St. Louis catcher Gus Mancuso and the alert rookie doubled Lopez off second. Score an assist for Commissioner Landis.

Third baseman Wally Gilbert followed with a single that should have scored the winning run in one of the most important games ever played in Brooklyn. It was too late. Herman flied out to end the inning.

In the top of the tenth Vance, undoubtedly tiring, surrendered a run on a double by Andy High (who came in in the eighth) and a single by Douthit, but closed out the inning without further damage. In the Brooklyn half, shortstop Glenn Wright led off with a thunderous double to left-center. All was not lost. Hallahan was tiring too, as he demonstrated when he issued his first walk of the game to Bissonette. Left fielder Harvey Hendrick laid down a perfect sacrifice, and suddenly Brooklyn had the tying and winning runs in scoring position with 1 out.

Thirty thousand necks craned to see whether Street would lift his starter. But the old optimist stayed with Hallahan and signaled Mancuso to put pinch hitter D'Arcy "Jake" Flowers on first to set up a double play. This brought up young Lopez, the hot hand, who had singled an inning earlier. Al drilled a terrific shot toward the hole and 30,000 throats contracted to emit the victory cry. Cardinal regular third baseman Sparky Adams, who had been moved to short when Gelbert was shaken up in an eighth-inning collision, dived to his right, made the stop, but had the ball bound away from him momentarily. It seemed certain that the tying run would score. Reporter Roscoe McGowen described what followed as "one of the fastest double plays on record." Adams coolly recovered the ball, fired from his knees to Frisch, who had already started his pivot at second. Frisch's relay doubled the hustling Lopez. The Cardinals had almost cleared the field before the stunned crowd realized what had happened. St. Louis had taken the league lead.

It's impossible to know how long it took for the tragic news to spread throughout the Borough. Unlike the situation in enlightened Chicago, there was no radio broadcast of baseball games in the New York area. Stations WEAF and WJZ featured scheduled sports reports at about seven in the evening. They were just five minutes long. If you weren't hovering over your Stromberg-Carlson or Philco console, you risked missing the whole program. In any case, only a minority of Brooklynites could afford a radio. Most fans got their baseball news from the newspapers. It meant waiting until morning or perhaps standing around the kiosks under the El platforms until trucks delivered the bulldog edition of one of the New York papers. On this terrible night, not even that news source was available, since the trucks were delayed by the weather.

Just as night fell, the record heat ended in a frightening storm. Hurricane-force winds uprooted trees, downed power lines. Storm sewers could not handle the volume of rain and streets flooded. Many injuries were reported, but no fatalities. On Brooklyn's Furman Street, facing the East River, a fifty-by-fifty-foot roof, weighing several tons, was ripped loose from a machine shop and carried intact over two rows of four-story tenements. Somebody up there was displeased with something—perhaps Steve McKeever's hubris.

Or maybe it was the "kidnapping" of Cardinal right-hander Flint Rhem. No account of that fateful Tuesday in September is complete without a nod to the mysterious disappearance of the eccentric South Carolinian, renowned both for his fastball and a passion for strong beverage. On the previous Friday, Rhem had beaten the Giants in the desperation series at the Polo Grounds to preserve a split for the Cardinals. Then, before the team could board the train for Boston, the mercurial right-hander vanished. The disappearance was especially worrisome for manager Street, since he had planned to pitch Rhem in the opener at Brooklyn.

On the eve of the Brooklyn series, Rhem surfaced, unshaven and bleary-eyed. He had, he reported, been kidnapped at gunpoint from in front of the team's hotel in New York and driven to New Jersey. In a remote cabin, the testimony ran, Rhem was held prisoner and "forced to drink tumblers of raw whiskey"—without a chaser. Other than the whiskey, the details of Rhem's story were sketchy. He offered no explanation of what his captors wanted. Or why they let him go. But one fact was unmistakable: Flint was in no condition to pitch. Contrary to plan, Street was forced to go with Hallahan. The switch sealed Brooklyn's fate.

Rhem stuck to his story, but no reporter believed him. A couple of years earlier the right-hander had explained a bender to his abstemious manager, William "Deacon Bill" McKechnie, by claiming that he had sacrificed himself by intercepting drinks intended for Grover Cleveland Alexander. As Rhem saw it, the gesture was an unselfish attempt to keep Alexander sober because "Aleck is more important to the club than I am."

On notice that they were out of favor with the baseball gods, the drooping Robins meekly bowed their heads to fortune. Two veteran Cardinal right-handers—Sylvester Johnson and Burleigh Grimes, a hero out of Brooklyn's own past—throttled the Flock on Wednesday and Thursday to sweep the series. The triple loss dropped Brooklyn to third place behind Chicago. Cruelly, the rejuvenated Pirates arrived on the weekend to pummel the reeling locals twice more. But the ultimate humiliation was to have the Giants administer loss number six on Tuesday and climb past Brooklyn in the standings. In one fateful week the proud Robins had plunged from first to fourth.

As Brooklyn played out the schedule in a dream state to finish fourth, 6 games behind the Cardinals and 1 behind the Giants, Robbie ruefully confided to reporters that it was not the late-summer hitting slump and certainly not unsteady pitching that had cost him what would prove to be his last chance to win another pennant. The manager put his finger instead on that old Brooklyn nemesis—capricious defense. He was probably right. Robbie was still bleeding from the 8 errors Brooklyn had made against the Pirates back on June 4.

Operating, as in 1924, with a mixed bag of baseball talent, the colorful manager had once again given it his best shot and once again come up short. Before turning in the last lineup card of his career, Robbie bumbled his way through the 1931 season, one in which hitting played a much-diminished role. In less than four years Robinson would be dead, just months after the funeral of his old teammate and rival John McGraw.

The 1930 season had not been without its compensations for Brooklyn. They drew 1.1 million fans at home, the most in the club's history and more than they would draw again until their championship season of 1941.

Fortune continued to smile on St. Louis. Following the crucial series in Brooklyn, the schedule makers had arranged for them to go straight to Philadelphia's Baker Bowl for 5 games against the last-place Phillies. Of course, you could never be sure that the free-swinging Phils would not rise up and engulf you in extra-base hits. On this occasion, however, Gabby Street's scoring machine racked up 53 runs to outlast Philadelphia and come away with 4 wins. In an unreal struggle on September 23, the Cards poured out 26 hits before subduing the Phillies, 19 to 16. At one point St. Louis enjoyed a 10-to-0 lead. Pure 1930.

The Cardinals were on a roll, but the second-place Cubs, having absorbed more than their share of bad luck during the season, were not disheartened. The defending champs still had plenty of pop in their bats. To illustrate how hard the Chicagoans were hitting the ball, on September 10, Brooklyn left fielder Rube Bressler had pulled in a line drive off the bat of Hack Wilson and suffered a broken finger—on his gloved hand. Still, fate seemed determinedly against the Cubs. On September 15, for the second time in the season, the Phillies' Lefty O'Doul came off the bench to pinch-hit a game-winning home run against them, probably causing owner Wrigley to reach for his Bromo-Seltzer.

Rolling with the punches, the plucky Cubs hung in there to the end, winning their last 6 to finish 2 games out of first. In their final game on September 28, when Guy Bush was blasted from the mound by Cincinnati, leaving his team trailing by 9 runs, the Cubs refused to surrender. Without benefit of a single home run, they rallied to beat the Reds, 13 to 11, sparing Bush what would have been a well-deserved eleventh loss.

A few days before the season ended, Wrigley made one of the dumbest moves an owner has ever made. Still smarting from the World Series loss in 1929, he announced that Joe McCarthy's contract would not be renewed and named Rogers Hornsby manager for 1931. The ensuing stampede to sign the jobless McCarthy was won by the Yankees' Jake Ruppert.

The Cards clinched the pennant two days before the close of the season. Since their loss to Brooklyn on August 8 in St. Louis, they had won 81 percent of their games. The team played admirably consistent baseball. In their seven-week stretch drive the

Cards had no winning streak greater than 6 games, no losing streak greater than 2. Finally able to rest his dog-tired pitching staff, Gabby Street was curious to find out how a loud, boastful nineteen-year-old right-hander, up from Houston for a look-see, would fare against major-league batters. Jerome "Dizzy" Dean (later called Jay Hanna Dean) could have told the manager before the game started. Dean closed the season by holding the hard-hitting Pittsburgh Pirates to 3 hits and beating them 3 to 1. The Cardinals' record for September was 20 and 4.

In 1930 the Philadelphia Phillies played out a scenario that might have come from Samuel Beckett. The club batted .315, the third highest major-league average of the twentieth century. They did it on 1,783 hits, the most ever by a major-league team. They hit 126 home runs, scored 944 runs, and had almost 2,600 total bases. The batting onslaught netted the Phils 102 losses as they finished last, 40 games behind the Cardinals. When the season closed a reporter asked manager Burt Shotton, "How could you conceivably finish last with such hitting?"

"I won't pretend that it was easy," Shotton replied. "It took a bit of second effort on the part of my pitching staff."

Shotton's pitchers had surrendered 1,199 runs in 156 games, a major-league record that seems safe for all the ages. Some of the worst teams in baseball history—a few playing a schedule of 162 games—have yet to come within hailing distance. The Phils' staff served up a record 1,993 hits and posted a Precambrian earned-run average of 6.7.

On the morning of December 4, 1930, Phillies principal owner William F. Baker died suddenly in the lobby of the Ritz-Carlton Hotel in Montreal, where he was attending the minor-league winter meetings. There may be a fragment of substance to the rumor that in the pocket of his overcoat was a copy of the recently released official National League pitching averages for the season past.

The situation in Philadelphia must have been discouraging for young Chuck Klein, playing his second full season. Klein, who hit safely in a record 135 games, batted .386. He also set the modern National League record for runs scored with 158 and drove in 170. His 445 total bases remain the fourth highest total ever recorded. Happily, Klein would eventually get to play on a winner. In 1934 the Phillies sold him to the Chicago Cubs.

Klein's teammate Lefty O'Doul, a bit off his feed after his big year in 1929, hit .383. Since the Cubs finished just 2 games behind St. Louis, he could take comfort in the thought that his pinch-hit homers probably had cost Joe McCarthy the pennant.

While the American League generated nothing resembling a pennant race after July, the Athletics' victory was far from the cakewalk of 1929. For half a season the Washington Senators, aided by the best pitching in either league, crowded the World Champions and held Philadelphia's eventual winning margin to 8 games. Washington manager Walter Johnson, the grand old master of the fastball, had somehow put together a staff of youth and age that produced five 15-game winners and registered the only ERA in the majors under 4.00. The Senators even outhit the Athletics, .302 to .294, but, of course, they did not begin to match Philadelphia's power.

The Yankees, in their first season under former pitcher Bob Shawkey, successor to the late Miller Huggins, wound up a disappointing third, 16 games out. It was not for lack of hitting. New York led the league with .309 and became the first American League team to score 1,000 runs. Their 1,062 runs established a modern major-league record, one they would better by a scant five the following season. The Yanks also led the league in hits, triples, home runs, and total bases. Most remarkable of all, the 1930 squad came within one-thousandth of a percentage point of tying the all-time slugging average of .489, set by Murderers' Row.

Actually, had a few breaks gone against them, the proud Yankees might have duplicated the noisy but futile performance of the Phillies. In two years Yankee pitching and fielding had eroded grievously. Manager Shawkey carried two starters with ERAs well above 5.00. Had Barrow not snaked right-hander Red Ruffing from Boston in May, there is no telling where the Yanks might have landed.

The thirty-five-year-old Babe Ruth, noticeably sobered by the death of Miller Huggins, started the season as if it were 1920 all over again. He hit 12 home runs in May, 8 against Philadelphia, and by July was on a pace that figured to carry him past his record 60. With the kind of pitching that was generally being offered up in 1930, it seemed as though nothing could stop the Babe. But on July 5, with his home-run total at 32, he tore a nail off a finger of his left hand while trying to make a circus catch against a wire fence at Washington's Griffith Stadium. The mishap not only put him out of action for ten days, but on his return to the lineup he had difficulty gripping the bat. Ruth finished the season with 49 home runs, disappointing to Yankee fans, perhaps, but still good enough to lead the league. In spite of Babe's failure to match the 1927 record, it was hardly a poor season.

Lou Gehrig, free from the aches and pains that had handicapped him in 1929, hit with the old gusto. He batted .379 to come within 3 percentage points of beating out Al Simmons for the league championship. Lou hit 41 homers and drove in 174 runs. As long as Shawkey could keep his twin crushers in harness, the Yankees were a source of worry for rival managers, weak pitching notwithstanding.

The Yankees' first series in Philadelphia in late May is worth a closer look as an illustration of what the American League race might have been like if New York had been stronger in the field and on the mound. On May 21 and 22, the teams split back-to-back doubleheaders and in the process scored 71 runs. In the opening game Ruth hit 3 homers, one of which went completely over the row houses on Twentieth Street. This was the game in which he came to bat right-handed, essentially robbing himself of the chance for 4 homers in one game. Miller Huggins probably would not have countenanced the prank, but Shawkey was a former teammate of Babe's and lacked Huggins's aura of authority. The Yanks wound up losing the game. In the only tame contest of the 4 in Philadelphia, left-hander Walberg held New York to 5 hits in the nightcap to win, 4 to 1. Between them the teams had hit 7 homers on the first day.

On May 22 it was the Yanks who swept 2. New York took the first game, 10 to 1, as Babe added 2 homers to his total. Even Yankee pitcher George Pipgras had a home run. But it was the second game that so richly characterized the season. The Yankees scored 7 runs in the top of the first, and after three hours had outlasted their hosts, 20 to 13. This time it was Gehrig's turn to hit 3 home runs in one game, the third time he had accomplished it in his career. Each team had 5 homers for the day. It was a record that would stand for twenty years. Ruth's homer in the second game brought his two-day total to 6.

Baseball researcher George T. Wiley has exhaustively tabulated the results of the tradition-rich New York–Philadelphia confrontations between 1927 and 1932. It was truly a clash of titans, since they shared six pennants equally. Arguably the two best defensive teams of the era, the Yankees and Athletics met 133 times in those six years and between them averaged 11.07 runs per game. Despite the wealth of pitching talent they enjoyed for much of the period, the clubs would sometimes generate more than 30 runs in a single game.

Neither team's sluggers showed much respect for the other's ace pitchers. Philadelphia's Lefty Grove, often rated history's greatest left-hander (according to sabermetrician Bill James, simply the greatest pitcher), was frequently manhandled by Ruth and his entourage. In 1930, when Grove was 28 and 5, he scored only 1 win over the Yankees and their heavily left-handed batting order. The *Spalding Guide* for 1931 observed laconically, "Grove never has been very successful against New York."

After the electrifying National League pennant race, the World Series had to be a letdown for St. Louis fans. The Athletics took the Cardinals, 4 games to 2, the first time since 1926 that a Series had gone as far as 6 games. Though the A's dropped Games Three and Four in St. Louis, during which they scored only 1 run, the Series was actually more certain in its outcome than it had been in 1929 and offered little excitement. Connie Mack's World Champions had too much of everything for the scrappy Cardinals, especially pitching.

In 1930, of all years, the Athletics and the Cardinals had come up with a pitchers' Series. Philadelphia's wan .197 batting average was matched by St. Louis's .200, two of the lowest team marks ever for a 6-game Series. In fact, they had come within 1 percentage point of the all-time World Series low, established by the Cubs and White Sox back in 1906—with a dead ball. But while the Athletics may not have hit often, more than half their hits went for extra bases, among them 6 home runs.

When weary statisticians completed their postseason chores for 1930, it was announced that Giant first baseman Bill Terry was the National League batting champion with an average of .401. He remains the last National Leaguer to reach the .400 level. Terry got 254 hits, to tie O'Doul's league record of 1929. It still stands. Three other National Leaguers—Herman, Klein, and O'Doul—batted over .380, and Giant third baseman Fred Lindstrom missed the goal by .00069.

In recent years Terry's achievement of 1930 has been much denigrated by baseball analysts. It is described as "soft," though I am not entirely sure what the term implies. I am more strongly persuaded by a comment made to Roger Angell by Hall of Famer Johnny Mize in the summer of 1987. "My worst day was when I got traded to the Giants," Mize said, "and I knew I'd have to hit in the Polo Grounds all year, with that five-hundred-foot center field. It was four hundred and twenty-two feet to right-center, where I liked to hit the ball. Bill Terry hit straightaway and he batted four hundred in the Polo Grounds before I got there, and to me that's five hundred, easy, in any other park."

Although Babe Ruth had temporarily surrendered the major-league home-run title to Hack Wilson, he was, at age thirty-five, still king of the hill in his own league. In addition, Babe batted .359 and drove in 153 runs. A dozen years after he had sparked the revolution in batting, Ruth remained a towering figure in baseball. Moreover, he had several good seasons ahead of him.

For the first time since 1924, the National League, without explanation, declined to make an award to the league's most valuable player. The American League had dropped out of the MVP business in 1929. The National League's action could be viewed as confirmation of a declining economy. The award traditionally carried a cash prize of $1,000 in gold, and by the autumn of 1930 gold was taking on new importance. In fact, many European countries with gold on deposit in the United States were hastily sending ships to fetch it home.

In the absence of league action, *The Sporting News* took it upon itself to appoint a special committee of baseball writers to name an MVP in each league. Bill Terry and Washington shortstop Joe Cronin topped the voting. There was no cash award. But the Baseball Writers Association, which chose Hack Wilson in a National League poll of its own, added a check for $1,000 for the winner. It was a prize richly earned.

The hero of 1930's tame World Series was without doubt Philadelphia's hulking right-hander George Earnshaw. He started 3 of the last 5 games, the finale on just one day's rest, winning 2 and losing none. Against a team that had scored more than 1,000 runs during the season, he gave up just 2 runs in twenty-five innings and struck out 19 batters.

Earnshaw came from a wealthy and socially prominent New York City family and was a graduate of Swarthmore College on Philadelphia's Main Line. The hero of the next World Series— between the same two teams—would be a lantern-jawed Oklahoma farm youth of scanty education, John "Pepper" Martin. As Earnshaw faded prematurely after three outstanding seasons, Martin would parlay an aggressive survivalist spirit and some modest talent into a Depression-era major-league career. In the early thirties Pepper sometimes rode the rods to training camp in order to save the train fare the Cardinals had advanced him.

While neither man can properly be styled typical of his baseball generation, in a curious way Earnshaw and Martin symbolize the transition between eras. The 1920s were characterized by extravagance and glitter, by optimism and merriment; it was the age of sixteen-cylinder sports cars, diamond-studded dog collars, and .400 batting averages. After the watershed year of 1930, the focus of attention in American life was economic survival. Things could never be quite the same again either inside or outside the ballpark.

EPILOGUE

In 1931 HITTING declined in the majors. The National League average dropped precipitously to .277; the American League slipped from .288 to .278. Home-run totals were down as well, off a startling 45 percent in the National League. The sudden drop should not have come as a surprise. At the major-league winter meetings in December 1930, it was apparent that in spite of record attendance in the season past, many owners were bent on curbing offense.

The principal target of reform was the home run, reflecting again a prejudice that had failed to die after a decade of evidence that the long ball was instrumental in winning new fans. Irving E. "Cy" Sanborn's grim editorial from *Baseball Magazine*, written as far back as 1924, still applied: "One of the most important matters the magnates of the major leagues have on their minds this winter," Sanborn declared, "is the rescue of the home run from the ranks of the commonplace and its restoration to the distinguished position it formerly held in the esteem of baseball fans."

In 1930 major-league batters had walloped a record 1,565 homers, almost 900 in the National League. Admittedly, it was a figure calculated to chill the blood of a baseball purist. On the other hand, purists had become a scarcely audible minority among baseball fans, who were, after all, paying the freight. Nevertheless, most of the joint meeting on December 10 was devoted to discussions of how to discourage the increase in home runs. No solution was found. Oddly, no one seems to have gone on record as opposed to the swollen batting averages. Apparently, only the flood of home runs was objectionable.

A few cynical writers present suspected that the owners were moved less by purist sentiments than by the fear that in a worsening economy, home-run hitters, taking their cue from Babe Ruth, would demand ever-larger salaries. Early in 1930 Babe had signed a much-publicized contract for $80,000 a year, more than President Hoover was paid. If the owners were in fact apprehensive about the greed of sluggers, the concern was groundless. As the Depression deepened, Ruth, like everyone else, took a cut in pay.

At their separate meeting on December 9, American League owners voted to make mandatory the numbering of players' uniforms, beginning with the 1931 season. The traditionally more conservative National League would resist making numbering mandatory until 1933, although individual clubs adopted the practice earlier on a voluntary basis.

When the winter meetings ended, the owners had arrived at no decision affecting the baseball. Before the opening of the new season, however, minor modifications were approved for adoption. At the spring scheduling meeting in February, the National League revealed that it had just approved a ball with a slightly thicker cover and raised stitches rather than the traditional countersunk ones. The American League joined the move to raise the seams, but stayed with the old cover. For the first time ever, the two major leagues would play with demonstrably different baseballs. Still, the difference was slight, and by 1934 the majors would again agree on a uniform ball.

Did the minor changes in the ball account for the falloff in hitting in 1931? It is the most probable conclusion, although it may be only part of the story. The late Carl Hubbell, whose earned-run average dropped by 1.10 between 1930 and 1931, told me that the change in the ball was immediately apparent to pitchers. "The ball just plain felt bigger in your hand," he said. "It was easier to grip." In addition to permitting the pitcher a better grip, the raised stitches almost certainly affected the flight of the ball to the plate.

If it was the intention of the owners to put a cap on home runs without at the same time lowering batting averages, they got the reverse of what they were after. While averages generally declined through the 1930s, especially in the National League, home-run figures held up very nicely. In any case, over time the traditional hostility to home runs seemed to get lost in the steam vapor of late-Depression soup kitchens. Or, possibly, Babe Ruth's retirement in 1935 removed the specter of swelling salaries.

Even before the winter meetings of 1930, reformers were in action. The official rules committee had met earlier to undertake the first major overhaul of baseball rules in many years. What the committee achieved was mostly streamlining of the wording. The rules were reduced in number by fourteen without greatly changing their substance. A strong urge to tidy things up can be seen in the new rule that no one out of uniform may appear on the field during a game. This even applied to the bat boys, who had hitherto worked in mufti.

Two changes in the rules directly impinged upon hitting. The sacrifice-fly rule was rescinded (to be partially restored eight years later) and fair balls that bounced into the stands were no longer scored as home runs but as ground-rule doubles. It is possible that the rewording of other rules exercised some subtle influence to curb offense, but it's difficult to pin down.

There can be no question that revocation of the sacrifice-fly rule affected batting averages. In fact, in 1931 an unofficial (and unidentified) statistician tracked the effect of the new rule from Opening Day through the end of June and calculated that at the midpoint of the season, the change was costing each league approximately 6 percentage points. As for home runs bounced into the stands, old box scores made no distinction. Original scorers' sheets might provide the best information, but they are not readily accessible. At all events, there is little evidence in the daily reporting of games to suggest that bounced homers made up a significant number of the total. Most outfield fences were either distant or high. We know, for example, that none of Ruth's record 60 was bounced into the stands.

Something else that may have contributed to the decline in hitting was a new spirit of frugality in the consumption of baseballs. Before the 1930 season, American League president E. S. Barnard ordered that a strict record be kept of the expenditure of balls and that everyone make an effort to avoid waste. Barnard ruled that no longer could a ball be thrown out of a game until it had first been inspected by an umpire and the umpire concurred. Further, the league president asked the cooperation of the players in keeping a ball in play as long as it remained in reasonably good condition. And apparently they complied. The Barnard policy may in part explain the 15-point disparity in batting average between the leagues that season.

It's safe to assume that the balls used in the American League in 1930 never approached the unspeakable condition of a game ball in the spitball era. At the same time, batters no longer enjoyed the luxury—as they had for ten years—of seeing nothing but gleaming white baseballs float up to the plate. In 1931 the National League would also adopt the economy move. Although in time the majors abandoned the policy of frugality, it remains the rule that an umpire must inspect a game ball before it is thrown out.

In spite of raised stitches on the ball and disadvantageous modifications in the rules, including subtle redefinitions of the strike zone, .300 hitters did not disappear in a puff of smoke after 1930. The very best batters—Gehrig, Ruth, Foxx, O'Doul, Klein, Simmons, Gehringer, Terry, Waner, Manush, and others—continued to hit for high though somewhat diminished averages and were succeeded by equally successful rookies, such as Joe DiMaggio, Hank Greenberg, Joe Medwick, and Ted Williams. Home-run hitters became more numerous than ever. But among journeymen in the lineup, batting steadily declined, especially in the National League, until by 1941 league averages were back down where they had begun in 1919.

Since the high noon of 1930 there have been plenty of virtuoso batting performances, among them Ted Williams's .406 average in 1941, DiMaggio's 56-game hitting streak in the same year, Maris's 61 homers in 1961, Gehrig's 184 RBIs in 1931, Jimmie Foxx's .749 slugging average and 438 total bases in 1932, and Williams's 162 walks in 1947 and 1949. However, most of them were entered in the book before World War II. Since 1941, no major leaguer has batted .400, only four men have topped .370, and only four have driven in as many as 150 runs. In a game increasingly dominated by night play, oversized pitchers, and relief specialists, fewer and fewer players can hope to hit .300 even once in a career. Equally, goals such as scoring or driving in 100 runs a season seem out of reach of all but a tiny handful of superstars.

Take it or leave it, we live in an age of modest run production, high strikeout totals, and the solo home run. I'll take it, naturally, because I love baseball and what matters in the end is not statistics but closely matched teams and exciting pennant races. Still, I hanker to see a pitcher hit .360 again, an infielder knock in 180 runs, and anyone at all strike out 4 times in a season instead of 4 times in a game.

INDEX